Eating Disorders
in Athletes

Eating Disorders in Athletes

Joaquín Dosil
University of Vigo, Spain

John Wiley & Sons, Ltd

Other Wiley Editorial Offices

John Wiley & Sons Inc., 111 River Street, Hoboken, NJ 07030, USA

Jossey-Bass, 989 Market Street, San Francisco, CA 94103-1741, USA

Wiley-VCH Verlag GmbH, Boschstr. 12, D-69469 Weinheim, Germany

John Wiley & Sons Australia Ltd, 33 Park Road, Milton, Queensland 4064, Australia

John Wiley & Sons (Asia) Pte Ltd, 2 Clementi Loop #02-01, Jin Xing Distripark, Singapore 129809

John Wily & Sons Canada Ltd, 6045 Freemont Blvd, Mississauga, Ontario, L5R 4J3

Wiley also publishes its books in a variety of electronic formats. Some content that appears in print may
not be available in electronic books.

Library of Congress Cataloging-in-Publication Data

Dosil, Joaquín.
    Eating disorders in athletes / Joaquín Dosil.
        p. ; cm.
    Includes bibliographical references and index.
    ISBN 978-0-470-01169-0 (cloth   ) – ISBN 978-0-470-01170-6 (pbk.   )
    1. Eating disorders.   2. Athletes–Nutrition.   3. Athletes–Mental health.   4. Sports medicine.
I. Title.
    [DNLM: 1. Eating Disorders.   2. Sports–psychology.   3. Sports Medicine. WM 175 D723e 2008]
    RC552.E18D67 2008
    362.196′8526–dc22

                                                                                        2007041617

British Library Cataloguing in Publication Data

A catalogue record for this book is available from the British Library

ISBN 978-0-470-01169-0 (HB)   ISBN 978-0-470-01170-6 (PB)

Typeset in 10.5 on 12.5 pt Minion by SNP Best-set Typesetter Ltd., Hong Kong

Contents

Foreword

Disordered eating and pathogenic weight control behaviours seem to be present in athletes across a wide range of sports, and not just in the aesthetic and weight division sports. Many athletes, however, remain in the disordered eating closet for a variety of reasons. Probably one of the top motivators for staying in that closet is shame. Athletes, coaches, parents, and the general public look upon practices such as binging and purging (e.g. vomiting, using laxatives) as more or less disgusting. That shame and disgust is often internalized in those athletes struggling with eating and weight control, and to avoid those negative emotional responses that would result from letting other people know about their difficulties, it is safer to remain in the closet.

Males with disordered eating will have an additional reason for keeping their difficulties secret. Added to the shame of eating disorders is the issue of having a 'girlie' problem. In the hypermasculinized world of sport, admitting to having difficulties that are perceived to be primarily present in girls' and women's sports is tantamount to saying 'I am a soft and weak male.' Several years ago, in that most masculine of male sports, Australian Rules Football, a professional player came out publicly about his long-term struggles with eating and weight. Although he was sympathetically received by the press, his 'confession' has not resulted in any other footballer revealing difficulties. I know several sport psychologists who work with professional Aussie Rules players, and all of them have told me that they conservatively estimate that 10 to 15 per cent of the men in the Australian Football League (AFL) have eating disorders, but no one is speaking up. In contrast, here in Australia in the past couple years, athletes of both genders have been outing themselves, left and right, about their experiences with depression. Depression is the 'common cold' of mental health, and there are plenty of support groups and organizations dedicated to helping people with depression. In Australia, we even have a depression support group headed by a well-respected former AFL player. The same situation cannot be said of support for athletes with disordered eating. The closet doors remain shut and locked.

On-going research on jockeys in the horseracing industry has revealed that a very high and worrisome number of currently racing young male jockeys exhibit signs of osteopenia (reduced bone mass) and osteoporosis. Young males, in general, are usually well protected (hormonally and nutritionally) from bone density pathology. Jockey practices, however, of fasting, laxative and diuretic use, time spent in saunas to lose water weight, alcohol and nicotine consumption, and low calcium intake, along with the possibility of never having the opportunity to re-hydrate on race days (they may have the lightest weight ride at the end of the day) have resulted in a population at serious risk. By most criteria of eating disorders or pathogenic weight control, many jockeys fit disturbingly well. Is this a problem that jockeys 'have'? Or is this a problem of the costly demands of a racing environment and culture that perpetuate pathogenic behaviour in the pursuit of glory and money and fame? The racing calendar in some countries is 360+ days a year. Top jockeys in the glamour positions may get a break (they are the money winners). The majority struggle all year long, and their struggles represent the consequences of the institutional abuse of human capital.

Sport psychology has a lot to answer for with its history of promoting the myth that athletes are more likely to be mentally healthy than the general population (see William Morgan and colleagues' work in the 1970s and 1980s) and that eating disorders in sport primarily manifest in girls and women (Roberta Sherman and Trent Petrie's work in the 1990s). It may be that the majority of eating problems manifest in women and girls, but being male assures no immunity. The head of the Australian Institute of Sport Performance Psychology Unit stated a few years ago:

People on the whole [in sport] tend to be far more functional . . . the natural selection process means that typically people who are dysfunctional don't get the opportunity to progress through in their sport. So that, as young athletes, they typically already can't cope at a lower level with the demands of training and all those types of things . . . we don't tend to see a lot of athletes coming through who have those clinical and counselling issues. (Fink, 2004, p. 75)

To his credit, the most visible sport psychologist in Australia has since recanted, but such myths about athletes are one reason closet doors remain bolted. We like to think our athletes are super-human heroes and heroines, and such fairy stories place unreasonable demands and expectations on all-too-human sport participants.

Much of the sport psychology literature focuses on eating disorders from the position that they are problems that athletes 'have', and the overwhelming foci have been treating the athletes and *their* problems. We need more attention paid to the pathogenic environment of sport (e.g. the horseracing industry), so it is good to see, in this book, a whole chapter dedicated to the problem of environments that help foster eating disorders. From over 20 years of service delivery, I have come to view many sport environments as abusive and dehumanizing. It is amazing to see what psychologically and physically abusive behaviours and practices by coaches that parents (and athletes) will tolerate in the name of sport. If those same behaviours (e.g. yelling, demeaning athletes, calling athletes fat) were brought into classrooms, parents would be calling for teachers' heads. Yet, we stand by and watch the abuse, and maybe we rationalize our inaction because the coach is famous and has a great track record of producing winners. Sport psychologists are no less guilty of being bystanders while abuse occurs, offering services to help athletes cope with the abuse. 'So the coach is being abusive. Here are some cognitive reframes to help you handle the coach calling you a "weak and worthless little shit." How does that sound?' It sounds like collusion with abuse to me and profoundly misses the point of where the problem truly lies.

How does one treat an athlete with an eating disorder? That's a reasonable but naïve question. Treatment is not a one-way street from practitioner to client. In the literature we see lots of team-treatment plans for athletes with eating disorders where several practitioners are involved (e.g. physicians, nutritionists, psychiatrists, psychologists) in a 'team approach,' and this tactic is viewed as good service. Is it? Maybe, maybe not. At the beginning of treatment is it really best for athletes to go to a bunch of other practitioners and have to tell their painful and shameful stories over and over again. The word 'abuse' comes to mind once more.

The working alliance

The core of treatment is not the athlete's 'problem' (e.g. bulimia); it is the working alliance or the relationship that evolves between the athlete and the practitioner. Change is effected not so much by charting one's eating behaviour or identifying cues to bingeing, but rather by the quality of the interpersonal landscape of the two people working together. One can treat athletes with eating disorders using a variety of methods (e.g. gestalt, psychodynamic, cognitive–behavioural), but the approach is not as important as the question: 'Do the athlete and practitioner really like each other and work well together?' We know from past research in psychotherapy that it is the quality of the working alliance that accounts for the most variance in treatment outcome (Sexton & Whiston, 1994). So how much time do we spend training sport psychologists in how to develop and deliver treatment plans for athletes with eating disorders versus time spent on how working alliances and relationships grow and thrive. Both are important, but the latter type of training is often impoverished at the expense of learning 'evidenced-based' intervention techniques. Unfortunately, much evidence-based intervention research is not really much evidence at all. People are never randomly assigned to treatment. Interventions are rarely consistently delivered 'by the book.' Therapy is, if anything, almost always idiographic, and the key components of treatment are often left out of research. Most randomized clinical trials are therapist-evacuated research with the personality of the therapist and the quality of the relationship between practitioner and client left out of the picture. Psychodynamic approaches to eating disorders (e.g. Sours, 1992) do take these personality and relationship factors as central issues in treatment, but dynamic or object-relations sport psychologists are rare in our field. I hope this book helps sport psychologists broaden their ideas about what treatment is really all about.

Sport is good!

Sport psychologists often have the prejudice that sport is good, and we need to help athletes adjust to the demands of sport so they can reap the benefits of this wonderful endeavour. Sport psychologists, if they are worth their salt, should have as their over-arching agenda the well-being and happiness of their clients. So we need to be mindful that leaving sport, and abandoning fantasy goals of glory (and elusive happiness), may be in the best interest of the athlete. In several cases I have come across, the central issues facing the athletes with disordered eating were the demands of the sport and the practices of the coaching staff. As one collegiate diver explained to me after she returned from a 2-week break 'When I was home and away from the pool, it [bingeing and purging] didn't happen once, but as soon as I got back on the boards, Boom! it started all over again.' Do we try and help athletes adjust to an abusive environment, or do we help them explore other avenues that may lead to better health and happiness, such as getting out of sport. The latter approach will not win us any popularity contests with coaches and administrators, and may cost us our jobs. Van Raalte and Andersen (2007) have discussed the issues sport psychologists face when what is best for the athlete is to leave the sport. These issues are not easy ones to resolve, but when health and happiness take a back seat to sport participation, performance enhancement, and more medals, then something is rotten in the state of sport psychology service delivery.

I hope this book will help clear away some of the secrecy, shame, and stigma of eating disorders in sport. Participation in sport can be a wonderful experience where many fine lessons about life may be learned. Too often, however, the lessons learned are pernicious ones. I always want to ask parents 'Would you want your sons or daughters to engage in an activity where there is a good probability that they will end up being ashamed of their bodies, having physically damaged their bones and organs, and becoming quite unhappy?' Maybe this book will help sport become a more healthy place for people to grow and learn good things about themselves.

Mark B. Andersen
Victoria University, Australia

List of Contributors

Joaquín Dosil, PhD, is a professor at the University of Vigo in north-west Spain and head of the doctoral course: 'Current perspectives of physical activity and sport psychology'. He is a foundation member and the former President of the Ibero-American Society of Sport Psychology (SIPD). Dosil is the Director of a Sport Psychology Unit in Santiago de Compostela, where he attends athletes and sport teams from various modalities and levels. He has authored or edited 12 books with the most recent being, *The Sport Psychologist's Handbook: A Guide for Sport-Specific Performance Enhancement*, and published over 60 articles and chapters in Spanish. He frequently participates as a lecturer in International and National Congresses, Masters and Doctoral Degree programmes. Dosil is also an avid runner, specializing in distance events, particularly the half-marathon.

Juan Jose Crespo
University of Vigo
Pontevedra
Spain

Luis Casáis
University of Vigo
Pontevedra
Spain

Isabel Díaz
University of Vigo
Pontevedra
Spain

Olga Díaz
University of Santiago
Santiago de Compostela
Spain

Olaia González
Eating Disorders Unit
Centro Libredon
Santiago de Compostela
Spain

Enrique J. Garcés de Los Fayos
University of Murcia
Murcia
Spain

Jacinto González-Oya
University of Vigo
Pontevedra
Spain

Introduction

Relationship between sport, society, and eating disorders

In recent years, eating disorders have become a cause for concern and debate in diverse sectors of society. Such was the concern, that in 1999 Spain created a special government Commission to study the matter in more depth. In the same year, the Spanish Ministry of Health and Consumption made public some alarming statistics regarding the prevalence of eating disorders, stating that 1.5% of youngsters aged between 14 and 24 years, approximately 80 000, suffer eating-related problems. Other sources, such as the Association for the Defence of Anorexia Nervosa (ADANER-Spain), indicate even more startling numbers, suggesting that some 500 000 people are affected by these diseases, 90% of these women aged between 14 and 18 years.

Nevertheless, these data are difficult to verify. The variety of behaviours linked to eating disorders is enormous, ranging from abnormal eating behaviours, which fail to comply with any particular pathology, to those diagnosable as a specific eating disorder, such as anorexia nervosa or bulimia. On the other hand, people suffering these illnesses rarely voluntarily seek professional help, failing to recognize they have a problem. Moreover, the pathological formation of these disorders makes their assessment, diagnosis, and treatment especially difficult. Consequently, three principal characteristics can be established, and are discussed in this book:

- *Eating disorders principally occur in the developed world.* Without a doubt, industrialized countries present the highest rates of eating disorders. The cultural reasons for this, such as passing fashions, body 'worshipping', etc., have been dealt with in previous chapters. This factor will be explained using statistics from Spain, since it is representative of all nations with similar socio-economic and political characteristics.

- *Accessing reliable information is complicated.* As previously highlighted, the predictive variables for eating disorders are usually disguised by the individuals suffering these problems, or denied in the face of help offered to them by friends and family. In accordance with the reality sports psychologists face, and for an optimum degree of accuracy in the final diagnosis, this factor should be considered when establishing psychological assessment systems.

• *The prevalence rates for these disorders are high.* Finally, although it is difficult to verify the data that confirms the incidence of psychological eating problems, it is clear that the occurrence of these problems is high. Even removing the 'reported' effect, which through the media has caused a greater detection of these disorders in recent years, it has become apparent that the frequency of anorexia and bulimia, as well as other more recent problems, such as bigorexia, is extremely elevated.

Following this line of analysis, a Spanish educative journal (*Nuestros Hijos,* edition 1999), offers the following statistics:

• The age of patients is gradually getting lower (more girls aged between 8 and 10 years are admitted into hospital refusing to eat for fear of becoming fat).

• 6 per cent of sufferers will lose their lives as a result of their obsession to be thin, and one in five patients will suffer the consequences of having stopped eating for the rest of their lives.

• Finally and perhaps more worryingly: the annual growth rate of these illnesses lies around 15–20 per cent.

The increase in psychological problems related to eating, such as anorexia, may be explained by a series of interrelated factors (Gordon, 1999):

• *The changing role of women*
  The improved social and professional role of women has made them very active members of society in every aspect. As with the beauty industry, many women are carried along with the 'tyranny' of imposed fashions, disguised somewhat ironically, as components of freedom of choice.

• *The increasingly difficult transition from adolescence to adulthood*
  The complex move from adolescence to adulthood affects many youngsters, especially girls. In addition to all the typical obstacles, the demands of trying to be a liberal and active woman, with enormous desires to progress professionally, have served to increase the difficulty of this changeover. These factors coincide to generate expectations that cannot always be met, and the consequent frustration regularly manifests in the form of psychological disorders, such as eating-related problems.

- *The importance society attributes to physical appearance*
  Being thin is the beauty ideal (a symptom of health and good physical form). Paradoxically, whilst being slim seemingly indicates good health, diminishing weight beyond the reasonable limits for a certain stature or physical constitution, increases the risk of health problems. Likewise, the continuous consumption and expulsion of food gives rise to physical stressors that can lead the body to deteriorate brusquely. However, changing the current state of affairs remains complicated whilst it is in the economic interests of certain business entities in the fashion and beauty industries to continue promoting an almost impossible to achieve 'ideal' body image. Two opposing examples may be cited: on the one hand, companies dedicated to marketing fast food have a bearing on the development of obese children; whilst on the other, businesses dedicated to fashion, generate media models, whose image encourages eating disorders such as anorexia.

In short, a series of psychological problems affecting an elevated number of people in the industrialised world is apparent. On the contrary, a study conducted by Nasser (1988) observed the non-existence of eating disorders in developing countries such as Sudan or Egypt.

One of the more tangible explanations for these geographical differences lies in the social pressures to be thin in the western world, an effect that has intensified in recent years. In today's western culture, people commonly go on diets and worry about their weight or being 'in fashion'. For many, this quest for the ideal body has become a way of feeling more secure and accepted in today's society, and such behaviours thrive amongst adolescents, especially the female gender. Nevertheless, the majority of people who follow diets and 'obsess' over losing weight actually weigh what they should for their age and size (Toro *et al.* 1988).

In addition to diets, people suffering from eating disorders commonly turn to physical exercise and sport as a way of losing weight. For this reason, physical exercise has been directly related to these problems. But can this relationship function in the opposite direction? That is to say, can athletes themselves 'fall into' an eating disorder? The results of various studies respond affirmatively to this question; there is a wide range of sportsmen and women who have fallen into the grasps of anorexia, bulimia, bigorexia, orthorexia and other eating problems. All of the studies detailed below have confirmed the sport-eating disorder relationship over the last 15 years:

- Warren *et al.* (1990) investigated how established competitive structures influence the development of eating disorders in female athletes.

- Pruitt *et al.* (1991) conducted a study relating excessive physical exercise and sport to anorexia and bulimia in athletes.

- Brownell and Rodin (1992) described the prevalence rates of eating disorders in athletes, and explained how these data relate to the parameters set by the modern society.

- Stoutjesdyk and Jevne (1993) analyzed the frequency of eating disorders and problematic eating habits in elite athletes.

- Thompson and Sherman (1993a) carried out a broad study into the origin and development of eating disorders in athletes, as well as the potential solutions.

- Estok and Rudy (1996) focused their study on eating disorders in female athletics, comparing the results with other types of sport.

- Virnig and McLeod (1996) analyzed how the attitudes of different athletes towards eating and doing physical exercise varies, establishing differences between runners and tri-athletes.

- Hulley and Hill (2001) focused their investigation on the prevalence of eating disorders in elite female athletics.

- Petrie and Rogers (2001) have recently warned about the increasing number of male athletes suffering from eating disorders, not originally considered a high-risk segment.

- Sila (2001) conducted a comparative study into the incidence of eating disturbances in Portuguese athletes.

- Brewer and Petrie (2002), in a generic study into psychopathologies in the sports world, described eating disorders as one of the most important problems in athletes.

- Dosil and Díaz (2002) highlighted the presence of eating disorder symptoms in sporting disciplines such as aerobics, relatively undocumented in the past.

- Dosil (2003) compared the frequency of eating disorders in various sports, differentiating between those considered as 'high risk' and those which, given their intrinsic characteristics, pose lower possibilities of athletes suffering from eating disorders.

- Cogan (2005) analyzed the elements to consider when defining eating disorders in athletes.

In this book, we will start with the importance of factors such as information, weight control and the sports environment, in determining the development of eating behaviour disorders. The following chapters describe the aspects to consider in the evaluation, diagnosis, and treatment of eating problems in sport, presenting the use of the new technologies and the relationship with eating disorders in athletes. Finally, we offer, in the last chapter, different approaches for working with athletes from high-risk sports.

1 Good Eating Habits in Sport

Joaquín Dosil and Juan José Crespo

Despite having reached a relatively high level in my sport, there is still a lack of nutritional guidance. Sometimes the conversation crops up at training and people give you the odd piece of advice about what you should eat, what you shouldn't, and any supplements they assure work wonders for them. But nobody puts all of this lose information together and applies it to you, as an individual athlete, in a structured manner. Coaches are often too quick to say when you are a little over weight, telling you to 'watch what you're eating', or even that you are too skinny, 'make sure you're eating enough'. What's the real practicality of these remarks? All too often the first comments I hear from fellow female athletes following a bad training session or race is 'I'm too fat'. Perhaps this indicates the constant underlying risk of eating disorders in sport.

International Athlete (middle-distance running)

1.1 Introduction

The demands of today's ever-increasingly professional sports world lead athletes to thrive for perfection in all aspects of their preparation. In this quest for peak performance, the traditional coach–athlete training model has become somewhat dated. Gradually sport is incorporating a wider range of professionals into teams and clubs (physical trainers, physiotherapists, doctors, psychologists, nutritionists . . .), recognising the need for specialist guidance in the different aspects of athletes' performance.

Eating Disorders in Athletes   Joaquín Dosil
© 2008 John Wiley & Sons, Ltd

Eating is a conscious and voluntary action, influenced by cultural, economic and social factors. Undoubtedly, nutrition has an impact on the health and can prove either detrimental or beneficial to an athlete's performance. Whilst doctors and nutritionists are responsible for prescribing the most adequate 'diets' for each individual athlete, psychologists work to prevent environmental influences from provoking eating disorders. Likewise, given their role as team/ group coordinators, coaches may act as *behaviour observers*, consulting the relevant specialists if they suspect eating alterations. This somewhat utopian vision is intended to form a vital link in the process of optimizing sports performance. Since the prevailing reality reveals many nutritional errors are still being made in sport, this chapter endeavours to provide a source of basic information for coaches and athletes alike, promoting the role of the many professionals working in this field.

1.2   A balanced diet in sport

Nutritional control evaluates the dietary intake of athletes, verifying its suitability for the physical demands of their daily sports activity. The principal aim is to avoid the deficiencies or excesses that can hinder performance and general health. Whilst the primary objective of any nutritional strategy is to attain the necessary energy intake for an athlete (quantity), the secondary objective is to nourish the organism with the 45 essential nutrients: 13 vitamins, 9 amino acids, 21 minerals and 2 fatty acids (quality).

1.2.1   What is a balanced diet?

To survive, the human body requires energy, certain substances to maintain and replace tissues, as well as regulating metabolic reactions, and water. These basic needs are met by nutrients found in the different foods we consume. The main nutrients are: *macronutrients* (carbohydrates, lipids and proteins) and *micronutrients* (vitamins and minerals).

Whilst the function of carbohydrates and lipids is principally energetic, proteins have an important structural role, and vitamins and minerals assist in the body's regulatory mechanism.

Regarding nutritional requirements, the World Health Organization (WHO, 2003) stipulates the following objectives for the general population: 55–75 per cent carbohydrates, 15–30 per cent fats, and 10–15 per cent proteins.

In terms of body tissues, muscles have the greatest capacity to produce and employ the energy generated through adenosine triphosphate (ATP), the organism's 'energetic currency'. Since the concentration of ATP in the muscles is extremely limited (5 mmol/kg), there are four metabolic methods for renewing it: phosphorcreatine, anaerobic glycolysis, aerobic glycolysis (glucose/glycogen), and lipolysis (fatty acids). These energetic substrata are produced by certain nutrients, found in the foods we consume (principally carbohydrates and lipids), and are stored within the organism.

Athletes present exceptional nutritional requirements, which vary according to age, gender and body composition, as well as the type, intensity, frequency and duration of the physical activity. Although diet had already been related to physical performance at the beginning of the twentieth century, it was not until well into the 1960s and beginning of the 1970s, that the physiological bases of sports performance were scientifically established.

Adequate nutritional intake is a factor determining sports performance (American Dietetic Association, 2000). Moreover, an adequate diet should provide the sufficient number of total calories, 10–15 per cent of which should originate from proteins (1–1.5 g/kg of weight) 20–30 per cent from fats, and 60–70 per cent from carbohydrates (Katch, 1985).

1.2.2 Energy requirements

The calorie requirements of each individual athlete may be determined by estimating the *base metabolism (BM)*, the *dynamic-specific action (DSA)* of the nutrients (10 per cent average for the three macronutrients), the *additional calorie consumption* during day-to-day activities, and the *calorie consumption during physical and/or sporting activity*. The BM can be estimated using the Harris–Benedict (1919) formula:

$$\text{Male base metabolism} = 66.5 + 13.8 \times \text{weight (kg)} + 5.0 \times \text{height (cm)}$$
$$- 6.8 \times \text{age (years)}$$

$$\text{Female base metabolism} = 65.1 + 9.5 \times \text{weight (kg)} + 1.8 \times \text{height (cm)}$$
$$- 4.7 \times \text{age (years)}$$

Recording the various daily physical activities and calculating the energy expenditure of each, consulting the relevant tables, is one way of estimating additional calorie requirements (Ainsworth *et al.*, 1993; McArdle *et al.*, 1991).

Athletes, compared with more sedentary individuals, present an average additional energy expenditure of 500–1000 kcal/h of exercise (Brouns, 1995). Therefore, an athlete immersed in a high-intensity exercise programme cannot operate off the same diet as the rest of the general population.

Finally, regarding energy requirements, nutritional evaluation is another relevant aspect. In the sports context, and particularly in sports medicine, the body mass index (BMI) is frequently employed to relate athletes' weight in kilograms to their height in metres squared:

$$\text{BMI} = \text{weight (kg)}/\text{height (m}^2)$$

The BMI allows coaches to objectively measure their athletes' physical state at any given point of the season. An individual is considered malnourished if the BMI falls below $18.5\,kg/m^2$, and normal if the reading lies between $18.5\,kg/m^2$ and $24.9\,kg/m^2$. Nevertheless, the characteristics of each sporting discipline must not be disregarded, since the physical biotypes of each may vary, altering the normal limits.

1.2.3 Forming a nutritional plan

Without imposing notable changes in athletes' eating patterns, a dietary plan may be elaborated through the following steps:

1. Estimate the athlete's energy requirements using the pertinent formulas and tables.

2. Divide the calories into macronutrient categories.

3. Convert the calories into grams (proteins, 4 kcal/g; carbohydrates, 4 kcal/g; fats, 9 kcal/g).

4. Divide the nutrients into food groups (dairy products, meat/fish/eggs, cereals/potatoes, vegetables, fruit, and fats). The nutritional pyramid and food composition tables prove useful here.

5. Prepare each mealtime (4 or 5 daily intakes).

6. Adapt the food quantities according to the reference measurements.

Despite being somewhat problematic, many professional athletes use reference-eating models, often provided by coaches and teammates. Athletes from different sports seek diverse objectives through their nutrition (see Table 1.1). For example, whilst cyclists aim to renew the energy lost through daily physical exertion, gymnasts seek a minimum ideal weight to compete more effectively.

In certain sports, in which athletes seek an extremely thin body, especially in predominantly female disciplines (e.g. gymnastics, synchronised swimming, artistic ice-skating, distance running, dancing, or horse riding), energy intake often fails to meet recommendations, producing nutritional deficits in the majority of cases (Otis *et al.* 1997; West, 1998; Hobart & Smucker, 2000). On many occasions, such insufficiencies oblige athletes' doctors to take correctional measures, including the employment of vitamin and mineral supplements.

In particular physiological conditions, such as adolescence, nutrition plays a vital role in growth and sexual development. Many athletes, especially females, already compete at elite level during their early adolescence (10–13 years of age), when they should be attending to three fundamental aspects: the pubertal growth spurt (higher protein and calcium requirements), changes in body composition (increased fat percentages in girls) and other individual alterations influenced by the social environment (Santrock, 2004). Up to 11 years of age, the recommended daily energy intake is the same for boys and girls; from 11 to 14 years, boys are recommended to consume 300 kcal/day more than girls; and between 15 and 18 years, this difference rises to 800 kcal/day. In Spanish adolescents, 10–15 per cent presents with an

Table 1.1 Factors influencing the pursued nutritional objectives in sport. The energetic consumption and proportion of macronutrients consumed in different sports

Objectives of diet in sport	Factors influencing diet in sport	Average daily energetic consumption in different sports: (% of carbohydrates, fats and proteins)
Replacement of energy resources	Prioritization of nutritional objectives	Cycling: 5000–7000 kcal (64% – 26% – 10%)
Provision of the 45 essential nutrients	Macronutrient absorption	Marathon: 4000–5000 kcal (50% – 36% – 14%)
Repair and maintenance of bodily tissues	Control of non-nutritional energetic elements, e.g. alcohol	Football: 3300–3900 kcal (45% – 40% – 14%)
Organic regeneration and growth	Daily distribution of total calorie intake	Skiing: 4900–7100 kcal (46% – 40% – 14%)
Maintenance of the immune system's capacity and response to exercise-induced stresses	Eating habits and availability of quality food items	Swimming: 4400–5500 kcal (47% – 42% – 11%)
Prevention of injuries and avoidance of hyper-calorie nutrition, dehydration, etc.	Number of daily training sessions: the time frame of food intake	Gymnastics/dance 1600–1900 kcal (49% – 36% – 15%)

Source: Villa and Navas (2002).

iron deficit, only 40 per cent of boys and 15 per cent of girls meet the recommended daily calcium intake, and 10–40 per cent fail to comply with the required ingestion of vitamins A, B, and folic acid (Lozano de la Torre & Muñoz, 1995).

Given the exceptional physical demands of elite sport, nutritional awareness is essential for everyone involved in this context. Moreover, such knowledge should be much more abundant and exhaustive than for rest of the general population. Nevertheless, given the lack of information and the physical stress placed upon their organisms, athletes often find themselves 'destitute' in this respect.

This chapter now proceeds to describe the most important elements in athletes' diets: macronutrients, micronutrients and liquids. Such basic nutritional knowledge should be common throughout the sporting community, helping to prevent eating disorders.

1.3 Nutrients required by humans and athletes

Unlike eating, nutrition is a combination of processes through which the organism receives, transforms and employs dietary substances contained within foods. In order to provide the necessary quantity of nutrients, each individual's food intake, whether an athlete or not, should be sufficient in energy, varied, balanced and, of course, enjoyable.

1.3.1 Macronutrients

There are three macronutrient groups: *carbohydrates*, *fats* or *lipids*, and *proteins*. The organism's two principal energy sources are fats and carbohydrates. In a state of rest, fat is the primary energy supplier, but as physical exercise increases, the role of carbohydrates becomes more significant, constituting the most important fuel in high-intensity physical activities, such as difficult training sessions and competitions (Table 1.2).

The main characteristics of each macronutrient group are described below.

Glycogen/glucides, or carbohydrates   Carbohydrates (CH) constitute one of the most important energy resources in human nutrition. For the majority of athletes, they represent the principal energy source for muscular contraction and even the general population are aware of the benefits of a carbohydrate-rich diet (e.g. pasta is often referred to as 'athletes' food'). Its components (carbon, hydrogen and oxygen) are linked in a formula, generally abbreviated as: $C_n(H_2O)_n$ – hence its classic denomination.

Carbohydrates may be distinguished according to their structure and chemical characteristics, or how easily they can be digested and absorbed into the body. From a structural perspective, the following classification can be made:

- Monounsaturated carbohydrates: the most commonly found are hexodes (six carbons), glucose, fructose and galactose.

- Saturated carbohydrates: two units of monounsaturated carbohydrates joined together. The most commonly found are: maltose, sucrose and lactose.

- Polyunsaturated carbohydrates: produced through the polymerization of ten or more glucose units. From a nutritional perspective, the following may be high-

Table 1.2 The approximate required proportions of macronutrients in different sports. Reproduced from Villa and Navas (2002), courtesy of McGraw-Hill, Madrid

Macronutrients	Athletes conducting short physical efforts at high intensities (sprinters, weight lifters) and technical sports (figure skating, rhythmic gymnastics)	Athletes conducting prolonged physical efforts at elevated intensities (marathon runners, cyclists, cross-country skiers . . .).
Carbohydrates	50–55%	60–70%
Fats	30%	18–28%
Proteins	15–20%	12%

lighted: starch, glycogen, dextrose and dietary fibre. These have a slower absorption rate than saturated and monounsaturated carbohydrates. Dietary fibre is composed of certain oligounsaturated carbohydrates (stachyose, raffinose) and polyunsaturated carbohydrates (cellulose, mucilage, pectin, insulin), which cannot be absorbed into the human intestine, but play an important role in intestinal functioning.

One of the classification criteria for carbohydrates, known as the 'glycaemic index' (Jenkins *et al.*, 1993) determines the increase in glycaemia above the base levels, which is produced 2 h after ingesting a food element containing 50 g of carbohydrate (compared to 50 g of glucose). Foods with an elevated glycaemic index (>85) include bread, rice, muesli, potatoes, glucose polymers, banana, and cornflakes. Foods with a moderate glycaemic index (60–85) comprise pasta, biscuits, grapes, pastries and cakes. Foods with a low glycaemic index (<60) are peas, figs, ice cream, and dairy products in general. The glycaemic index varies according to gastric emptiness, protein and fat contents of the foods, the size of the starch molecule and even how the food has been prepared (hence, the nutritional impact of cooking methods).

Carbohydrates are directed towards the digestive tract before being converted, almost exclusively, into glucose (fructose and galactose are also absorbed). Glucose is then distributed around the organism through the blood, with two main destinations (Barbany, 2002):

- One part is accumulated as glycogen reserves in the liver (80–100 g) and muscular fibre (400–500 g).
- Another part is used in certain cells (neurons and **haematites**), as a form of fuel.
- The rest is directed to fatty tissues, where it is transformed into triglycerides to stimulate the insulin hormone (lipogenesis).

At rest, the consumption of glucose is extremely low. However, it is used constantly during physical activity. During prolonged periods of exercise at intensities surpassing 60 per cent of the *maximum oxygen consumption* (VO_2 max), there is a lineal relationship between the exercise intensity and the muscular glycogen consumption rate. Moreover, in physical activities around 80–85 per cent of the VO_2 max, this material constitutes the principal substratum (Coyle, 1995). During intermittent physical exercise at maximum intensities, the work capacity may be enhanced through a carbohydrate-rich diet, or hindered by a diet lacking in this macronutrient (Maughan & Poole, 1981; Jenkins *et al.*, 1993). According to various authors (Saltin & Karlsson, 1972; Bergstrom & Hultman, 1967; Bergstrom *et al.*, 1967; Hermansen *et al.*, 1967; Karlsson & Saltin, 1971, and Stepto *et al.*, 2001), at exercise intensities around 65–90% of the VO_2 max, the appearance of fatigue is directly related to the diminishment of muscular glycogen. Furthermore, Del

Castillo (1998a) considers that carbohydrates should constitute 50–70 per cent of the daily energy provision in the diets of endurance athletes. Today, the importance of a high carbohydrate diet during the 3 days prior to a competition has been demonstrated (Noakes, 1993), since it increases the glycogen reserves, directly improving physical performance.

When physical exercise is carried out for more than 45 minutes, it is preferable to have previously ingested foods containing 20 g of carbohydrates for each hour of exercise. Nevertheless, it may also be necessary to take in hydration during the physical activity itself, such as some form of liquid preparation containing 4–8 per cent glucose.

Prior to a competition, numerous studies (e.g. Brotherhood, 1984) recommend an easily digestible low-in-fat snack, containing a moderate level of carbohydrates, which should ideally be eaten 3–4 h beforehand.

Jimenez et al. (1998) offers a detailed description of certain foods with high and low carbohydrate contents (Table 1.3).

Table 1.3 The glucose contents of some foods

Food	Carbohydrate content (g per 100g)
Sugar	99.5
Rice	77.0
Pasta, semolina.	76.5
Honey, biscuits, flour, raisins	75.0
Dates	73.0
Jam	72.0
Chocolate	65.0
Beans	60.0
Chickpeas, lentils	58.0
White bread	55.0
Chestnuts	40.0
Peanuts	26.0
Bananas	20.0
Potatoes	19.0
Grapes, cherries	17.0
Peas	16.0
Hazelnuts, walnuts	15.0
Pears	14.0
Apples, peaches, pineapple	12.0
Plums, apricots, onions	10.0
Mandarins, oranges, carrots	9.0
Beetroot, Brussels sprouts	8.0
French beans, strawberries	7.0
Melon	6.5
Grapefruit	6.0
Mushrooms	4.0

Training induces changes in the enzymatic activity (above all, those related to glycogen synthesis), which assists the storage of muscular glycogen (Acheson *et al.*, 1998; Bloom *et al.*, 1987), and provokes an increase in energy resources, principally employed in high-intensity physical efforts. Therefore, given their better-developed enzymatic systems, athletes engaged in training regimes have a greater capacity to accumulate glycogen than non-athletes.

Figure 1.1

Lipids and fats   Lipids, principally energetic nutrients, have a variable chemical structure and are insoluble in water. In the human body, 95 per cent of these are *triglycerides* (the combination of a glycerol nucleus and three fatty acids). Depending on the length of their chain, fatty acids may be classified in the following manner: short chain (4–6 carbon atoms), medium chain (8–10 carbon atoms) and long chain (12 or more carbon atoms). These may then be divided into two groups, according to whether there are double links between the carbon atoms: saturated and unsaturated. If they present a double link, they are termed *monounsaturated fats* and if they comprise two or more double links, they are termed *polyunsaturated fats*. Saturated fats are solid or semi-solid and have a higher fusion point (they mainly originate from animals: egg yolk, margarine, lard); whilst unsaturated fats have a lower fusion point, meaning they are liquid at room temperature (they mainly originate from vegetable sources). Likewise, it is important to highlight the existence of fatty acids, which cannot be produced in the organism and therefore, must be provided by the diet. The essential fatty acids are: *alpha-linolenic* and *linoleic*.

In addition to triglycerides, other substances have similar characteristics, but contain phosphor, nitrogen or glucides (combined lipids: phosphor-lipids, lecithin/ pectin, glucolipids and sterols).

Fats constitute an important energy source (9 kcal/g). Moreover, they are a vital part of the human diet, since they contain essential fatty acids, a vehicle for ingesting liposoluble vitamins. Some of these fatty acids, such as cholesterol, are precursors of hormones. In addition to carbohydrates, fats represent the principal source of energy during prolonged exercise, although their mobilization is much slower. The organism has three forms of depositing fats: in the fatty tissues, in the intermuscular areas and in the circulating triglycerides.

For sportspeople engaged in a high-intensity training regime, fats should not constitute more than 25 per cent of total calorie intake, and saturated fatty acids should not surpass 10 per cent of total calorie intake, in order to avoid hypercholesterolemias (Williams, 1995). Moreover, it is recommended that the intake of cholesterol is limited to around 300 mg/day.

Taking supplements containing medium-chain triglycerides, in order to save carbohydrates, has been proved useless and even damaging, failing to improve the use of fatty acids; this favours weight loss in strength sports.

Resistance training induces a metabolic adaptation, tending towards an increase in the oxidation of triglycerides, hence reserving carbohydrates.

Table 1.4 details a series of commonly consumed foods and their corresponding fat contents expressed in percentages (Jiménez et al., 1998).

Regarding plasmatic lipids, it is widely recognised that regular exercise (training) significantly increases the levels of high-density lipoprotein (HDL) cholesterol when an individual carries out moderate to intense training sessions (Durstine & Haskell, 1994; Elwood et al., 1993; Lakka & Salonen, 1992; Word et al., 1988). Likewise, habitual exercise induces beneficial effects on cardiovascular health.

Proteins   Proteins are formed by amino acids, molecules containing carbon, hydrogen, oxygen and nitrogen (Wooton, 1988). Since amino acids are necessary for synthesizing hormones, enzymes and antibodies, as well as assisting in growth processes and the development of organs and tissues, they may be considered an essential element in any diet. Human life is not possible without proteins. They constitute

Table 1.4   The fat contents of some foods

Food	Fat content (per 100g)
Butter	83.0
Vegetable margarine	83.5
Egg yolk	33.0
Cream	30.0
Pork	16.0
Eggs	12.0
Ox meat	7.4
Full-fat milk	3.9
Chicken	3.0

the basic substrata of any living cell and are responsible for a diverse range of functions, such as transporting oxygen and hydrogen, or the formation of contractile material in the muscles, etc. As with fats, there are a series of amino acids that the organism is unable produce naturally, and which must be consumed through the diet. These are therefore denominated essential amino acids (isoleucine, leucine, lysine, methionine, phenylalanine, threotine, tryptophan and valine). Others, although generated in the organism, do not reach sufficient quantities (arginine and histidine), and must also be provided by the diet, since a lack of these substances can provoke diverse neurological disorders: spasms, altered muscular coordination, atrophies, developmental disorders in some organs – such as the liver or the testicles – or alteration to growth patterns, etc. (Muñoz & López Meseguer, 1998).

Figure 1.2

Adults require approximately 0.8–1.0 g/kg of weight a day of proteins, in order to compensate for daily losses. Nevertheless, athletes generally require a higher protein input compared to more sedentary individuals. In strength and speed athletes, these requirements rise to 1.2–2.0 g/kg a day; whilst in endurance sports, this amount is in the region of 1.2–1.4 g/kg, reaching figures of around 1.5–2.0 g/kg

Table 1.5   Foods with elevated protein contents

Food	Protein contents (per100 g)
Chicken	26.0 g
Lentils	24.0 g
Prawns	22.0 g
Lean meat, cheese	21.5 g
Cold meat	21.0 g
Almonds	20.5 g
Chickpeas, tuna, liver	20.0 g
Beans	19.5 g
Salmon	19.0 g
Squid	18.0 g
Anchovies	17.0 g
Hake	16.0 g
Sole, cereals	15.0 g
Walnuts	13.5 g
Eggs	13.0 g
Pasta	12.0 g
Brown bread	9.0 g
White bread, condensed milk	8.5 g
Rice	8.0 g
Milk	3.5 g

Source: Muñoz & López Meseguer (1998).

when training sessions last for more than 3h, or in ultra-resistance competitions (Ecónomos *et al.*, 1993). Expressed in terms of total calorie intake, proteins should constitute 15 per cent, reaching 20 per cent in strength and speed athletes. Daily intakes exceeding 2–2.5 g/kg, so common in bodybuilding, do not appear to provoke an increase in body mass nor muscular strength (Lemon, 1995), although adequate strength training would serve this purpose (Girard, 2000; Roy *et al.*, 2000). Moreover, such an elevated protein intake could potentially lead to altered calcium levels, as well as hepatic and kidney overload.

The oxidation of proteins provides 3–18 per cent of the energy consumed during prolonged physical effort (Decombaz *et al.*, 1979), especially once glycogen reserves have been used up.

Table 1.5 contains some common foods containing elevated protein content per 100 g.

1.3.2 Micronutrients

Micronutrients comprise vitamins and minerals. Their main functions are regulatory and they provide no energetic value. In developed countries, the majority of micronutrients are met through the diet, although some situations demanding higher intakes (sport, pregnancy . . .) can produce deficiencies. Consequently, the use of vitamin and mineral supplements amongst sportspeople is very common.

Vitamins   Vitamins are organic substances required by the organism in very small amounts in order to carry out specific functions. The discovery of the 13 essential vitamins for the organism culminated in 1941 with the recognition of folic acid as being essential (Bässler *et al.*, 2002).

Vitamins are usually classified as fat-soluble or water-soluble. Fat-soluble vitamins include vitamins A, D, E and K. These are stored in body tissues, principally in the liver, and excessive intakes can produce cellular damage in the liver, kidneys and heart. Water-soluble vitamins include the B group vitamins and vitamin C. These are not stored within the body and in the case of excessive ingestion can usually be eliminated through the urine. However, if the organism is unable to eliminate the B group vitamins, an overload can lead to numbness, altered movement or even limb paralysis; and in the case of vitamin C, the consequences may include gastroenteritis, diarrhoea, colitis and kidney stones.

An adequate and varied diet should cover all the body's vitamin requirements. Nevertheless, in certain circumstances, such as defective absorption, or excessive expenditure, vitamin deficiencies may appear, provoking negative effects on sports performance. Therefore, in some cases, an increased ingestion of vitamins is justified, whether this implies altering the diet or complementing it with vitamin supplements. For example, in weight division sports (wrestling, horse riding, etc.), or those requiring low weight for successful performance (gymnastics, dancing, etc.), it may become necessary to complement the normal diet with extra vitamin supplements. Moreover, given their important role in producing haemoglobin and red blood cells, a combined iron and vitamin C supplement may be required by female athletes who suffer from heavy menstruation (vitamin C facilitates the absorption of iron into the body).

Table 1.6 describes the fat-soluble and water-soluble vitamins, the body's daily vitamin requirements, and the foods rich in each (Arnhein, 1994).

The consumption of certain vitamins may prove insufficient for some elite sportspeople (Burke & Read 1993; Mataix 1992), who suffer more easily from the most common vitamin deficits than the non-sporting population. The most widespread deficiency is a lack of the B group vitamins, especially in low-calorie diets (Delgado, 1998). Administering vitamin supplements has not yet been proved to improve physical performance (Burke & Read 1993; Williams 1995). Nevertheless, a lack of any vitamin almost certainly heeds sports performance (principally vitamin B1 and vitamin C) (Belko *et al.*, 1983).

Minerals   Around 5–6 per cent of the organism is made up of minerals. The main dietary mineral elements may be classified in two groups:

- *Macronutrients*: calcium, magnesium and phosphorus. These must be ingested on a daily basis in relatively large amounts.

Table 1.6 Vitamin requirements and corresponding food sources

Fat-soluble vitamins	Requirements	Food sources
A Pro-vitamin A (β carotene) Vitamin: Retinol	Male adult: 1000 µg Female adult: 800 µg Children:400–1000 µg	Liver, cream, butter, whole milk, egg yola, green and yellow vegetables, yellow fruit, enriched margarine
D Pro-vitamins: ergosterol, 7-dehydrocholesterol Vitamins: D2 and D3	5–10 µg	Enriched milk, enriched margarine fish oils, sunlight on the skin
E Tocopherol	Adults: 8–10 mg Children: 3–10 mg	Vegetable oils
K K1 K2 K3	Adults: 65–80 µg Children: 15–65 µg	Cheese, egg yolk, liver, green leafy vegetables

Water-soluble vitamins	Requirements	Food sources
Thiamine (B1)	1.1–1.5 mg	Pork, beef, liver, whole or integral seeds, pulses
Riboflavin (B2)	1.2–1.7 mg	Milk, liver, pulses, fruits
Niacin (nicoinic acids, nicotinamide), vitamin B3	15–19 mg	Meat, peanuts, integral cereals
Vitamin B5	4–7 mg	Liver, eggs, milk, integral cereals
Vitamin B6	1.6–2.0 mg	Corn, wheat, meat, liver, eggs, fish
Biotin, vitamin B8	30–100 µg	Egg yolk, liver, meat and fish
Folic acid – B9-	Adults: 150–180 µg Children: 50–180 µg	Liver, green leafy vegetables
Vitamin B12	2.0 µg	Liver, meat, dairy products, eggs, cheese
Ascorbic acid (vitamin C)	60 mg	Citrus fruits, vegetables

Source: Arnhein (1994).

- *Micronutrients* or *oligoelements*: iron, iodine, cobalt, copper, fluoride, manganese, and zinc. These elements are required in much smaller quantities.

- *Electrolytes*: including sodium (Na^+), potassium (K^+) and chlorine (Cl^-).

- *Trace elements*: these exist, and are required, in tiny quantities, e.g. selenium, molybdenum.

Iron plays a vital role in maintaining the system responsible for transporting oxygen around the body and assists the body's capacity to conduct muscular work. It is the most commonly lacking mineral in the diet of the general population, especially amongst women. Anaemia, produced through an iron deficiency, the most frequent in female athletes, has negative repercussions on physical performance (Hinton *et al.*, 2000), particularly in resistance activities (Malczewska *et al.*, 2000). Various factors contribute to an iron deficiency and a reduction in haemoglobin levels in athletes, including: profuse sweating, abundant menstrual flow, reduced iron absorption in the digestive system, an increase in the destruction of red blood cells due to mechanical trauma, low iron consumption, etc. It is important to highlight a true anaemia termed *pseudo-anaemia*, shown by some athletes (Newhouse & Clement, 1990), which is caused by an increase in plasma volume linked to physical activity itself. On the other hand, when there is an iron deficiency (inadequate intake and absorption), it becomes important to boost iron levels through the diet, and when this measure proves insufficient, with iron supplements under medical supervision.

Another important element is calcium. The human body contains approximately 1200 g of calcium, of which 99 per cent forms part of the skeletal system and 1 per cent is contained in intra- and extracellular fluids. This small proportion represents the metabolically available reserve. As with iron, when calcium intake is reduced, the plasma levels are maintained at the expense of a reduced absorption rate into the bones. Hence, the plasma levels are never a true indicator of the state of calcium reserves. During physical exercise, calcium plays an important role in muscular contraction. Its intake depends on the diet, the consumption of calcium-rich foods, as well as the total energy and nutrient intake. Although physical exercise has a stimulating effect on bone mineral density, female athletes with low-energy diets or those engaged in weight loss programmes can suffer amenorrhoea and low bone density, accompanied by an increased risk of stress fractures (Beshgetoor *et al.*, 2000).

1.3.3 Water

Water is the main component of the human body, constituting 50–70 per cent of total body weight (2/3 intracellular water and 1/3 extracellular water). It is the principal substance in metabolic processes (it transports oxygen, nutrients, and hormones; assists the dissipation of internal heat, determines arterial tension and the cardiovascular function). A decrease in body water of just 20 per cent can cause death (Delgado *et al.*, 1999). In order to maintain the daily balance of water in the organism, intake should be equivalent to loss. A daily liquid intake of 1 ml per calorie spent is recommendable (Del Castillo, 1998a). For example, if an individual spends 3000 kcal/day, the suggested water intake is 3 litres.

During physical exercise, and especially in conditions of extreme heat, the body protects itself from overheating through the evaporation of sweat. During this process, a large quantity of liquids and electrolytes are lost, more so in humid atmospheres, and in order to avoid dehydration, athletes must replace these through the consumption of water, juices or isotonic and hypotonic drinks. The quantity of liquid lost through sweating can range from hundreds of millilitres to over 2 litres per hour. In competition, high-resistance athletes, such as those participating in ultra-marathons, present the most significant weight loss through dehydration (Noakes *et al.*, 1988). However, playing other sports such as football can also produce significant liquid losses (Maughan & Leiper, 1994). The degree of liquid reduction depends on various factors: age, sex, climate and acclimatization, level of training, exercise intensity, and body surface area (the number of active sweat glands).

Dehydration increases the muscle temperature, which in turn increases the use of glucose in the muscles, favouring a reduction in the generation of free fatty acids (González-Alonso *et al.*, 1997). Body temperatures above 41°C can cause death.

The effects of advanced dehydration (−4 per cent of body weight) cause the lactic threshold to appear prematurely at lower exercise intensities, accelerating the appearance of fatigue (Kenefick *et al.*, 2002). However, despite this being common knowledge, a recent study (Gonzalez-Gross *et al.*, 2001) showed that approximately 32% of athletes do not drink anything at all during training sessions.

Figure 1.3

The more evident symptoms of dehydration, such as having a dry mouth, appear once 3% of fluids have been lost; a fluid loss of 4 per cent produces a 20–30 per cent reduction in physical capacity (Greenleaf, 1992). Nonetheless, an adequate liquid intake in athletes engaged in training or competition serves to prevent the emergence of dehydration-related fatigue (Sawka *et al.*, 1984). Based on these facts, the following guidelines are recommended before, during and after a competition (modified from American College of Sports Medicine (ACSM), 2000):

- Two hours beforehand: drink 500 ml of water, isotonic drinks or juices.

- 5–10 minutes beforehand: drink 200 ml of water.

- During: for competitions lasting less than an hour, the fluid intake rhythm should be 200 ml per 15–20 minutes; in competitions lasting 1–1.5 hours, 150 ml per 15 min; and in competitions lasting over 3 hours, 200 ml per 20 min. The composition of the liquid ingested should include 0.5–0.7 g/litre of sodium, and 1.1 g of carbohydrates per kg of body weight, per hour.

- Whenever possible, the liquid ingested should contain 5–7.5 per cent carbohydrates per 100 ml of water, since they have a similar gastric emptying rhythm to water (Epstein & Armstrong, 1999; McArthur & Feldman 1989; Maughan & Noakes, 1991; Maughan, 1993; Taylor *et al.*, 1999).

- The temperature of the drink should be cold (between 7 and 13°C)

- Liquids should be consumed before the sensation of thirst appears, in order to maintain hydration.

- Immediately after each competition it is advisable to drink 500 ml of water, or a carbohydrate-rich drink (isotonic drink or diluted juices), continuing with 250 ml every 15 min. The quantity of liquid consumed should equal the weight loss produced through exercise.

- Post-competition hydration can be improved by consuming foods rich in water (fruit, vegetables, salads, soups).

Specialists affirm that an adequate pre-competition diet does not compensate for an inadequate one during the prolonged training process (USOC, 1998). Therefore, athletes must be nutritionally aware and maintain these basic 'nutritional rules' throughout the training cycle, not just prior to an important competition.

1.4   Ergogenic aids

Ergonic assistance is defined as any method (nutritional, physical, mechanical, psychological or pharmaceutical) used to improve the body's capacity to carryout a determined physical effort or to enhance overall sports performance (McArdle *et al.*, 1991). In competitive sport, involving heavy training and competitive workloads, it is logical for athletes to use legal and harmless ergogenic aids to counteract the potential nutritional deficiencies produced through such intensive physical efforts. However, this should always be done under medical supervision. Nevertheless, in recreational sport, a balanced and varied diet, sufficient in calories and nutrients, should be enough to cover the additional demands of physical activity. Approximately 50 per cent of the general population have reported taking some form of dietary supplements, while 76 to 100 per cent of athletes in some sports are reported to use them (Ahrendt, 2001).

With the exception of caffeine, creatine, sodium bicarbonate, carbohydrates and the correct hydration in situations of caloric stress, few nutritional supplements have been proved to be effective (Burke *et al.*, 2000). Moreover, the World Anti-Doping Agency (WADA) prohibits none of the aforementioned substances.

Creatine is a combination of amino acids and is found in animal food sources. Additional intake and the organism's own capacity to produce creatine serve to replenish the body's phosphor-creatine reserves (95 per cent in the muscular cells). A supplement of 20–25 g per day, during 5–7 days, has been proved to effectively increase the amount of creatine in the muscles (Maughan, 1995, Kreider *et al.*, 1998), as well as improving performance in short intermittent physical effort (Balsom *et al.*, 1993; Greenhaff, 1995). Its most common side effect is fluid retention, frequently causing body weight to rise by 1–3 kg. Juhn (2003) indicates that creatine is ergogenic in repetitive anaerobic cycling sprints but not in running or swimming.

Caffeine is a methylxanthine, which produces stimulating effects on the central nervous system, increasing an individual's alertness (Clarkson, 1993). An additional supplement of 3–9 mg/kg does not produce any noticeable side effects, except in cases of gastrointestinal intolerance. What is more, caffeine produces the following ergogenic effects: greater resistance to fatigue (Graham and Spriet, 1991; Spriet 1995), enhanced performance in certain aerobic activities (Juhn, 2003) and in short sports events (Wiles *et al.*, 1992). In sports carried out in hot conditions, it is important to consider the diuretic effects of caffeine. Positive effects may be noted on performance by taking a dose of 1.4–2.7 mg of caffeine per 0.453 kg, 1–2 h prior to the physical effort. Therefore, a 79 kg man will need 245 to 472 mg of caffeine. This level can be obtained by drinking 680 g of tea or two cups of coffee (Michela, 2007). Caffeine is found naturally in chocolate, coffee, and tea, and is frequently added to foods such as soft drinks (Table 1.7).

Table 1.7 The average amount of caffeine in beverages

Beverage	Average caffeine (mg)
Coffee, brewed, drip method, 8 ounces (0.24 l)	165
Coffee, instant, 8 ounces (0.24 l)	95
Tea, 10 ounces brewed (0.30 l)	80–120
Iced tea, 12 ounces (0.35 l)	70
Hot cocoa, 8 ounces (0.24 l)	5
Diet Pepsi	35
Pepsi Cola	40
Coca-Cola	45
Diet Coke	45

Source: Michela (2007).

Given its capacity to neutralise the pH of lactic acid, sodium bicarbonate is used in high intensity physical effort lasting 1–10 min, which produce high quantities of this substance in the muscles (Bouissou *et al.*, 1988; Matson & Tran, 1993). Some of the mild side effects, such as diarrhoea or nausea, can be avoided by using sodium citrate (McNaughton & Cedaro, 1992).

Other ergogenic aids, whose benefits have not been proved scientifically, include: amino acids, arginine, ornithine and lysine, as well as antioxidants and hydroxyl-methyl-butyrate. A wide range of supplements, which have not been scientifically tested, are freely available, such as ginseng, chromium picolinate, carnitine, coenzyme Q10, inosine, or medium-chain triglycerides (Burke *et al.*, 2000). In order to avoid the abusive use of these legal substances, which on rare occasions contain illegal ingredients, such as hormones and/or precursors of anabolic steroid hormones, athletes should always follow the guidance of a sports doctor and/or nutritionist, who is fully aware of their nutritional requirements and is qualified to recommend the use of such ergogenic aids.

1.5   The need for nutritional information for athletes

In many cases, the much-needed nutritional control for athletes is non-existent. Along the road to high performance, athletes adapt their diets according to the 'advice' they acquire from the sporting context itself, which as will be seen in the corresponding chapter, is not always adequate. Nutritional guidance is vital to prevent eating disorders, and coaches and parents should know it (Gilbert, 2005).

Figure 1.4

Nutritional guidance is absolutely necessary throughout an athlete's sports career, even more so once submitted to the demands of elite competition, where careless-ness in the nutritional aspect can be enough to provoke periods of low performance. Therefore, it is recommended that coaches, who usually constitute the main refer-ence point for athletes (given the lack of economic resources in the majority of cases), have the adequate knowledge of the basic nutritional requirements of their athletes, applying it accordingly and consulting with the relevant professionals where necessary.

In a previous study (Dosil, 2003), a survey was conducted with nine of the most practised sporting disciplines in Europe, in which athletes were asked about the degree of nutritional information they had received throughout their sports career. The results of this survey are detailed in Table 1.8.

In general terms, and in light of these results, the lack of nutritional information in the majority of sports may be highlighted. Two-thirds of the sportspeople sur-veyed had not received any information about nutritional aspects, a worrying sta-tistic considering how important it is for athletes to follow an adequate diet. This apparent shortfall of information is similar to that encountered by Dosil (2000) in a survey with 267 athletes participating in aerobics, athletics, basketball, judo, physi-cal conditioning, rugby and taekwondo. This study showed how 56.8 per cent of subjects claimed to have received no nutritional guidance of any sort. Focusing further on the results in Table 1.8, it may be noted that rhythmic gymnastics obtained the worst results in terms of nutrition-related guidance. This result proves somewhat contradictory to the participatory predominance of very young athletes, in a sport characterised by its strict aesthetic criteria, which provokes a tendency towards eating disorders. Other sporting disciplines such as athletics, basketball, bodybuilding or swimming also present some elevated results, reflecting a more general lack of information. Nevertheless, in those cases where athletes had received some form of nutritional guidance, it is important to identify where this came from. Dosil (2000) forms the following conclusions:

Table 1.8 The degree of nutritional information received by athletes in different sports

Sport	No information received (%)	Information received at some point (%)
Football	58.7	41.3
Swimming	69.2	30.8
Judo/wrestling	62.7	32.8
Aerobics	59.1	40.9
Athletics	72.5	27.5
Basketball	72.1	27.9
Rhythmic gymnastics	79.2	20.8
Body building	77.8	22.2
Rowing/canoeing	50	50
Total	66.8	33.2

- In all of the sports studied, the coach/monitor provides the most nutritional guidance to athletes. Sherman *et al.* (2005) support this statement, indicating how the coach plays a fundamental role in identifying and managing athletes with disordered eating.

- Doctors/nutritionists are not usually active in grass-roots sport, and few athletes resolve their nutritional doubts with the help of the adequate professionals.

- Families (parents and siblings) have more influence over eating habits in fitness sports such as aerobics, whilst in other disciplines; it is the coach who provides the most nutritional guidance.

- Although relatively low, other individuals/sources appear to have some influence over athletes' nutrition: books, television, the Internet, partners, psychologists, conferences, etc.

1.6 Conclusions

Together with physical, technical and psychological capabilities, nutrition is fundamental for adequate sports performance. The incorporation of nutritionists and/or sports doctors in teams and clubs, and the consequent elaboration of personalised diets, would constitute an important achievement, undoubtedly improving the health of athletes and increasing their performance.

Advances in physical activity and sports science have brought to light a series of conditioning aids, which have lacked the deserved recognition in the past. Old beliefs, still rife in some sectors of sport, that defend the principle that what makes athletes perform better is hard work and physical repetition, have been dismissed, opening the doors to new concepts of more integrated training methods.

Specialists in this field agree that in order to reach peak performance, an exhaustive multi-faceted preparation is required. The degree of professionalism in sport is increasing, demanding more hours of competition preparation. Part of this process includes so-called 'invisible training', which refers to the variables affecting and complementing physical training. Hence, nutrition, rest, or social relationships, etc. have been proved to have a direct effect on training and competition performance. Therefore, it is imperative for athletes and coaches alike to attend to these aspects, increasing their awareness where relevant and avoiding the potential consequences of neglecting them.

Inadequate diets or eating-related disorders negatively affect sports performance and what is worse, the lives of athletes. Informing about these issues, with a view to preventing and eradicating these problems, represents the ultimate aim of this publication.

2 The Importance of Weight in Some Sports

Joaquín Dosil and Olga Díaz

Both as a taekwondoka and a coach, I have followed various diets. During the months prior to a competition, I normally went on special diets to lose enough kilos so I could compete in the weight division I considered best for me. Taekwondokas in heavyweight divisions generally try to lose weight by burning excess fat, whilst those in lightweight divisions prefer to sacrifice muscular fibre rather than fat. In the latter case, it's much more difficult to maintain the desired weight.

Each weight division spans 4 kilos. Coaches tend to study the individual possibilities of each taekwondoka, according to their physical characteristics, selecting the most adequate weight division. If a taekwondoka stands out more for his/her speed than for his/her strength, then we'd generally consider maintaining the same category or dropping down a division. So, we normally employ two types of diets: gradual diets and express diets. Initially, nutritionists and sports doctors guide gradual diets over a prolonged period of time, eliminating those foods that cause weight gain. On the other hand, express diets aim to lose a specific quantity of weight quickly, often employing hyper-protein regimes, combined with special supplements. These express diets frequently provoke serious health problems. We don't recommend that these diets are maintained for more than two or three weeks, since they can cause excess cholesterol and uric acid. Other classic weight loss methods include the sauna, exercising in plastic clothing to induce sweating, laxatives or vomiting. The most commonly used methods are plastic clothing, saunas and fasting, in order to lose the necessary 2 or 3 kilos to compete in a lower weight division; laxatives or vomiting are less frequent. I would like to highlight that this type of diet diminishes a competitor's physical capacity, perhaps even becoming counteractive. The ideal scenario is to conduct a study of each individual athlete and apply a balanced diet in the long term'.

Taekwondo Coach

Eating Disorders in Athletes   Joaquín Dosil
© 2008 John Wiley & Sons, Ltd

2.1   Introduction

Sports nutrition has gained a more important role in recent years. Advances in the field of sports medicine have allowed athletes to attain better results, partly thanks to the exhaustive control over their nutritional requirements.

In certain sports, weight and its relation to nutrition, are especially important. This chapter deals precisely with these sporting disciplines, focussing on the risks and consequences of inadequate nutrition and weight control.

Depending on the sport, body mass becomes more or less important. In many cases, adequate nutritional assessment and guidance on behalf of coaches would prove sufficient to avoid problems in this domain. Nevertheless, there is a notable lack of information and training in nutritional matters in the sports world, which frequently translates into to weight-related 'problems' in certain disciplines. What is more, from a very young age and without any form of related knowledge, it is not uncommon to come across athletes carrying out drastic dietary measures in order to please their coaches, parents and teammates.

Body weight is a matter concerning the majority of elite athletes. In this respect, Guthie (1986) – quoted by Swoap and Murphy (1995) – surveyed a group of 384 athletes from various universities, questioning them about their reasons for wanting to lose weight. The following conclusions were formed:

Athletes want to lose weight because:

- it is essential to execute peak performances

- it is necessary for the aesthetic beauty ideals valued in certain sports

- they are influenced by weight-related comments from technical staff

- it allows them to compete in a lower weight category.

The results of this study reflect the importance of weight control in sport. Depending on the speciality in question, it becomes increasingly or decreasingly relevant. The following section describes those sports, in which the influence of weight is extremely high. Therefore, these disciplines have been denominated 'high-risk' sports in terms of eating disorders. The second part of the chapter details the most commonly used weight loss methods in sport, analysing a survey carried out with athletes from so-called 'high-risk' disciplines; and the final section distinguishes between 'real weight', 'ideal weight' and 'sports weight'.

2.2   High-risk sports

In high-risk sports, maintaining a specific weight or being thin is a principal factor of peak performance, requiring athletes to constantly monitor this aspect. In these disciplines, the pressure to lose weight is such that athletes are at greater risk of developing eating related disorders compared to other sports. Coaches and professionals working with athletes play a fundamental role in the prevention and development of such disorders, making it essential that they are informed of the risks involved in the sporting disciplines they manage.

Based on the given definition of high-risk sports and following the criteria stipulated by the United States Olympic Committee (USOC, 1998), the following classification is presented (Table 2.1).

In *aesthetic sports*, the physical appearance of participants is fundamental and forms part of the judges' point-scoring criteria. The predominant body types sought within female disciplines share some common characteristics: pronounced thinness, long and toned legs, a small bust and thin hips. Bachner-Melman *et al.* (2006) studied the symptoms and personality profiles of female athletes in aesthetic sports and their relation to eating disorders. The results showed that whilst most of the athletes displayed excellent psychological health, one subgroup revealed signs of non-specified eating disorders (see Chapter 4) and did not appear to receive the appropriate treatment. On the other hand, males generally desire a different body type, reflecting muscularity and elasticity. Nevertheless, in either case, nutrition and weight control play an important role, on many occasions becoming cause for concern. In these sports, it is necessary for coaches to regularly monitor their athletes' weight, informing them when they need to shed a kilo or two. Therefore, to avoid problems, they must be capable of expressing the facts with appropriate messages, achieving the correct weight objectives without provoking the use of pathological weight loss methods. Adequate daily nutrition, guided by specialists, along with an objective evaluation of how to maintain the ideal weight for the sporting discipline in question, are key factors in the prevention of eating disorders.

Table 2.1 Classification of high-risk sports

Type of sport	Description of the sport	Examples of sporting disciplines
Aesthetic sports	Sports in which the required bodily aesthetics demand thinness	Rhythmic and artistic gymnastics, ice-skating, dance, etc.
Weight division sports	Sports in which athletes' weight determines the category they compete in	Judo, boxing, wrestling, etc.
Gym sports	Sports pursuing muscular development and/or a reduction in body fat	Bodybuilding, aerobics, fitness, etc.
Endurance sports and low weight performance sports	Sports demanding resistance and a thin body to reach peak performance	Athletics (middle-distance and distance), cycling, swimming, horse racing, motorcycling, etc.

Figure 2.1

Weight division sports are also considered high risk. For several decades now, athletes in certain sports regularly lose weight rapidly prior to a contest, in order to compete in a division below their natural weight, believing that facing lighter opponents will make winning easier (Swoap & Murphy, 1995). For this purpose, they turn to 'express diets' involving significant periods of fasting, to lose several kilos prior to competition weigh-ins. Following the competition, they may indulge in uncontrolled ingestion or 'binge-eating'. With this fast–binge system, athletes lose and subsequently regain considerable quantities of weight during competition periods. Needless to say, this rapid weight loss entails physiological risks. One study conducted at Ithaca College (USA) demonstrated the potential neurological problems of athletes who submit their bodies to drastic weight oscillations in such short spaces of time, which include the loss of short-term memory, for example. These physiological risks should serve as a dissuader to athletes competing in weight division sports. Once again, adequate and structured nutrition throughout the competitive season allows athletes to maintain an appropriate weight for a determined category. Along these lines, coaches, together with sports psychologists and nutritionists can programme an eating and weight control system, with which athletes can perceive that they are constantly working towards peak performance.

The third type of high-risk sports includes those specialities practised in the gym setting. Within this group of disciplines, we must highlight a fast growing problem known as *muscle dysmorphia, bigorexia* or *Adonis complex* (Pope *et al.*, 2002). Typically, those suffering this disorder are male gym-users, with an almost obsessive concern for muscular development. Muscle dysmorphia is a type of body dysmorphic disorder in which individuals develop a pathological preoccupation with their muscularity (Olivardia *et al.*, 2000). Their primary objective is to attain a perfectly sculptured body, not only leading to bigorexia, but also other associated disorders such as anxiety, depression and certain forms of addiction. Bodybuilders (Goldfield *et al.*, 2006) and weightlifters (Hildebrandt *et al.*, 2006; Choi *et al.*, 2002) display the highest prevalence of muscle dysmorphia and problems related to body image and eating. Similarly, the typical environment surrounding general keep-fit activities, such as step or body-jump, which urge participants (mostly female) to become more concerned about their figure and weight, may increase the risks of eating disorders (Dosil & Díaz, 2002). Moreover, the beauty ideals of today's society revolve around the need for a slender body, encouraging participation in gym-based activities, such as fitness classes. Consequently, it would be a step forward to introduce nutritional assessors and specialist psychologists into this setting, assisting gym-goers to participate in fitness activities without compromising their sense of well-being, and perhaps more importantly, minimizing the risks of potential eating-related disorders.

Figure 2.2

Endurance sports and disciplines in which increased weight does not help per- formance constitute the fourth type of high-risk sports. Broadly speaking, in these specialities, the lower an athlete's weight the greater the sports performance. For example, in horse racing or motorcycling, jockeys and riders must maintain the lowest weight possible, allowing them to reach higher speeds. The characteristics of these disciplines, along with the desire to win, lead numerous sportspeople to resort to extreme diets or weight-loss methods during competitive periods. This concern for weight is also rife in endurance sports. Athletes from these disciplines, such as long-distance running or cycling, often turn to strict diets, since the loss of body fat equates to better performances. Various studies have dealt with this aspect; for example, Hulley and Hill (2001), examined the presence of eating disorder syn- dromes in elite female distance runners (track, road, cross-country, and fell/moun- tain running) in the United Kingdom. Nevertheless, on many occasions, not only do athletes lose body fat, but also body mass, which is not maintained when the weight loss is very fast. This reduction in body mass can prove counteractive during heavy training sessions. When weight loss surpasses certain limits, athletes no longer receive the necessary quantity of nutrients, causing diminished performance, per- sistent fatigue and increased injury-recovery time (Barbany, 2002). Therefore, in endurance sports, it is important to consider the advice provided in Chapter 1. A nutritionist (or coach) can develop an appropriate dietary plan for each individual athlete, based on his/her constitution and training/competition workload, translat- ing these requirements into daily mealtimes.

2.3 Weight loss methods in sport

When it comes to performance, the prevailing principle for many athletes is 'the thinner, the better'. This belief often leads sportspeople to employ inadequate weight loss methods in an attempt to reduce body fat, despite the fact that medical studies have yet to demonstrate a clear relationship between thinness and improved per- formance. Byrne and McLean (2002) examined the importance of such pressure to be thin, discovering that athletes competing in sports that emphasise the value of a thin body shape or a low body weight are particularly vulnerable to developing eating disorders.

The most commonly used weight loss methods are usually dealt with in most texts referring to eating disorders in athletes (ANRED, 2007; Davis & Cowles, 1989; Garner & Garfinkel, 1979; USOC, 1998; etc.). However, generally speaking, the most frequently employed techniques include:

- thermal methods: sauna or covering oneself in plastic material

- laxatives and diuretics

- vomiting

- fasting

- fluid restriction
- slimming pills
- excessive physical exercise.

The weight-loss method employed depends on the objectives an athlete seeks. In some sports, such as judo, taekwondo or wrestling, athletes require rapid weight-loss methods prior to competition weigh-ins, which determine the category they can compete in. Along these lines, Alderman *et al.* (2004) indicate that excessive running, using saunas, and wearing vapour-impermeable suits were cited as the most commonly used methods to achieve rapid weight loss. In other disciplines, such as rhythmic gymnastics, running or gym-based activities (aerobics, step, etc.), the weight-loss methods employed are not aimed towards a rapid weight reduction, but intend to maintain a low weight over a prolonged period of time.

The different types of weight loss techniques can prove detrimental to an athlete's health, provoking a series of physical or psychological complications. Rankin (2002) states that athletes who use drastic food or fluid restriction to lose weight may experience negative consequences, including the loss of lean tissue, hormonal disturbances and performance impairment. In the majority of cases, such physical difficulties disappear if the lost weight is recovered and the individual resumes healthy eating habits. What is more, rapid weight reduction can also cause mental problems, which may negatively affect the competition following a weigh-in. In a study with 43 judokas, Yoshioka *et al.* (2006) examined the mood responses before and after weight reduction, finding significant mood changes that can negatively affect competition performance. This investigation coincides with that of Degoutte *et al.* (2006), which concluded that the combination of energy restriction and intense exercise training before a competition, have adverse affects on an athlete's physiology and psychology and impair physical performance.

Figure 2.3

Regarding the diversity of weight loss methods used, and their relation to sporting disciplines, a study conducted by the United States Olympic Committee (1998) produced the following results:

- In weight division sports, such as karate or judo, the use of plastic clothing is the most commonly used weight loss method (73 per cent). The other weight loss methods are distributed in the following manner: fluid retention (71 per cent), sauna (63 per cent), fasting (52 per cent), laxatives (15 per cent), diuretics (13 per cent) and vomiting (13 per cent). NB: individuals may employ more than one method simultaneously.

- In so-called aesthetic sports (rhythmic gymnastics, synchronised swimming . . .), the predominant methods are slimming pills (17 per cent) and vomiting (20 per cent).

On the other hand, Rosen *et al.* (1986) conducted a study with 182 female athletes aged between 17 and 23 years, finding that 25 per cent continuously used slimming pills, 16 per cent consumed laxatives and 14 per cent used vomiting as their preferred weight loss method. In a later investigation, Rosen and Hough (1988) established that 62 per cent of all gymnasts used some form of pathogenic weight loss method: vomiting, laxatives/diuretics, fasting, slimming pills or liquid retention.

In order to identify which weight-loss methods are most frequently used in high-risk sports and contrast the results against previous investigations, a study has been conducted with 256 athletes from both 'high-risk' and 'low-risk' disciplines (Table 2.2).

The obtained results are detailed in Table 2.3, and are then compared with those of similar studies in order to help clarify the most frequently used weight-loss methods and their repercussions on athletes.

Various conclusions may be formed from these results, allowing us to become more familiar with the use of weight-loss methods in different sports:

1. All of the weight-loss methods are used to some extent in the majority of sports, with the exception of vomiting, to which none of the subjects admitted using

Table 2.2 The sports selected for the study of weight-loss methods

Type of sport	Selected sporting disciplines
Aesthetic sports	Rhythmic gymnastics
Weight division sports	Judo/wrestling
Gym-based sports	Bodybuilding/aerobics.
Endurance sports and sports requiring low weight	Athletics (middle-distance/long-distance) and swimming
'Low-risk' sports	Football and basketball

Table 2.3 Weight loss methods used in different sports (*each subject may choose more than one method)

Weight loss method	High-risk sports					Low-risk sports		
	Rhythmic gymn.	Judo/wrestling	Body-building	Aerobics	Athletics	Swimming	Football	Basket
Fasting	4.2%	11.6%			2.2%		1.6%	5.7%
Eating less	29.2%	30.4%	16.7%	50%	29.7%	30.8%	9.5%	40%
Calorie restriction	33.3%	30.4%	50%	18.2%	22%	30.8%	17.5%	21.4%
Increased training	29.2%	44.9%	44.4%	54.5%	33%	30.8%	31.7%	42.9%
Fluid retention					1.1%			1.4%
Laxatives	4.2%	5.8%			2.2%			
Sauna		13%	16.7%	18.2%	1.1%		3.2%	10%
Plastic clothing	12.5%	14.5%			2.2%		6.3%	2.9%
Vomiting								
Slimming pills			5.6%					
Other	12.5%	1.4%	5.6%		2.2%			
None	41.7%	27.5%	22.2%	22.7%	51.6%	46.2%	53.22%	40%

(contradictory to other investigations; e.g. Rosen & Hough, 1988). Supposing that some subjects do employ this method and chose not to admit to it, it becomes feasible to hypothesise about the social stigma connected to vomiting and its relationship with eating disorders. Along these lines, it may be reasonable to presume that a proportion of the subjects falsify their results, so to maintain social desirability and avoid criticism.

2. Sauna is a widely accepted weight-loss method amongst the sporting population. Aerobics, bodybuilding and judo/wrestling participants most frequently employ this technique. This statistic may be explained by the fact that these specialities are normally practised within sports centres, where access to a sauna is likely. On the other hand, the nature of weight division sports, such as judo/wrestling (13 per cent), may explain the use of sauna in these disciplines. The 'pressure' to compete in an inferior weight category means athletes try to rapidly lose weight prior to competition weigh-ins. Dale and Landers (1999) confirmed these results, showing that in-season, athletes exert great weight control, but out of season, there are no significant differences between athletes and non-athletes. Therefore, the sauna, which reduces weight through the loss of bodily fluids, stands out as a likely candidate. Likewise, the sauna reduces the quantity of water in the skin, helping bodybuilders to accentuate the network of veins, so highly valued by judges (Yates, 1991).

3. Judokas/wrestlers most frequently use fasting as a weight-loss method (11.6 per cent). Combining this technique with the sauna constitutes the most popular method for losing weight quickly prior to weigh-ins. In a similar investigation, Kiningham and Gorenflo (2001) studied the weight-loss practices of 2532 wrestlers, obtaining the following results: 72 per cent of wrestlers engaged in at least one potentially harmful weight-loss method each week of the wrestling season; 52 per cent used at least two methods each week; and 12 per cent used at least five methods each week. Weekly use of laxatives, diet pills, or diuretics was reported by 2 per cent of wrestlers. Vomiting to lose weight was done at least once a week by 2 per cent of wrestlers. Wrestlers who engaged in at least one rapid weight loss method per week lost more weight, began wrestling at an earlier age, and reported more binge eating compared with wrestlers who did not report weekly rapid weight loss. The majority of wrestlers engaged in at least one potentially harmful weight loss method each week of the wrestling season. Fasting and various methods of dehydration were the primary methods of rapid weight loss. Wrestlers who lost weight each week were more likely to binge eat. Potentially harmful weight loss practices were found to be common at all levels of the sport.

4. In this study, only subjects from bodybuilding claimed to use slimming pills. Bodybuilding is a sport in which protein preparations and other substances are commonly used to increase muscular volume and reduce fat. Diuretics, which

Table 2.4 The most frequently used weight-loss method in each sport

Sport discipline	Weight-loss method
Rhythmic gymnastics	Calorie restriction (33.3%)
Judo/wrestling	Increased training (44.9%)
Bodybuilding	Calorie restriction (50%)
Aerobics	Increased training (54.5%)
Athletics	Increased training (33%)
Swimming	Eating less, calorie restriction and increased training (30.8%)
Football	Increased training (31.7%)
Basketball	Increased training (42.9%)

eliminate liquids from the body, also constitute slimming pills. In an important research investigation, Goldfield *et al.*, (2006) showed that 22.5 per cent of competitive male bodybuilders and 16 per cent of recreational male bodybuilders use laxatives and diuretics, but none resort to vomiting as a weight-loss method. It should also be highlighted that in both groups, 50–60 per cent employ vigorous exercise and strict dieting in order to rapidly lose weight.

5. All the sports analysed in this study present one predominant weight-loss method. Table 2.4 details the most commonly used technique in each discipline. As can be seen, three methods in particular stand out: increased training, calorie restriction and eating less.

6. Surprisingly, some 'low-risk' sports (football and basketball) produced high usage percentages in certain weight-loss methods. In the case of football, the majority are male players, employing weight-loss techniques to stay in shape. Basketball produced notable differences between male and female participants. Whilst male players do not employ any weight-loss methods, female players generated some high percentages, boosting the sport's overall result. This outcome may be explained by the fact that many female players take up basketball to lose weight through exercise.

2.4 The difference between 'real weight', 'ideal weight' and 'sports weight'

The general population can relate to two types of weight: 'real weight' and 'ideal weight'. *Real weight* is an individual's objective weight, that is to say, what a person weighs in reality. On the other hand, *ideal weight* is marked by a series of medical criteria, established in terms of height, sex, age and body constitution. However, it is important to indicate that the weights recommended by medical tables do not always correspond with what people *desire*. In other words, along with these medical criteria, other factors influence a person's ideal weight: beauty ideals, fashion, or peoples' perceptions of their own bodily image (this may be termed as 'ideal mental weight').

In sport however, another type of weight may be added to the equation: the *sports weight*, defined as the ideal weight for participating in a specific sporting discipline. In other words, it is the 'ideal' weight for a determined sport.

In order to understand the eating disorders that can potentially emerge in the sporting context, it is necessary to sufficiently comprehend these types of weight and how they relate to one another. In the majority of cases, an athlete's ideal weight does not correspond with the sports weight (e.g. in peak condition, a marathon athlete displays some excessively marked physical characteristics: protruding cheek bones, extremely thin arms and legs, something medical criteria would never recommend in normal circumstances, and perhaps somewhat aesthetically undesirable). Sometimes athletes seek sports weights that do not correspond with their physical constitution, age and sex (ideal weight), favouring the appearance of inadequate eating behaviours. Consequently, in some sports, it is easy to encounter athletes who, despite reflecting a physical aspect that favours peak performance in their discipline, are not in a good physical state.

Therefore, to discern the difference between real, ideal and sports weight, the following sections present the results of an investigation carried out with so-called high-risk sports (comparing the results with low-risk discipline). The objective of this study is to provide guidelines, highlighting the importance of identifying the real, ideal and sports weight of each individual athlete. Hence, the following sections compare the different types of weight, in order to examine the variations between each one.

2.4.1   Ideal weight vs. real weight

The difference between an individual's real weight and the weight he/she considers ideal constitutes a significant factor in the development of eating disorders. Being unsatisfied with one's weight has been proved as a variable provoking eating related problems. For this reason, analysing this factor in different sports has been deemed necessary.

Along these lines, Table 2.5 compares the real and ideal weight of athletes, creating three different categories:

- *Ideal weight = real weight*: subjects who believe their current weight is inline with their ideal weight. They conform to the weight they see on the scales, and have no intention of losing or gaining weight.

- *Ideal weight < real weight*: in these cases, subjects consider they weigh *more* than they should do. Their aim is to lose weight in order to attain their ideal.

- *Ideal weight > real weight*: this final group encompasses subjects who believe they weigh *less* than they should do. Some consider putting on weight to reach the ideal that best corresponds to them.

Table 2.5 The relationship between ideal weight and real weight in different sports

Sport / Weight	Football	Basketball	Judo/wrestling	Aerobics	Athletics	Swimming	Rhythmic gymnastics	Bodybuilding	Rowing
Ideal weight = real weight									
Total	33.3%	24.2%	28.8%	0%	16%	36.4%	10.5%	31.3%	35.7%
Ideal weight < real weight									
1–2 kg	25%	12.1%	8.5%	5.3%	27.1%	9.1%	21.1%		14.3%
3–4 kg	6.3%	22.8%	15.3%	42.1%	18.5%	18.2%	42.2%	12.5%	14.3%
5–6 kg	10.4%	12.1%	13.6%	5.3%	17.2%	18.2%	5.3%	6.3%	7.1%
7–8 kg	9%	9%	8.5%	10.6%	1.2%		5.3%		
>9 kg	2.1%	9%	6.7%	26.5%				6.3%	
Total	43.8%	65%	52.6%	89.8%	64%	45.5%	73.9%	25.1%	35.7%
Ideal weight > real weight									
1–2 kg	4.2%	7.6%	5.1%	10.6%	11.1%	18.2%	5.3%	18.8%	14.3%
3–4/kg	6.3%	1.5%	5.1%		5%				
5–6 kg	4.2%	1.5%	3.4%		2.5%		5.3%	18.8%	7.1%
7–8 kg	6.3%				1.2%			6.3%	
>9 kg	2.1%		1.7%				5.3%		7.1%
Total	23.1%	10.6%	15.3%	10.6%	19.8%	18.2%	15.9%	43.9%	28.5%

Using the sample of athletes represented in Table 2.5, the aforementioned relationships between ideal weight and real weight have been analysed, reaching the following conclusions:

1. In five of the nine sports represented, 50 per cent of subjects are unhappy with their real weight, considering it is higher than it should be. The degree of discontent is directly related to the sporting discipline, given that the highest results were produced in specialities in which weight and figure are important for competing successfully: in sports such as rhythmic gymnastics, the bodily figure is a criteria valued by judges; in long-distance athletics, weighing little helps improve performance; or in judo, weight divisions form part of the competition structure.

2. Of all the sports, aerobics, with 89.9 per cent, has the greatest proportion of participants who are unhappy with their real weight and wish to reduce it. This elevated proportion may be explained by the typical profile of participants, females who take part in aerobics in an attempt to lose weight (Dosil & Díaz, 2002). Furthermore, it is one of the sporting disciplines in which participants aspire to lose the most kilos, with 26.5 per cent considering their real weight exceeds their ideal weight by 9 kg or more. This longing to lose weight is reconfirmed in the 'ideal weight = real weight' category, in which only aerobics produces a 0 per cent result. This outcome further corroborates the extent of weight dissatisfaction amongst the subjects of this sporting discipline.

3. Rhythmic gymnastics also generates elevated levels of dissatisfaction with real weight. In these cases, gymnasts establish their ideal weight according to the sports weight required for their speciality, in which an exceptionally thin body is a valued asset. Therefore, after aerobics, rhythmic gymnasts express the greatest degree of concern, with only 10.5 per cent of gymnasts claiming to be satisfied with their real weight.

4. At the other end of the spectrum, bodybuilding is the only sport in which a higher proportion of subjects consider their real weight to be *lower* than their ideal weight. This is due to the fact that this speciality demands increased and exaggerated muscle mass, as opposed to weight loss. What is more, any weight loss proves counteractive for participants, since it reduces their much-valued muscular development. Along these lines, only 25 per cent of bodybuilders believe they need to lose weight. Consequently, compared to other sports, bodybuilding has the lowest proportion of participants claiming they weigh more than they should (ideal weight < real weight).

5. In judo, 52.6 per cent of subjects are unhappy with their real weight. This may be explained by the characteristics of the sport's competitive structure. Given

the presence of weight divisions, losing weight rapidly to compete in a lower category is believed to facilitate victory. Therefore, over half the subjects interviewed desire an ideal weight that is lower than their real weight.

2.4.2   Real weight vs. sports weight

The contrast between real weight and sports weight is considered relevant to the development of eating disorders in sport. As with the previous analysis, three possibilities may arise:

- *Real weight = sports weight*: subjects consider their real weight (objective) as 'ideal' for their particular sporting discipline.

- *Real weight > sports weight*: from a subjective perspective, athletes believe their real weight is higher than their ideal sports weight. Consequently, to compete more successfully in their sporting discipline, they consider it necessary to lose weight.

- *Real weight < sports weight*: subjects consider their real weight is less than the ideal weight for performing well in their chosen sport.

Using Table 2.6 as a guide, the following conclusions may be drawn:

1. Aerobics has the highest percentage of participants, some 94.1 per cent (predominantly women), who believe they need to lose weight in order to attain their ideal sports weight. Moreover, 29.4 per cent claim that their real weight exceeds their sports weight by 9 kg or more. These extremely high proportions and the fact that none of the subjects considers their real weight to be lower than their sports weight confirms the theory that the majority of those participating in this activity principally do so to lose weight.

2. Similarly, an elevated degree of dissatisfaction with weight may be observed in rhythmic gymnastics, with some 77.2 per cent of subjects claiming their real weight to be higher than their sports weight. This high proportion reflects the pressure to lose weight in this particular sport, provoked in part by the fact that competition judges reward a thin body. This strain is reflected in the results, where only 18.2 per cent of the gymnasts consider their real weight as adequate for competition.

3. Bodybuilding is the only sport in which more subjects consider their real weight to be *lower* than their sports weight. Once again, these results reflect bodybuilders' desires to increase their muscular mass, represented in this case, in terms of weight.

Table 2.6 The relationship between real weight and sports weight in different sports

Sport / Weight	Football	Basketball	Judo/wrestling	Aerobics	Athletics	Swimming	Rhythmic gymnastics	Bodybuilding	Rowing
Real weight = sports weight									
Total	44.9%	18%	19%	5.9%	11.3%	25%	18.2%	29.4%	15.4%
Real weight > sports weight									
1–2 kg.	10.2%	14.8%	20.7%	11.8%	13.8%	16.6%	9.1%	5.9%	
3–4 kg.	14.3%	11.5%	10.3%	41.1%	31.3%	16.6%	36.4%	5.9%	30.8%
5–6 kg.	4.1%	4.9%	19%	11.8%	21.3%	8.3%	13.6%	5.9%	7.7%
7–8 kg.	2%	6.6%	6.9%		3.8%	8.3%	4.5%		
>9 kg.	6.1%	9.8%	10.3%	29.4%	1.3%		13.6%	11.8%	
Total	36.7%	47.6%	67.2%	94.1%	71.5%	49.8%	77.2%	29.5%	38.5%
Real weight < sports weight									
1–2 kg.	6.1%	8.2%	1.7%		8.8%	25%		17.6%	15.4%
3–4 kg.	6.1%	8.2%	5.2%		3.8%				7.7%
5–6 kg.		6.6%	3.4%		2.5%		4.5%	17.6%	7.7%
7–8 kg.	4.1%	6.6%	1.7%						
>9 kg.	2%	4.9%	1.7%		2.5%			5.9%	15.4%
Total	18.3%	34.5%	13.7%	0%	17.6%	25%	4.5%	41.1%	46.2%

4. Athletics is another sport in which there is a broad dissatisfaction with real weight. A high proportion of athletes consider their real weight as being heavier than their sports weight. This elevated percentage is normal considering it is a sporting discipline in which concern for weight and body fat is commonplace. Moreover, the use of strict diets is normal in athletics.

5. Judo is one of the sports in which weight is considered extremely important; 67.2 per cent of the subjects claim their real weight as being higher than their sporting weight. This degree of dissatisfaction is due to the rules of the sport, in which weight divisions form part of the competitive structure. Along these lines, Pérez Recio *et al.* (1992), demonstrated how athletes from weight division sports obtain higher point scores on the Body Dissatisfaction Scale on Body Dissatisfaction Subscale (see Chapter 4).

2.4.3 Ideal weight vs. sports weight

The final analysis compares ideal weight with sports weight. Initially, it seems logical to expect the ideal and sports weight to correspond. Surely athletes will desire the most beneficial image and weight for their sport? The results of this analysis are shown in Table 2.7, which reflect the proportion of subjects who consider their ideal weight to be the same as their sports weight.

In light of these results, the following comments may be highlighted:

1. Bodybuilding, football and swimming produce the highest proportion of subjects who claim their ideal weight is equal to their sports weight. These results may be related to the physical demands of these disciplines, and the fact that the sports weight required to compete successfully in these sports are considered 'socially ideal'.

2. On the other hand, rhythmic gymnastics and athletics produce the lowest percentages. One possible explanation may be that the sports weight required to

Table 2.7 The relationship between ideal weight and sports weight in different sports

	Ideal weight = sports weight	N	%
High-risk sports	Rhythmic gymnastics	25	27.8
	Judo/wrestling	35	41.7
	Bodybuilding	25	73.8
	Aerobics	37	41.2
	Athletics	36	33.8
	Swimming	26	60
Low-risk sports	Football	40	65.2
	Basketball	32	36.7

compete successfully in these disciplines, differs greatly from the ideal weight for the normal population. Along these lines, if an athlete achieves their ideal weight in terms of medical and aesthetic criteria, it probably won't be sufficient to compete at a high level in these sports. Or inversely, if an athlete attains their sports weight, perhaps it will not result so attractive in terms of social aesthetic ideals.

3. The majority of sports selected for this investigation (judo/wrestling, aerobics, athletics, basketball, rhythmic gymnastics and rowing/canoeing) produced percentages below 50 per cent, revealing clear differences between ideal weight and sports weight. Interestingly, by analysing the specific data for each sporting discipline, we may observe how even in so-called 'low-risk' sports (principally basketball), differences were detected amongst female participants (the majority of male players believe their ideal weight equals their sports weight).

2.5 Conclusions

Undoubtedly, the importance of weight in some sports increases the risks of eating disorders. Throughout this chapter, various 'high-risk' sports have been described, specialities in which weight represents a key determinant of high performance (the goal of any elite athlete). The demands of training and competition lead athletes to employ diverse weight-loss methods in order to control this factor, on occasions becoming pathogenic.

From grassroots through to elite sport, both coaches and parents should be fully aware of the potential risks. Being responsive to these hazards assists the prevention and early detection of potential eating related problems, as well as aiding the rapid employment of resources to confront them.

In the sports world, there is an extremely fine line between the three types of weight (real, ideal and sports). The pressures to maintain a certain weight are not only limited to the training and competition environment, but tend to invade all aspects of an athlete's life. There is a clear predisposition for athletes from so-called 'high-risk' sports to be much more demanding about their ideal weight (they believe their real weight greatly exceeds their ideal weight).

In light of these conclusions, given this great concern for weight, sportspeople are much more prone to developing eating disorders at some point of their lives compared to the general population.

3 Eating Disorders and the Athlete's Environment

Joaquín Dosil and Jacinto González-Oya

Throughout my coaching career in athletics I have come across many cases of eating disorders. The environment athletes operate in exerts many pressures related to weight and eating. More specifically, I think the most influential figure in an athlete's life is the coach; whatever he/she says has its effects, and perhaps coaches should be more careful with the negativity of their comments.

Within athletics, middle-distance and long-distance athletes are more likely to suffer eating disorders, given the context within which they train and compete. The predominant physical model desired by these athletes is excessively thin, often too much so. Therefore, athletes in these events are generally more obsessed with their figure and weight than in any other discipline. Likewise, training mates play a crucial role in this aspect, potentially benefiting or damaging an athlete's perception of their own body figure. Taking all of this into account, I strongly believe that the role of parents should be to educate their children from a young age in matters related to food and eating, arming them with the sufficient knowledge to survive the negative influences they will face throughout their athletic career.

Athletics coach

Eating Disorders in Athletes   Joaquín Dosil
© 2008 John Wiley & Sons, Ltd

3.1   Introduction

All too often, the dominant aesthetic models of today's society dictate that a person's physical aspect is the most important tool for success. Although this 'social imposition' affects everybody, youngsters are especially vulnerable to the negative pressures of the prevailing body types transmitted by the media. In an investigation highlighting the influence of this 'body culture' amongst the general population, Marzano (2001) relates the habits 'imposed' by society to the development of eating disorders, directly linking physical exercise into the relationship.

In the treatment of eating disorders, the environment surrounding a patient is a key piece in the 'puzzle'. Moreover, high expectations on behalf of the family (mainly parents) and pressures from the coach and teammates are amongst the principal factors causing these illnesses. Therefore, as defended in other texts (Dosil, 2004), in the development and treatment of eating related problems, sport in itself may prove either positive or negative depending on the specific context and its variables, and can be considered a neutral factor. Along these lines, the environment surrounding athletes and the focus of their sporting activity are two factors converting sport into a potentially beneficial or damaging element.

In grass-roots sport, parents and coaches constitute the greatest source of pressure on young athletes. A report by the USOC (United States Olympic Committee) in 1998 revealed how both these actors significantly influence the development of unrealistic expectations related to food intake and weight. In relation to this report, Hausenblas and Carron (1999) present some conclusions:

- Today's society demands physical thinness and form, to such an extent that individuals are under constant pressure to attain an 'ideal' body through diets and exercise.

- In addition to these social influences, athletes are exposed to the internal pressures of their sport, which often demand a determined weight to achieve peak performance.

- Doing sport and excessive physical exercise play an important role in the development of eating disorders.

- Vulnerability to developing eating disorders may be increased by certain psychological characteristics, such as perfectionism, compulsiveness, or high self-expectations, etc.

This chapter describes the role of certain actors who potentially influence the emergence and development of eating behaviour disorders in athletes. Likewise, it explains the initiatives for preventing these illnesses, which may be applied by the numerous individuals involved with athletes on a daily basis, encouraging the active participation of parents, coaches, directors and other related professionals.

3.2 Pressures in the athlete's environment

Social imperatives have become an authentic mass phenomenon, and the sports context is no exception, often becoming a stage for individuals seeking a body weight and figure that goes beyond the normal limits for their physical constitution.

When analysing the pressures exerted by different sporting contexts, the intrinsic characteristics and competitive cycles of each discipline constitute two important elements. Generally speaking, coaches establish certain objectives, which athletes try to achieve, forcing themselves to the maximum and exhausting all the possible strategies. Many sportspeople go on diets throughout the sporting season, resorting to 'extra' weight loss methods when they see fit. Similarly, it has been noted that in the sporting context, women find it more difficult to interrupt a determined diet at the end of a competitive cycle, whilst men are more flexible when it comes to resuming more ordinary eating habits (Dosil, 2003). As seen in previous studies (Díaz *et al.*, 1998), the proportion of women suffering from eating disorders is considerably higher than men. Notably, Brownell *et al.* (1992) reported that the overall prevalence of eating disorders is higher amongst female athletes (95 per cent) than male athletes.

Figure 3.1

These circumstances, added to the current social culture, exert greater pressures on women to possess certain physical aesthetics (even in the sports context): physical form, clothes, hairstyles, accessories, etc. This reality makes it more likely for women to develop a distorted body image, which can lead to eating disorders. As detailed in the previous chapter, the importance of body image and physical composition in certain sports is such that it can determine the success or failure of an athlete. Therefore, endurance athletes, dancers, gymnasts or artistic ice skaters are at particular risk of developing eating disorders. For example, in a study by Taylor and Ste-Marie (2001) with 41 artistic ice-skaters, 92.7 per cent perceived a sport-related pressure to lose weight.

The influence of the context surrounding athletes has been analysed in previous studies (Dosil, 2003). In a survey with 420 sportspeople from various disciplines (rhythmic gymnastics, judo, bodybuilding, aerobics, athletics, swimming, wrestling, rowing, football, and basketball), subjects were asked which individuals or entities most influence their weight loss behaviours. The results confirm that the pressure to lose weight is greater in some sporting disciplines than others, whilst coaches, parents and the athletes themselves, constitute the most influential actors (Table 3.1).

The athletes participating in this study consider that their weight loss behaviour is most influenced by the pressure they exert on themselves, followed by parents and the coach, who press them through comments suggesting or encouraging the need to lose weight. From this study, it also becomes clear that environmental forces vary from one sport to another. Therefore, in sports such as swimming, judo/wrestling, rowing, athletics and rhythmic gymnastics, it is the coach who most sways the choice of weight loss methods; whereas in other sports, like bodybuilding, books have more influence. Somewhat curious results were obtained in aerobics, in which parents, family and boyfriend were cited as being most influential.

In order to assist the development of eating behaviour disorder prevention programmes, this data may be used to study the importance of the different actors implicated in the sports context. For example, it has become clear that the coach is the most important figure when it comes to weight loss in athletics (Table 3.2).

Hence, what these individuals think about eating disorders, whether or not they are familiar with these problems and how to deal with them, etc., are factors that must be addressed. Along these lines, in order to decipher the specific characteristics of each sport, their relation to eating disorders and the degree of existing knowledge about these illnesses, various interviews have been conducted with coaches from a broad range of disciplines (Dosil, 2003). The majority of coaches confess to having basic knowledge about eating behaviour disorders, but feel they lack the capacity to adequately confront them. In light of this discovery, the final section of this chapter focuses on the development of eating behaviour disorder prevention programmes, whose principal objectives are to provide a practical solution to this apparent lack of awareness amongst sports professionals.

Table 3.1 The individuals or entities that influence weight loss in different sports

| | High-risk sports | | | | | | | Low-risk sports | |
	Rhythmic gymnastics	Judo/wrestling	Bodybuilding	Aerobics	Athletics	Rowing	Swimming	Basketball	Football
Myself (M)	45.9%	26.1%	22.2%	68.2%	27.5%	6.3%	38.5%	30%	17.5%
Coach (C)	20.8%	21.7%		4.5%	15.4%	6.3%	15.4%	12.9%	3.2%
Parents (P)		10.1%		9.1%	2.2%		7.7%	8.6%	1.6%
Siblings (S)	4.2%	7.2%		4.5%	1.1%		7.7%	4.3%	
Family (F)		4.3%		9.1%				2.9%	
Books, journals (BJ)		7.2%	5.6%		4.4%			8.6%	
Television (T)		4.3%			2.2%			1.4%	
Boy/girlfriend (BG)		2.9%		9.1%				10%	1.6%
Teammates (TM)	8.3%	15.9%			6.6%	6.3%		8.6%	1.6%
Others (O)		1.4%	5.6%			6.3%			3.2%
Nobody (N)	41.7%	50.7%	66.7%	27.3%	58.2%	87.5%	53.8%	51.4%	73%

Table 3.2 The individuals or entities that most influence weight loss in different sports

High-risk sports							Low-risk sports	
Rhythmic gymnastics	Judo/ wrestling	Bodybuilding	Aerobics	Athletics	Rowing	Swimming	Basketball	Football
Coach	Coach	Book/journal, others	Parents, family, nobody	Coach	Coach, team-mates, others	Coach	Coach	Coach, others
Team-mates	Team-mates	Coach, siblings		Nobody		Parents, siblings	Team-mates	Parents, nobody, team-mates

The causes of eating disorders are a combination of elements: biological (genetic and biological tendencies), psychological (family influences and psychological conflicts) and cultural–social (social influences and expectations). Within this model, individuals inside the sports context can develop an important role in the prevention or development of eating disorders.

3.2.1 The role of the family

The age at which an individual commences and develops a sporting activity implies a series of circumstances that may increase the risks of developing eating disorders. For example, a certain biological 'vulnerability' exists amongst adolescents, given the many body changes that must be assumed during this period; and peers begin to gain more importance in the lives of young athletes, especially when accompanied by the desire for independence from the family unit. These factors, in addition to the expectations generated around athletes, often manifest in inappropriate eating behaviours in adolescent athletes. Nevertheless, when attempting to identify an age at which athletes are more at risk, it is important to consider that every individual is different and not everyone matures at the same rate, nor do they react in the same manner to the various pressures they are exposed to.

The role of the family is fundamental in the prevention of eating behaviour disorders in athletes. Morandé (1995) suggests the family is the basic element and is closely linked to the surfacing of eating disorders. Nevertheless, only a simplistic analysis would maintain this theory without including other individuals within the athlete's context, who can exert as much, if not more pressure. Along these lines, a broader framework should be established, in which all members of an athlete's social and family life play an important role, not only in terms of treating eating disorders, but also for general psychological and physical training. In this sense, a study by Taylor et al. (2006), with 455 university females, demonstrated how negative comments from the family regarding weight, shape, and eating directly affect the development of eating pathologies.

Numerous authors support the influence of the family in the development of eating disorders. Amongst others, Gomez (1996) highlighted the existence of a causal correlation between different parental attitudes, the diverse structures of family functioning and the development of determined psychopathologies, such as depression, neurosis or eating disorders. Similarly, Stein et al. (1999) revealed very strong familial aggregation amongst the female relatives of women suffering from bulimia nervosa. Other authors, the majority of them clinical psychologists, have highlighted different alterations in the family relationships of patients suffering from eating pathologies. For example, Haworth-Hoeppner (2000) studied the critical family environment, coercive parental control, and a dominating weight-related discourse in the household and their effect on the development of eating disorders. All these studies note the existence of excessively close relationships with too many interpersonal implications, such as poor relationships between parents.

Although family factors can provoke eating disorders or worsen an already exist-ing eating pathology, it is the combination of these characteristics with the personal-ity traits of an athlete, and the prevalence of certain socio-cultural factors, which make an individual more susceptible.

Without 'labelling' specific family types, some common traits may be noted in families affected by eating disorders (Dosil, 2003):

- poor communication between family members

- incapacity to resolve conflicts

- overprotective parents

- unwillingness to confront new situations

- absence of generational limits

- exaggeratedly high parental expectations

- family history of depression or alcoholism

- the existence of sexual and/or physical abuse within the family unit.

As demonstrated by systemic and structural family theories (Becvar & Becvar, 2000; Gladding, 2002; Minuchin, 1977; Minuchin *et al.*, 2006), certain types of family organisation and functioning are characteristic of patients suffering from eating disorders. Family members find themselves 'trapped' in patterns of interac-tion, in which the child's symptoms serve to cover up the real family conflict. Therefore, the patient maintains the family 'equilibrium', consciously or uncon-sciously perceiving themselves as a key piece in the family dynamic. Moreover, when a child practises sport, this situation intensifies. Family members often get involved with their child's sporting activity, attending training sessions and com-petitions, which often results in the young athlete 'assuming' the role of 'being the one to blame' for the family's problems.

On a general level, the families of athletes suffering from eating behaviour dis-orders tend to accept the different measures they use to lose weight, considering them as just another part of their sporting activity (e.g. 'she needs to take care of her physique, she has to make some sacrifices in what she eats'), and something necessary to achieve improved performance. In fact, sometimes they even admire their willpower ('he can hardly eat, but that's what his sport demands'). Families' acceptance of these circumstances stems from them habitually seeing and sharing the different moments and processes their children undergo throughout a season. On many occasions, depending on the sport in question, individuals feel the need to maintain a determined weight or figure, which the family naturally accept and consider as something normal, perhaps lacking the sufficient knowledge to identify when a problem exists. Consequently, it becomes complicated for families to dif-ferentiate between a potentially harmful alteration in eating behaviour and a 'normal' adjustment as part of a sports regime. Therefore, in order to prevent eating disorders, communication between coaches and families becomes fundamental, as well as the guidance of sport psychologists and nutritionists.

Another family-related problem is the degree of autonomy an athlete has, or perceives. Those athletes who present certain difficulty in functioning independently from their family unit are usually more likely to develop an eating behaviour disorder. Similarly, when athletes' security is based exclusively on exterior agents, they try to adjust to the image others may form of them. In these cases, feeling personal inefficiency, a reduced capacity to solve problems and continuous self-doubt, become inevitable. It is important for families to emphasise and support the independence of their children, trusting in their aptitudes and capabilities to succeed. This confidence should spread to other areas of the athletes' life, minimising the overprotection that is so often present in those individuals suffering from eating disorders. Even in cases where an eating disorder has already taken hold, the family should gradually increase the confidence in the athlete's capabilities to overcome the illness. It is typical for families to swing from one extreme to the other, to go from having total confidence in the athlete ('everything they do is to improve their sporting performance'), to losing all belief (the sensation of having been 'fooled', and difficulty accepting the illness). Therefore, the work of sport psychologists should focus not only on the athlete, but also on how the family can help the patient recover their self-esteem and self-confidence, seeking strategies to assist the family unit to feel more 'comfortable' within the 'new' situation.

Likewise, it is important to highlight the role of the family in seeking professional help. Athletes suffering from an eating disorder are not usually fully aware of their illness, and frequently fail to believe they need to attend a psychologist and/or doctor/nutritionist to assess their problem. Therefore, it is often down to parents to make the decision to seek professional help. Nevertheless, on occasions, influenced by their child, parents fail to recognise the need for expert attention, reassuring themselves with statements such as 'she isn't eating, but her coach must have told her that she can't', or 'my child would never suffer from an eating disorder'. It is also common to come across athletes who use one of their parents as an accomplice, who in turn rejects professional help and brings into disrepute those who insist on doing so. This typical denial is an important barrier to treatment and allows the disorder to further take hold. If both the athlete and parents fail to accept the problem exists, the treatment process is blocked and the recovery delayed. It is imperative to recall that the earlier an illness of this type is diagnosed, the easier it is to cure.

Thus, the information families receive about healthy eating habits is considered of the utmost importance, reminding them that athletes' performance is directly related to the diet they maintain. Although an adequate diet is not enough on its own to improve results, an inappropriate diet can have a detrimental effect on performance (Olmedilla & Andreu, 2001). From extracurricular activities and grassroots sport, through to elite level, adequate eating habits should be taught and encouraged, providing athletes with the sufficient energy for their activity and acting as a preventative measure against the development of atypical eating behaviours. To achieve this ideal, not only the family, but an athlete's entire social context should be made aware of the serious consequences poor nutrition can entail.

3.2.2 The role of the coach

The influence of the coach in the sports context is undeniable. The coaching figure usually directs and coordinates the team and the individual athletes. Consequently, athletes tend to turn to them for advice on most matters, including eating and nutrition. According to Govero and Bushman (2003), the majority of coaches have relatively high knowledge in terms of identifying an eating disorder. Similarly, in an investigation with 236 coaches from the National Collegiate Athletic Association, Vaughan *et al.* (2004) found that 91 per cent had dealt with a female athlete with an eating disorder at some point, but only 27 per cent felt confident identifying an illness of this type, and merely 38 per cent felt secure asking an athlete if she is suffering an eating-related problem. This reality shows that coaches not only require the capacity to identify eating disorders in athletes, but also the skills to effectively approach and deal with the problem when it arises.

Along these lines, Moriarty and Moriarty (1997) emphasise the facts all coaches should be aware of, summarising them into what they call the five P's:

- Predisposition: the types of personality prone to the development of eating disorders

- Prediction: the instigation of certain high-risk practices (diets, use of laxatives . . .)

- Perpetuation: the repeated practice of high-risk activities

- Professional help: for an adequate diagnosis and treatment

- Prevention: the best approach for dealing with eating disorders.

The pressure some coaches exert over weight control has been noted in numerous studies. For example, Harris and Greco (1990) chose a sample of 28 gymnasts, who considered they weigh more than their coaches would like. Through studying their responses, it was shown how 56 per cent were under direct pressure from their coaches to lose weight. Furthermore, they were weighed six times a month as a group and 14 times a month on an individual basis. These figures corroborate the extent to which coaches can pressurise their athletes in those sports where weight control forms an accepted part of the training regime. Many use the scales as a rigid evaluation system, a way of obtaining 'objective' data to see whether an athlete is progressing or has come to a standstill. This method is based on the idea that athletes' weight should diminish at certain stages of the season, and if this fails to occur, then performance will surely drop. Becoming obsessed with the weight–performance relationship, as well as exerting excessively strict control over athletes' lives, constitute a source of pressure that often leads to unsuspected consequences, which frequently go unnoticed by coaches. Kerr *et al.*, (2006) suggest that whilst many coaches admit to being aware of the use of unhealthy weight control practices in sports such as gymnastics, few recognise using them themselves.

On occasions this pressure may be indirect. For example, athletes sometimes form unfounded beliefs about what their coach wants in terms of weight, carrying out strict diets or adopting inadequate weight loss methods in an attempt to please them. Hence, adequate and effective communication between coaches and athletes is essential, since it allows trainers to effectively interpret their athletes' behaviours, feelings and sensations. Moreover, coaches should be careful with *how* they express weight-related comments, as well as their nonverbal language. In a study with 42 female gymnasts conducted by Rosen and Hough (1988), 67 per cent stated that their coach had told them they were too heavy on some occasion, and consequently, 75 per cent of these gymnasts employed pathogenic weight-loss methods (vomiting, laxatives, diuretics, diet pills, fasting, or fluid restriction). This study highlights the fact that something as insignificant as a simple gesture towards the belly of an athlete, indicating they are a few pounds over weight, may prove enough to trigger an eating disorder. Similarly, Heffner *et al.* (2003) found that many coaches have encountered disturbed eating patterns amongst their athletes, and some of their coaching attitudes and behaviours can inadvertently increase the risk for such disturbances.

Figure 3.2

In Chapter 2 endurance events were listed under high-risk sports. Coaches frequently press athletes to lose weight in order to increase their performance. Nonetheless, since the relationship between weighing little and increased performance is common knowledge in these events, athletes do not often need much motivation to maintain a low weight over long periods of time. Coaches should be aware of this situation and can develop an important function in the avoidance of potential eating problems. In other sports, such as aesthetic disciplines, athletes constantly monitor their weight because any alterations in their figure could prove crucial during competitions. Along these lines, in gymnastics, certain styles of coach insist their athletes weigh themselves on a daily basis, with the intention of controlling everything and anything concerned with their performance. However, coaches need to understand that this 'increased control' over gymnasts' weight often incites 'reduced control' over their eating habits. When a gymnast becomes obsessed with food and weight, with comments regarding body figure, etc., the likelihood of developing an eating disorder multiplies. Therefore, the role of sport psychologists is to teach coaches how to adequately explain the importance of weight and the need to maintain a controlled diet, whilst avoiding the excessive behaviours that can lead weight-related concerns to surface in the form of eating disorders.

Coaches' characteristics also play a crucial role in the prevention or provocation of eating disorders. On the one hand, athletes of *authoritarian coaches* (unidirectional relationship) rarely have the opportunity to express their concerns, and the 'recommendations' they receive are seldom open to discussion. Therefore, it is easy for them to become passive in certain situations, incapable of exchanging opinions and points of view with their coach. This type of relationship is risky when athletes face weight-related comments. If they have no social framework to turn to, and no way of conveying their concerns, it becomes easy to resort to inadequate eating behaviours. Conversely, *democratic coaches* maintain fluid and open communication with their athletes (bi-directional relationship), who are able to freely transmit their points of view. The coach's opinions are 'relative', seeking the wellbeing of the athletes through discussion and joint agreements. More specifically, when it comes to making weight-related comments, the athlete is able to participate in the dialogue, giving ideas and sharing their concerns. Hence, coaches can prevent potential eating disorders through offering profound communication on any matters that may be worrying their athletes.

Although the approach to coaching constitutes an important dynamic in the prevention of eating-related problems, it is insufficient if coaches lack the adequate training and knowledge to deal with these problems. On this note, Garner et al. (1998) stress the advice coaches should be given about the physical, psychological and behavioural symptoms of eating disorders. Likewise, in a more applied study, Harris (2000) analysed 107 tennis players and 26 tennis coaches, concluding that the coaches had a very limited knowledge of weight-loss methods. This author also observed how both coaches and players considered physical image as highly important, deeming tennis to be a high-risk sport in terms of eating disorders.

Prevention is difficult without the adequate training. It is not enough to conform to a secondary prevention system, aimed at shortening the length of an eating disorder through early diagnosis and treatment. The only true prevention is primary avoidance, which implies providing up-to-date, truthful, comprehensive and clear information to coaches, parents and athletes, about the causes and most common consequences of eating disorders, as well as the risks of high-risk dietary practices. Turk *et al.* (1999) carried out a study with 258 coaches, identifying a clear lack of knowledge in the majority of cases and demonstrating the importance of educating them in matters regarding eating disorders and their prevention. Coaches themselves have manifested these circumstances. For example, Vaughan *et al.* (2004) indicate that almost all athletics coaches (93 per cent) feel that increased attention needs to be paid to the prevention of eating disorders amongst female university athletes.

Coaches are in a perfect position to detect potential eating-related problems early. Coaches constantly follow the physical evolution of their athletes, and this close monitoring can also be employed to spot any anomalous behaviours. Getting to know athletes in a more general manner, which goes beyond their sports performance and collaborating with parents, will favour this task.

3.2.3 The role of team-mates

As with any aspect of life, the influence of peer groups in sport is undeniable. At the ages when eating disorders typically appear (adolescence), the self-perception of body image is highly conditioned by the opinions and comments of others (Santrock, 2004). Therefore, not only do peer groups influence behaviours, values and ideas, but also body image and physical appearance. Carron and Hausenblas (2000) studied how group influences can manipulate eating and dieting behaviours. Of the 131 athletes interviewed, the majority (60 per cent) did not perceive any form of influence from their peers, whilst 30 per cent reported team-mates had a positive influence and 10 per cent a negative influence. These results can prove somewhat confusing, as they suggest peers have little influence over eating and weight. Nevertheless, on many occasions, athletes are simply unaware that their eating habits have been altered by the 'recommendations', 'comments' or conversations of their team-mates.

The degree of interaction between athletes varies from one sport to another. Therefore, a distinction can be made between the role of peers in team sports and the role of training colleagues in individual sports. In the latter, athletes usually train alone or accompanied by a reduced group of people, who have less influence over one another given the lesser level of communication (greater external pressure). However, in team sports, comments related to image, weight and figure, are often commonplace within the group itself (internal and external pressure). The effects of such remarks are more or less significant depending on the personal characteristics of each individual athlete and his/her situation within the team.

The nature of competition and the pressures it entails also vary between individual and team sports. Whilst in individual sports, all the responsibility to perform well falls upon the athlete (being in good shape, maintaining the correct weight to compete in a certain category, carrying out diets to increase performance, etc.), in team sports, these tasks are shared between the group, and the individual player does not feel so personally responsible for the end result (except when the group exerts direct pressure on one individual). Good team cohesion usually constitutes a fundamental pillar in the physical and psychological well being of its comprising athletes.

Figure 3.3

Professionals working with athletes must consider some key aspects, such as the stage of the season, the characteristics of the sport and individual athletes' personal development. Athletes often find themselves trying to conform to both their sporting results, as well as their physical image, tending towards perfectionism (a common trait amongst individuals suffering from eating disorders). Healthy eating habits are fundamental for high performance and any variation in this aspect can negatively influence results. Correctly informing athletes of how to carry out a healthy and balanced diet is essential for averting the development of eating related disorders. The pressure suffered by many athletes to maintain an optimum weight is a key factor in the emergence of eating behaviour disorders, and the influence of peers becomes so important (along with coaches and parents) that they can help to both prevent or trigger these illnesses.

Fellow athletes who have already reached 'elite' level are often extremely influential over other athletes' choices of eating behaviours. A 'model' athlete who comments on certain diets or methods to maintain/lose weight, may condition others to adopt the same techniques. Therefore, athletes' 'references' (directors, coaches, parents and athletes with certain status) should always encourage healthy sporting practices, carefully considering the information they choose to transmit and the repercussions their comments could have.

Finally, when doubts arise about eating or diet, the team/group allows athletes to openly vent their concerns. In the case of team sports, athletes can share their apprehension with colleagues, allowing them to feel listened to and understood. However, the downside arises if the responses received are based purely on personal experiences, inappropriate and lacking any form of scientific backup. On the other hand, for athletes in individual sports, it may prove more difficult to find someone to share their worries with, and faced with a lack of support, they may inadequately 'self-respond' to their circumstances without consulting anyone at all.

Whatever the sport, all athletes should have access to adequate information regarding healthy eating habits from the beginning of their careers. Likewise, athletes need to count on 'references' they can trust (coaches, parents, etc.), so they never have to confront stressful situations alone (including the influence of teammates' comments). Therefore, a support network, which offers information and encouragement during these critical moments, is fundamental.

3.3 The prevention of eating disorders in sport

In every sport, developing an environment in which eating disorders are less likely to develop should constitute a basic objective. The prevention of these illnesses not only depends on coaches and parents, but also requires the collaboration of society as a whole.

In today's culture, we are constantly bombarded with messages about the need to be thin and 'in shape'. Along these lines, nearly one in four adverts, seen by a predominantly female public, directly or indirectly promote weight loss or make weighing little appear desirable (Toro, 1995). It is feasible to say that society values weight more than other characteristics, often regarding it as a synonym of self-control. As previously established, the pressure to be thin is constant in some sports. Byrne and McLean (2002) highlight that athletes in sports that put emphasis on the importance of a thin body shape or a low body weight are more vulnerable to eating disorders. In these cases, prevention becomes fundamental.

Moreover, coaches can greatly influence both the prevention and development of eating disorders. Comments or suggestions to athletes regarding weight loss can easily trigger an eating disorder, or result in athletes turning to unhealthy weight-loss methods. Therefore, if there are no other professionals who can intervene (psychologists, doctors, etc.), it is fundamental for coaches to have the correct information about the risks of eating disorders in sport, being fully aware of their symptoms and consequences. If this were the case, coaches would be able to act on a preventative level, detecting the relevant signs and taking the necessary steps when problems arise (turning to qualified professionals if the dilemma goes beyond their competencies).

A multidisciplinary team within every sporting organisation would be the ideal scenario for effectively preventing and treating eating disorders. Some of these professionals, adequately trained in nutritional matters, can apply and supervise diets, giving advice on healthy weight-loss methods (when an athlete needs to lose a kilo or two). Olmedilla and Andreu (2001) uphold the need to place athletes at the centre of this process. Nevertheless, however important the role of a multidisciplinary team, the implication of the remaining members of the sporting context (parents, team-mates, coaches, etc.) remains essential, for without their collaboration, it would be impossible for athletes to achieve physical and mental equilibrium.

Parents also influence athletes' eating behaviours. Being part of a family in which healthy food and balanced eating habits are encouraged, makes it easier for athletes to maintain the correct nutritional regime and helps avoid potential eating problems. Toro and Vilardell (1987) stress the family as the basic pillar in the development and prevention of these illnesses.

In the state of Wisconsin, USA, other prevention strategies for eating behaviour disorders have been implemented in weight division sports (judo, taekwondo, boxing). Here, athletes' body fat percentages are measured on a regular basis, imposing a minimum category within which they are authorised to compete, barring the use of additional weight loss methods to move down a category (Davis *et al.*, 2002).

Figure 3.4

In light of the aforementioned aspects, some guidelines to prevent the development of eating disorders in athletes have been proposed (Díaz *et al.*, 1998):

- Individuals involved in sport should put weight into perspective, teaching athletes to objectively analyse this aspect.

- Athletes should be taught a series of general guidelines to develop a healthy and balanced eating culture. Moreover, they must understand the consequences of weight in their sport, being able to evaluate a weight increase with detachment and put into practice the correct weight-loss methods to regain their normal form, avoiding becoming excessively influenced by potentially harming comments from team-mates (and even coaches) such as: 'you're very fat', 'you should lose 5 or 6 kilos', 'you need to eat less' . . . .

- Coaches and parents should be made aware of these disorders, allowing them to detect potential situations in which athletes are exerting too much pressure on themselves.

- Coaches must seek support from the relevant specialists to design training sessions and elaborate guidelines for each athlete to follow. Likewise, parents who want their children to compete from a young age are encouraged not to exert too much pressure, teaching them the positive values of sport and avoiding treating thinness as a tool for success. Similarly, it is positive for them to accompany their child to some training sessions, especially when starting out, monitoring the coach's methods. Moreover, effective coach – parent communication serves to constantly help the child, rewarding effort rather than results, both in training and competition. No parent should accept a coach who focuses solely on success, who encourages athletes to develop unhealthy routines, or who is overly rigid in their approach, putting too much pressure on young athletes.

In conclusion, it is important to prevent eating related problems from a young age, encouraging adequate eating habits in children and increasing their knowledge of nutrition as they grow up. If this were achieved, along with the participation of a multidisciplinary team, these types of disorders could become a thing of the past.

3.4   Eating disorder prevention programmes for athletes

A state of adequate nutrition is the result of maintaining healthy eating habits over time. Sport should go hand in hand with a healthy lifestyle, in which deliverance, perseverance, consistency, effort, achievements and goals form part of a universal concept that cannot be broken down (Dosil, 2004).

Olmedilla and Andreu (2002) carried out a psychological intervention proposal in sports clubs, encouraging the involvement of the principal psychosocial actors: parents and coaches. According to these authors, it is essential to implant an awareness campaign within clubs, working in a multidisciplinary manner, with doctors, nutritionists, psychologists and coaches, and covering the following aspects:

- *Meetings with sports directors and coaches*: the sports psychologist and doctor should explain the aims and objectives, getting team managers involved in developing an eating habits programme with the athletes.

- *Establish contact with parents*: this serves to explain the work that is to be carried out, the objectives of the project and the role they are expected to assume as parents. The aim is to achieve greater parent involvement and awareness.

- *Carry out diverse informative talks about 'eating well'*: these talks should be directed towards parents, coaches, directors and athletes alike.

- *Training sessions with coaches and parents*: to explain the procedures athletes should follow in properly filling out their diet self-records.

- *Notice boards*: these can be used to summarise principal ideas, as a reminder of what has been covered in the sessions and talks. These notice boards should be positioned in the meeting place and in changing rooms, where athletes will see them regularly.

- *Provide parents, coaches and athletes with a healthy eating guide*. The multidisciplinary team, in order to guide athletes' eating habits and behaviours, should design this reference material. This technique has two functions: on the one hand, it provides precise information about healthy eating, adapted to each individual athlete; whilst on the other, it works as a preventative measure against risky eating behaviours, offering detailed information about the negative consequences of a poor diet and the different types of eating behaviour disorders.

The objective of this initiative is to train and inform those in contact with athletes on a daily basis, so they are capable of preventing and detecting changes in athletes' eating behaviours. This increased control allows these individuals to encourage the development of 'healthy eating habits'. This process not only affects the athlete, but also indirectly increases the awareness of a healthy lifestyle in all individuals related to the sporting context.

Amongst the eating disorder prevention programmes for athletes, the proposals developed by Díaz (2005), Govero and Bushman (2003), and Vaughan *et al.*, (2004), may be highlighted. All of these emphasise the importance of adequate training for coaches, who should be directly involved in the prevention of eating disorders

Table 3.3 The general and specific objectives of an eating disorder prevention programme for athletes

General objectives	Specific objectives
Reduce the prevalence of eating disorders in sport	Identify the symptoms of eating disorders
Increase coaches' knowledge of eating disorders	Recognise the risk situations that potentially provoke eating disorders
Educate coaches and athletes in basic nutritional aspects	Increased awareness of the high-risk behaviours (of coaches, parents and athletes), which favour the development of eating disorders
Encourage healthy habits in coaches and athletes	Provide information and training in sports nutrition
Improve athletes' quality of life and well-being	Learn to carryout a diet and control eating in a healthy manner
	Work on the social relationships within the training group
	Encourage a democratic coaching style
	Develop effective communication between coaches, parents and athletes.
	Establish a healthy lifestyle: sufficient sleep, hygiene, weight control, etc.

Source: Díaz (2005).

within the sporting context. These programmes are developed through weekly workshops, each lasting two hours, which deal with coaches' knowledge of eating disorders, as well as their communicational skills with athletes and parents. The general and specific objectives of these workshops are summarised in Table 3.3.

As a worked example, Table 3.4 details some sessions conducted with coaches and athletes.

Another course that has achieved some positive results, and deals with more than just eating disorders in athletes, is the ATHENA Programme (Athletes Targeting Healthy Exercise and Nutrition Alternatives) (Elliot *et al.*, 2004). The ATHENA curriculum aims to prevent young female high-school athletes from entering into disordered eating and abusing body-shaping drugs. The Programme, which is team-based, has eight weekly 45-min sessions, and covers topics such as healthy sports nutrition, effective exercise training, drug use and other unhealthy behaviours, as well as their effects on sports performance, media images of females, and depression prevention. Given the success of this programme, it becomes clear that sports teams are effective natural vehicles for gender-specific, peer-led curricula, to promote healthy lifestyles and to deter disordered eating, athletic-enhancing substance use, and other potentially harmful behaviours.

Summing up, the introduction of eating disorder prevention programmes in the sports environment is fundamental. Depending on the circumstances and available resources, coaches and athletes may opt to attend a prevention programme directly,

Table 3.4 Specific sessions with coaches and athletes

Module 1. General information about eating disorders

Objectives	Contents
Identify the symptoms of eating disorders Recognise the high-risk situations that potentially provoke eating disorders Increased awareness of the behaviours (of coaches, parents and team-mates) that can favour or deter the development of an eating disorder	1. Group presentation 2. Initial group assessment (specific questionnaire and questions about awareness of nutrition, eating disorder symptoms and communicational skills) 3. Psycho-education: explanation of eating disorder symptoms in athletes 4. Presentation of eating disorder risk factors, emphasising the differences between sporting disciplines and the relevance of the various stages of the sports season 5. Description of the coach's role in the prevention and development of eating disorders 6. Activities with individuals or in small groups: case studies to analyse the symptoms, high-risk moments and negative attitudes 7. Session summary

Module 2. Sports nutrition (taught by a nutritional specialist)

Objectives	Contents
Receive information about sports nutrition Learn how to distinguish and calculate real weight, ideal weight and sports weight Learn how to design a specific diet for the sporting discipline	1. Brief overview of the nutritional aspects relevant to the sport in question 2. Introduction of a weekly eating register 3. Distinguish between real weight, ideal weight and sports weight throughout the season 4. Individual activity: calculate real weight, ideal weight and sports weight 5. Group and individual activity: development of a suitable diet for the sport and a specific diet for each individual athlete 6. Session summary

Module 3. Team cohesion and eating disorders

Objectives	Contents
Identify the importance of team cohesion Distinguish between social cohesion and group cohesion Work on team cohesion and respect towards teammates	1. Presentation of 'cohesion' and its dimensions 2. Teach the factors that affect cohesion and individual differences within groups 3. Presentation of cohered and conflictive groups 4. Group activity: learn to value group relationships through a sociogram and establish action guidelines from within the group 5. Session summary

Table 3.4 (*Continued*)

Module 4. The democratic coach and the prevention of eating disorders

Objectives	Contents
Identify the different types of coach and their relation to eating disorders Encourage a democratic coaching style	1. Psycho-education: presentation of the different coaching styles (authoritarian, democratic and passive), providing examples 2. Description of the implications each coaching style has on the prevention and development of EDs 3. Group activity: role-playing with the different coaching styles 4. Session summary

Module 5. Effective communication in sport

Objectives	Contents
Differentiate between verbal and non-verbal communication Develop effective communication with athletes and parents	1. Present the effective forms of verbal and non-verbal communication 2. Explain the use of communication at the different moments of training sessions and competitions 3. Communication with parents and athletes 4. Activities in small groups: planning a meeting with parents 5. Group activity: role-playing discussions with parents and with athletes 6. Session summary

Module 6. Promoting healthy habits in the sports context

Objectives	Contents
Promotion of healthy habits: sleep, organising one's time, weight-control and menstruation	1. Information about how to organise one's time, combining work/studies with sport and free time 2. Explain general hygiene, sleep, weight-control and menstruation guidelines 3. Individual activity: write a diary, plan out the different activities during a day 4. Session summary

going to sessions as part of their training routine. Or, alternatively, coaches may receive guidance from specialist sport psychologists, and then transmit this acquired knowledge and skills to their athletes indirectly. On many occasions, when it is not feasible for athletes to attend a prevention programme in person, the latter option proves much simpler, since it only requires coaches to show interest in enhancing their awareness and dexterity in this aspect.

3.5   Conclusions

The social framework of athletes is a necessary element in the assessment of their eating habits. The ideas athletes harbour about being thin and weighing little to compete effectively, combined with the pressures of socially 'fashionable' diets and weight-loss regimes are factors contributing towards the emergence eating disorders in sport. This reality calls for nutritional re-education, both for those who practise sport, as well as those related to athletes (Thompson & Sherman, 1993a).

Changes in attitudes and behaviours are required to reduce the risks in those sports with higher eating disorder prevalence rates. These changes should not only be directed towards athletes, but cover a wider social context. Taking a short glimpse at television advertisements is sufficient to appreciate the degree to which today's civilization has developed a dominating body culture. Converted into victims of socially imposed beauty ideals, many people (predominantly women) are unsatisfied with their body image and weight. Although this fact does not predict future eating disorders, it serves to reflect the extent to which the culture and environment surrounding an individual influences self-perception. Therefore, society creates certain conditions that may increase a person's vulnerability to suffering an eating disorder. These circumstances, in addition to certain personal, family and sporting variables, can prove sufficient to trigger an eating-related pathology.

Corroborating this theory, Tiggemann et al., (2005) carried out an investigation with women in Australia and Italy, demonstrating that the factors provoking eating disorders vary between different cultures. Most intriguingly, this study discovered that fashion magazine consumption predicted body dissatisfaction and disordered eating only for Australian women, but not for Italian women. Pernick et al. (2006) conducted a similar study with three ethnic groups (73 African Americans, 277 Caucasians, and 103 Latin Americans), discovering that Caucasians and Latin female high-school athletes may be at greater risk from eating disorders than their African American peers.

The cultural character of eating disorders is also justified by the reality that these illnesses affect ten times more women than men (Pate et al., 2003). The changes that occur during puberty make it an especially alarming period in terms developing eating disorders. Frequently, youngsters lack the mental skills to overcome these changes, and individuals within their social context do not have the sufficient training to know how to help them through this time of transition. Along these lines, an interesting investigation by McCabe and Ricciardelli (2005) with adolescents concluded that messages from parents, above all fathers, were strong predictors of both strategies to lose weight and increase muscles among boys, with the media and best male friend playing a limited role. For girls, the strongest influences were mothers and best female friends, with little influence from fathers or the media.

In the sports context, at these ages, young athletes usually start deciding whether to continue their sporting activity in a more serious manner, or whether to give it up, a decision that serves to further increase the pressures they endure. Many youngsters feel unable to overcome this period of physical change and abandon sport altogether. Others, who decide to continue, train and compete in a 'dangerous' environment, undergoing constant, potentially harming comments (from the coach or team-mates). This reality is reflected in the results some studies, such as that carried out by Malinauskas *et al.*, (2005), who noted that the participation in regular physical activity is associated with a higher degree of body satisfaction, compared to non-athletes. In order to maintain a higher degree of control over this situation, the advice developed in this chapter should be taken into consideration, procuring a greater level of involvement of those individuals within the sports context.

4 The Assessment and Diagnosis of Eating Disorders in Sport

Joaquín Dosil and Enrique J. Garcés de Los Fayos

I go to the gym whenever I can. If I have a couple of free hours I make the most of them and go to some of the classes they offer throughout the day. I really don't mind what type of class or who the teacher is, the most important thing for me is to stay in shape, and the more exercise I can do the better! I'm managing to lose weight through hours of sacrifice, and I consider myself a healthier person for it. One of my secrets to stay in shape is to increase the amount of exercise I do when I have a heavy meal. For me, this is one way of compensating what I have eaten without having to turn to other weight-loss methods, such as slimming pills, miracle diets, laxatives, etc. . . . People are a very much mistaken in this aspect, and if they just did more sport they would stay in shape. I recommend my approach: I make the most of any spare hours in the morning and evening to go to the gym.

A regular gym user

4.1 Introduction

Does the person in the above example suffer some type of eating pathology? According to the information given, no pathogenic weight-loss methods are employed, but

Eating Disorders in Athletes   Joaquín Dosil
© 2008 John Wiley & Sons, Ltd

this individual uses exercise as a way of compensating for the food eaten, allowing him/her to stay in shape and maintain a certain body figure.

Analysing the factors that trigger eating disorders in sport is fundamental for their prevention. Perhaps the person described above is simply looking after their health through exercise. Nevertheless, depending on certain factors, which are discussed throughout this chapter, the words he/she uses may indicate a certain degree of obsession with physical activity and the gym setting. To give an accurate diagnosis, it is important to analyse both the person suffering from an eating disorder (the athlete), as well as other individuals implicated in the sports context (coaches and parents). This chapter explains the key elements psychologists must consider in order conducting an accurate assessment and diagnosis of eating disorders in sport, as well as guidelines to help parents and coaches detect these illnesses in their children and athletes.

The following pages describe the aspects to consider in the evaluation and diagnosis of eating problems in sport, presenting a psychological assessment system for eating disorders in athletes. Such a system must meet the following criteria:

- The use of comparable assessment techniques. As in any environment where a process of psychological assessment is to be established, the techniques used must be broadly tried and tested. Therefore, not only must the techniques have undergone empirical contrasting with reliable and valid indicators (questionnaires, for example), but also from a qualitative perspective, the subjective parameters should display a significant diagnostic potential.

- The use of an integral assessment system. Whilst for purely formal reasons, an analysis of each assessment proposal is conducted separately here; the process should be consistently based on the concept of a unified psychological assessment. This principal requires sport psychologists to employ a collection of complementary techniques, as well as constantly considering the possibility of adopting other forms of analysis where necessary, in order to consolidate the obtained results (for example, a physical evaluation).

- The use of innovative assessment techniques. Within the realms of possibility, and depending on recent advances in scientific literature, the most innovative methods of psychological assessment for eating disorders must be adopted. 'Innovative' does not always imply using the most recently developed assessment techniques: the effectiveness of not so recent strategies may have been proved in current research. The key is to draw on the techniques confirmed to be successful by up to date investigations.

- Rigorous development of the techniques. Whether the techniques employed are quantitative or qualitative, the aim is to support the overall study with methods that display a consistent development as analytical instruments (consistent, rigorous and supported by theories recognised by the scientific community).

• The use of characteristic assessment techniques from the sporting environment. Finally, wherever possible, psychological assessment systems developed and tested in the sports environment should be used, rather than turning solely to assessment instruments from the general field of psychology.

4.2 Diagnostic criteria for eating disorders in sport

In the University of Michigan, USA, they still remember when Jeff Reese collapsed just as he got on the scales. Reese, a third grade student and member of the wrestling team (an Olympic sport with great tradition in the USA), had arrived at the gym that day with glazed eyes, looking very weak and pale. This was the result of three days of sauna, strenuous exercises with a waterproof jacket over his cotton sports clothes, and almost inhumane fasting. His objective was none other than to lose the eight kilos he needed to shed to compete in the 150 lb weight division.

Romo, 1998

This scenario, which may shock some readers, is common in weight division sports, such as wrestling. As competitions get nearer, athletes employ various techniques to lose the necessary weight to compete in the most suitable division for their physical and technical characteristics. Weight is the only criteria for competing in one category or another, and all is decided during pre-competition weigh-ins. Normally, wrestlers are 1 or 2 kg over the allowed weight for a determined division, and try to rapidly lose them prior to competing. Although this is a familiar practice, it rarely reaches the extremes of the example shown here. When athletes reach these limits, their health and well-being is at risk, provoking negative consequences or even fatalities.

Athletes are at more risk of developing eating disorders in particular sports. Therefore, in weight division sports, or in disciplines in which being thin is essential to achieve the right aesthetics, or to meet physical demands, it is necessary to conduct a more specific psychological assessment than normal. Along these lines, with a sample of 78 female athletes at competitive level, Picard (1999) demonstrated how the time demands of doing excessive physical exercise correlate with the presence of psychological eating disorders. On the other hand, and more recently, Ackard *et al.*, (2002) studied a broad sample of 586 young females, verifying that the execution of excessive physical exercise is often associated with the presence of eating disorders, stressing once again the general idea that links disproportional physical activity with attempts to achieve certain weight-related goals (often irrational).

Anorexia, bulimia and eating disorders not otherwise specified (EDNOS) are the most frequently occurring eating pathologies. To the aforementioned conditions, other eating-related problems called bigorexia and orthorexia may be added (amongst other observed psychopathological conditions). In recent years, there has been a tendency to adapt the characteristics of each of these disorders to the sports context (Dosil, 2003). In the following sections, the principal aspects related to the psychological assessment of these conditions are described, both from a general perspective, as well as from a sports standpoint.

4.2.1 Anorexia in sport

The criteria for defining anorexia are described in any Handbook of Modified Behaviour or eating disorders texts, for which this section does not profoundly explain the general elements of this condition. According to the *Diagnostic and Statistical Manual* (DSM-IV-R) and the CIE-10, a series of basic characteristics displayed by individuals suffering from anorexia may be identified. More specifically, the characteristics displayed by anorexic athletes are:

- Significant weight loss (below 85 per cent of the minimum normal weight according to sex, height and age), and total refusal to maintain it above the minimum value (or trying to reduce it even further).

- Weight loss is voluntarily sought through the employment of certain weight loss methods, all of which are harmful to the body (vomiting, for example).

- Intense and irrational fear weight gain. Generally, sufferers are only able to maintain a relatively clear emotional stability when they lose weight.

- Distorted perception of all or some body parts. It is interesting to demonstrate how sufferers continue regarding their bodies as 'overweight', whilst others view a 'skeletal' frame.

- Organic symptoms may become evident, such as amenorrhoea in women or lack of sexual interest in men. Along these lines, if the disorder commences prior to puberty, the expected growth at this age is usually delayed or detained.

Some investigations show how excessive weight loss is related to a greater degree of physical activity. Szmukler *et al.* (1985) have demonstrated the relationship between anorexia nervosa and ballet. Although ballet is not a 'sport' in strict terms, it displays some definitive characteristics of being such; the great amount of hours dancers (principally children and adolescents) spend training and learning the different dance and ballet routines, and the immense physical strain this demands of them.

Toro (1995), referring to an experiment conducted by Routtenberg and Kuznesof (1967), showed how this 'weight loss–excessive physical activity' relationship also exists in animals. This investigation was carried out with rats, which were placed in a cage containing only a spinning wheel. The animals were allowed to freely access the wheel, but were only given food during 1 h a day. It became clear that the more the rats walked on the wheel, the less they ate, and their consequent weight loss further increased their physical activity. Eventually, this progressive starvation resulted in the death of all the rats. On the contrary, the control rats, which did not have access to a spinning wheel, but were placed under the same feeding regime, stabilised and survived the experiment.

Epling's research team at the University of Alberta, gathered and reinterpreted these experiments, concluding that animals submitted to restricted feeding regimes diminish their food consumption if they are given the opportunity to practise a locomotive activity (Epling *et al.*, 1983).

In humans, an increase in physical activity whilst embarking on restricted eating is a frequently observed practice in anorexics. There is a need to further develop the experiments conducted by Routtenberg and Kuznesof (1967), in order to establish whether the increase in physical activity is due to the diminished food consumption, as a biological process, or whether it results from a voluntary decision to lose more weight.

Along these lines, Epling and Pierce (1996) discuss the possibility of defining a new type of exercise-induced anorexia, based on the premise that physical activity produces a reduction in the ingestion of food as part of a biological process. This possible 'activity anorexia' is not yet recognised by any diagnostic category. The only types of anorexia specified are: the restrictive type, where an individual loses weight through voluntary starvation, diets or intense physical activity; and the compulsive/purgative type, where an individual turns to purgatory behaviours, inducing vomiting or the excessive use of diuretics, laxatives or emetics (DSM-IV-R) (Table 4.1).

Similarly, Draeger *et al.* (2005), in agreement with these concepts, coin the term *obligatory exerciser*, referring to subjects who practise sport to the point of it becoming an obsession (sport becomes a basic necessity). Other commonly used terms related to this phenomenon include: *activity disorder, compulsive athleticism, excessive exercise, exercise dependence, obligatory exercise, running addiction* and *obligatory running*. This form of exercise addiction may even entail symptoms of the abstinence syndrome when sufferers are unable to work out (this exercise dependence is further discussed in the section on bigorexia). These are individuals who want to improve every time they embark on physical activity and are never satisfied with their achievements.

Obligatory exercisers, just as anorexics, restrict the quantity of food they consume, believing that losing weight will improve their performance. Here the question may be asked: what makes these subjects any different from anorexics? In both cases, there exists an excessive concern for the body, and frequently, what drives sufferers to run so frequently is their own failure to conform to their weight and physical makeup.

As may be observed, a certain overlap of symptoms exists between these disorders, making it difficult to place subjects within one determined diagnostic category, such as anorexia or any other non-specified condition, such as obligatory exercise. Yates (1991), quoted by Toro (1995), in an attempt to unite the two disorders, proposed another category: *activity disorders*, in which the characteristics of anorexia and obligatory exercise unite to form a new condition, described by the following indicators:

Table 4.1 Summary of the diagnostic criteria for anorexia nervosa and bulimia nervosa, in accordance with the DSM-IV-R (American Psychiatric Association, 2000)

Anorexia nervosa	Bulimia nervosa
Refusal to maintain body weight above the minimal normal value according to age and height	Recurring binge-eating episodes, defined by: *Eating discretely for a period of time (for example, 2 h)*
Weight falls below 85% of the established level	Consuming a greater quantity of food than the majority of people would ingest in a similar period of time and under similar circumstances
	Sensation of loss of control
Intense fear of gaining weight or becoming obese	Repetitive employment of inappropriate compensatory behaviours to avoid weight gain, such as: self-induced vomiting, abuse of laxatives, diuretics, enemas or other pharmaceuticals, starvation and excessive exercise.
Altered perception of body weight or figure	A minimum of at least two binge-eating episodes and compensatory behaviours a week, during a period of 3 months
Self-assessment is excessively influenced by body shape and weight	
Amenorrhoea – menstruation assisted by hormonal treatments is also counted as amenorrhoea	Alterations do not occur exclusively during the course of the anorexia nervosa
Subtypes	
The restrictive type: the individual does not regularly employ 'binges' or other purgatory behaviours	*The purgative type*: the individual regularly provokes vomiting or uses laxatives, diuretics or enemas to excess
The compulsive/purgative type: the individual regularly conducts 'binges' or other purgatory behaviours	*The non-purgative type*: the individual employs other non-purgative conducts such as starvation or intense exercising

Source: Dosil (2003).

- *Qualitatively, the employment of physical activity defers from the norm.* Physical activity is not used for leisure, nor to maintain fitness and health, but solely as a means of achieving weight related objectives.

- *Sufferers experience high levels of arousal and unease when trying to relax or rest.* Any periods of inactivity create a sense of nervousness and discomfort, since the sufferer associates them with a failure to execute the aforementioned objectives.

- *Physical activity establishes the emotional state.* As with drug addictions, in which sufferers experience the abstinence syndrome (discomfort) if they cease

Figure 4.1

consumption, carrying out physical activity is the only way sufferers feel emotionally at ease.

- *Once the illness has taken hold, the disorder is self-perpetuated and sufferers resist change.* As with any psychological disorder related to modify eating, this disorder is difficult to amend, regardless the psychological therapy applied.

- *Some sufferers use primitive defence mechanisms to justify doing physical activity, such as idealisation, omnipotent control, grandeur fantasies, etc.* This indicator may be linked to other specific eating or personality disorders, which may prove the real 'breeding ground' for the appearance of this psychological problem.

- *Only the excessive use of the body produces the physiological effects of deprivation, an important component in an activity disorder.* The physiological effects of deprivation are generated through excessive muscular use of the entire body. This concept is further described in the section on bigorexia.

- *The provoked physical deprivation perpetuates the process and contributes significantly to the psychopathology.* As indicated earlier, the psychopathology is not only linked to eating pathologies, but to personality disorders too.

- *The extent to which subjects acquire self-control through physical activity is inversely related to their capacity to reduce control and receive gratification in their personal relationships.* As with all eating disorders, sufferers focus exclusively on developing the means to achieve their weight objectives and specific physical state, abandoning family and social interactions to the point of isolation.

- *Sufferers display a specific personality profile.* As will be seen with bigorexia, although sufferers do not fit perfectly into any one psychopathological profile, it is possible to describe the underlying personality traits of these individuals to a certain degree of accuracy.

- *Individuals with this disorder may attain academic and career success thanks to their orientation towards personal achievement.* One of the indicators linked to this psychological problem is obsessive behaviour. Since sufferers are able to direct their behaviour towards other activities, such as studying or work, psychologists often face individuals with great achievements in these fields, or in fact, in any area they decide to point their efforts towards.

Finally, Del Castillo (1998b) proposes the term: *athletic* or *sports anorexia* as a prevailing condition amongst athletes, characterised by an intense fear of gaining weight or becoming obese. In addition to normal training, these athletes carry out exercise in an excessive or compulsive manner so to purge their bodies of the effects of eating. As this type of disorder is closely related to the previous description by Yates (1991), the majority of the previously analysed indicators are applicable.

4.2.2   Bulimia in sport

Research studies into the symptoms of anorexia in the sports environment are ever more frequent. This may be partly explained by the increasing efforts to clearly and concisely catalogue the rising eating behaviour problems in athletes and, as with the non-sporting population, anorexia appears to be the most common eating disorder amongst athletes.

Bulimia, the other clearly defined eating psychopathology, may also be directly related to the sports context. As with anorexia, sufferers seek weight loss goals that can be achieved more quickly through adopting bulimic behaviours. Uniting the characteristics of the DSM-IV-R and the CIE-10, and adding a brief description to each proposed indicator, the following essential diagnostic criteria for bulimia nervosa may be cited:

- *Recurrent episodes of binge eating, in which sufferers voraciously consume large quantities of food, mostly high calorie items, in a short period of time.* Two aspects clearly characterise this type of behaviour: first, the array of thoughts and emotions sufferers endure in preparing the event, as well as in conducting the behaviour itself; and second, the undeniable compulsive and obsessive component.

- *Binge eating episodes are linked to sensations of loss of control (e.g. the sensation of not being able to stop eating), guilt, shame and desperation.* People suffering from bulimia describe how once the voracious consumption behaviour commences, they feel an uncontrollable desire to eat, leading to enormous consumption and subsequent feelings of guilt.

- *The employment of inadequate compensatory behaviours, aimed at impeding weight gain and undoing the consequences of binge eating.* The most commonly used method is self-induced vomiting. Shortly after engaging in binge eating, and as a consequence of the negative thoughts and emotions it provokes, sufferers try to compensate for their behaviour through self-induced vomiting, and in some cases, excessive exercise during long periods of time.

- *Persistent preoccupation with weight and body shape (a central symptom of anorexia and bulimia).* As with anorexia, the main motivator behind any of the described conducts is to maintain a certain body weight, usually within distorted or excessive parameters for a sufferer's height and physical constitution. Consequently, on many occasions, the symptoms of anorexia and bulimia coincide in the same individual.

Essentially, the prevalence of bulimia in athletes is lower than anorexia (as with the non-sporting population). The two disorders display certain characteristics that allow them to be distinguished from one another. For example, bulimic sufferers usually fall within the margins of their 'normal weight', something that does not tend to occur with anorexia, in which one of the principal criteria is a weight loss beyond the established weight limits.

However, with both disorders sufferers go 1 or more days without eating and/or do intense physical exercise, although in bulimia this conduct is carried out to compensate for the calories consumed during binge eating episodes. Bulimic behaviour is frequent in athletes who have suffered some form of setback during a season (for example, an injury), which has obliged them to rest and consequently gain weight. In these circumstances, the appetite usually increases and athletes feel 'guilty' for having to consume more food. This sensation is often the origin of binge eating practices, and many athletes have confirmed this as the main factor triggering bulimia.

To clarify the issue, Table 4.1 contrasts the diagnostic criteria for anorexia and bulimia.

The use of diverse and often inappropriate weight-loss methods is frequent in sport. On many occasions, the demands of training and competition 'force' athletes to introduce this sort of behaviour into their normal training routines, which can lead to non-premeditated eating problems.

Similarly, in certain sporting disciplines, when confronted with the physical impossibility of eating (prior to or during competitions), it is common for athletes to lose control in the post-competition period, and binge-eating episodes may constitute a form of 'freeing competitive tensions' afterwards, in turn inducing inadequate compensatory weight-loss methods. During these 'rituals', athletes generate non-adaptive responses to situations of excess anxiety, potentially establishing a 'viscous circle', which must be confronted by the therapy applied.

4.2.3 Bigorexia and orthorexia

Bigorexia and orthorexia are two 'new' eating behaviour disorders, both of which have been linked to the sports context, with cases occurring in athletes from a diverse range of disciplines. Although these conditions are not officially recognised by the DSM-IV, numerous studies have been published in recent years, relating them to the sporting environment.

Bigorexia   Bigorexia, *muscle dysmorphia* or *reverse anorexia* (different terms for the same condition) fit into a group of obsessive–compulsive disorders that are more specifically subcategorised as body dysmorphic disorder, suffered by individuals who are not at ease with their own bodies and obsess over improving certain physical defects (Garcés de Los Fayos & Vives Benedicto, 2003; Leone *et al.*, 2005). For some, bigorexia constitutes the reverse of anorexia: whilst anorexia appears mostly in young girls who never feel sufficiently thin, for however much weight they lose; in the majority of cases, bigorexia affects young men who crave for a more muscular body (Table 4.2).

Pope and research colleagues initiated the study of bigorexia (Pope *et al.*, 1993, 1997, 2000a, b), defining it as a mental disorder, provoking an exaggerated obsession with gaining muscular mass and losing non-lean weight. In the Laboratory of Biological Psychiatry at the Mclean Hospital, Pope directed an investigation into the use of anabolic steroids by men, selected from various gyms where weight-lifting was conducted. A significant number of subjects from this sample perceived themselves as small, thin and not very muscular, despite the extraordinary muscular development they displayed. Hence, the foundations were laid for what would later be termed 'reverse anorexia', given its initial association with an inverse form of the well-known eating disorder. Afterwards, the disorder was renamed bigorexia or, currently, 'Adonis Complex' (Pope *et al.*, 2000), which in its present form, refers to the muscular dismorphia observed in those suffering this problem.

Table 4.2   The principal differences between anorexia nervosa and bigorexia

	Anorexia	Bigorexia
Self-perception	Obese	Thin and weak
Predominant sex	Women	Men
Auto-medication	Diet pills, laxatives, etc.	Anabolic steroids, etc.

Bigorexia is related to any activity carried out excessively, to the point of making sufferers' daily lives more difficult. Along these lines, Zmijewski and Howard (2003) have researched into physical exercise dependence, an addiction that, without being termed Bigorexia, clearly refers to this disorder. In this study, it was demonstrated that young adults are most affected by this problem.

Figure 4.2

The essential characteristic of this psychological disorder is a chronic preoccupation for not being sufficiently muscular and, in some cases (especially in women), a self-perception of being too thin. As with the previously described eating problems, certain common personality variables play an essential role in compensating this syndrome. Hence, the primary personality traits that may be observed in people suffering from bigorexia, as indicated by Garcés de Los Fayos and Vives Benedicto (2003) are the following:

- *Low tolerance, bordering on frustration.* Sufferers fail to accept anything that goes against what they, as an individual, interpret as personal success. This explains their frustration at being quizzed over their activity and, above all, at failing to achieve their own exaggerated goals.

- *Difficulty expressing feelings.* To an alarming extent, sufferers display at least one dimension of the *alexitimia* syndrome, or more specifically, incapacity to express emotions and feelings, making it difficult for them to establish personal relationships outside of the gym setting.

- *Emotional somnolence.* In general, the emotional state of sufferers is 'low', with difficulty in feeling and expressing emotions (alexitimia). It is common to encounter individuals who are excessively self-focused.

- *Lack of barriers.* Sufferers do not appreciate the concept of limits when it comes to the muscular development of their bodies, not even their own health is a barrier to their obsessive corporal development.

- *Feelings of loneliness and pertinence.* As previously indicated, sufferers are usually solitary individuals. They frequently establish some personal relationships in the gym environment, the majority of which are superficial and serve only to highlight their loneliness.

- *Difficulty relating present actions to future events, such as utopian projects.* It is complicated to observe bigorexia sufferers planning future projects in function of a solid present reality. On many occasions, such a reality does not exist, since their whole life revolves around their excessive gym activity. Likewise, when some type of future project does appear, it is usually utopian, or related to physical activity and their exaggerated muscular development.

- *Avidity for power and control.* Sufferers display the need to feel powerful and in control of the few situations they experience. They associate 'power' with force, symbolised by an ever-increasing muscular frame.

- *Empty interior pseudo-identity.* These individuals possess a false identity, based on their bodies. Consequently, the more muscular they become, the more they are able to identify with themselves. This process is carried out with a feeling of strength and 'power', as previously described, but since they are practically never truly at ease with their bodies, their 'false' identity seldom becomes satisfactory.

Finally, according to Caracuel *et al.* (2003), an individual cannot be considered bigorexic for simply going to the gym a lot and lifting weights. Indeed, they must also display a series of behaviours which, when associated with the aforementioned personality variables, allow them to be diagnosed as suffering from this disorder. Such diagnosable conducts include the following:

- *Self-perception of being excessively thin, despite having a muscular frame.* These individuals enter a 'vicious circle', practising exercise intensively with the aim of increasing their muscular volume. However, continuing to perceive themselves as thin leads them to believe they are not doing the sufficient amount of exercise, hence further increasing their activity (logically, without success).

- *Excessive concern for the body.* For bigorexics, life revolves around their bodies and they try to sculpture it just as they imagine in their minds. Of course, it is generally impossible to attain the limits they envisage, leading to further frustration.

- *Many hours a day spent thinking about the body.* These individuals spend a great deal of time mulling over what they want to accomplish with their bodies (how they want it to look and when they are going to achieve it). These thoughts are recurring and obsessive, becoming unpleasant for athletes.

- *A considerable number of hours spent in the gym.* To achieve the desired objectives, sufferers carry out a lot of exercise, spending hours in the gym executing high intensity exercises.

- *The frequent abandonment of other habitual activities.* For bigorexics, the almost exclusive dedication to a life spent in the gym makes it difficult to rationally maintaining other areas of their lives (work and/or family). Moreover, if they deem their physical activity is being hindered, they often totally neglect or abandon other areas of their life.

- *Strict diets and the consumption of substances, such as anabolic steroids.* Realising it is impossible to develop the muscular body they desire with exercise alone, sufferers turn to other strategies. These usually include restrictive diets and the consumption of substances to increase muscular volume, both of which interfere with the functioning of the vital organs, such as the heart, liver and pancreas.

- *Repetitive obsessive behaviours related to physical activity.* Amongst other behaviours, sufferers may weigh themselves several times a day or look at themselves frequently in the gym mirror, comparing their bodies with those of others around them (fellow gym members), etc. These compulsive behaviours provide clues as to the existence of a deteriorating perceived body image.

- *Repetitive rituals that become tics.* Certain postures, accentuated poses when interacting with others, or movements reflecting the gym exercises carried out, are some of the rituals that can become nervous tics.

- *The sensation of failure.* In not being able to achieve exactly what they want, the everyday behaviour of sufferers reflects feelings of failure and unhappiness.

Orthorexia Bratman coined the term orthorexia in 1997, in an article published in *Yoga Journal*. People suffering from this condition are characterised by a pathological obsession with consuming healthy foods (Bratman & Knight, 2001). This fixation reaches the point that the individual scrutinises the ingredients and nutritional value of each and every food item, excluding those they consider damaging to the health. Compared to other eating disorders, such as anorexia or bulimia, in which the principal obsession of sufferers is the *quantity* of food consumed, orthorexia is related to the *quality* of the food item. An interesting investigation carried out by Catalina *et al.* (2005) describes the characteristics of orthorexia through case studies and explains the principle differences from other eating disorders.

There is still little research into this disorder, and existing studies tend to focus on the general population. These investigations conclude that orthorexic subjects attribute characteristics to food that reflect their specific 'feelings': 'dangerous' to describe a conserved product, 'artificial' for industrially produced items, and 'healthy' for biological produce (Donili *et al.*, 2004), as well as using food as a self-assessment instrument, ORTO-15 (Donili *et al.*, 2005). On all accounts, a greater number of investigations are required before being able to confirm orthorexia as a scientifically accepted disorder.

In the sports context, no studies have yet been conducted to establish the prevalence of this disorder. Nevertheless, experience working with elite athletes has revealed how many obsess over the ingredients of food items, evaluating them according to what they can contribute to training and/or competition tasks. Therefore, given this apparent 'food fixation', the sports environment should be studied as a 'high-risk' population in the future.

4.2.4   *Eating disorders not otherwise specified (EDNOS)*

Having analysed the two principal psychological problems associated with eating (anorexia and bulimia), and two 'novel' eating behaviour disorders (bigorexia and orthorexia), it is fitting to give a brief description of some non-specific eating disorders, including irrational eating habits. Those eating pathologies, which do not comply with the diagnostic criteria of anorexia, bulimia, bigorexia or orthorexia, may be placed within this category. The prevalence of these conditions amongst the general population is higher than other eating disorders, as demonstrated by Machado *et al.* (2006): in a sample of 2028 female students from Portugal, 0.39 per cent were found to be suffering from anorexia and 0.30 percent from bulimia, whilst an elevated 2.37 per cent had some form of EDNOS.

EDNOS present the following characteristics:

- Women, who meet all the criteria for anorexia, but have regular menstruation.

- Individuals who comply with all the criteria for anorexia, but do not deviate from the normal minimum weight limits.

- Individuals, who meet all the criteria for bulimia nervosa, but engage in binge-eating episodes and inappropriate compensatory behaviours less than twice a week, or during less than 3 months.

- Individuals with a normal weight whom; having ingested small quantities of food, regularly employ inappropriate compensatory behaviours.

- Chewing and expelling, but not swallowing, important quantities of food.

- Compulsive disorder: recurring binge-eating episodes with the absence of the typical inappropriate compensatory behaviours associated with bulimia nervosa.

- Behaviours reminiscent of physical exercise addiction, without the physical complexion of those suffering from bigorexia.

- People with extremely developed muscles and some incorrect eating habits, but who do not display obsessive and/or compulsive behaviours related to physical exercise and eating.

- Any non-reasonable eating habit that does not fit within the diagnostic criteria of the four described eating disorders.

Perhaps the eating pathologies represented in this list are the most frequently found in sport, although they are often confused with the most well known disorders: anorexia, bulimia, bigorexia, and orthorexia. EDNOS can easily go unnoticed by coaches and others involved in sport, making their diagnosis even more complicated. For example, an athlete who displays almost all the symptoms of anorexia, but who maintains a normal menstrual cycle or body mass index can be diagnosed with EDNOS. Therefore, in order to establish an effective psychological assessment and assist an accurate diagnosis, it is important for sport psychologists to be fully aware of all the diagnostic criteria (both for the 'classic' eating disorders, as well as those which are less documented in scientific literature).

Along these lines, as will be detailed in the following section, in addition to interviews and questionnaires, observation is one of the basic assessment techniques, allowing psychologists to make a correct diagnosis and provide accurate therapeutic proposals to help athletes suffering from these problems.

4.3 Methods for diagnosing eating disorders in sport

The psychological assessment and diagnosis of eating behaviour disorders in athletes has been much studied in recent years. Although the techniques and methods are varied, three strategies remain predominant for assessing aspects related to negative eating habits: interviews, observation, and specific questionnaires.

While *self-report questionnaires* are very helpful instruments, they should never be used alone. The information they provide, combined with that supplied by interviews and observation proves more definitive when it comes to forming an accurate diagnosis.

4.3.1 Interviews

Interviews should be designed to assess the presence of eating disorder symptoms. The interview guide by Kutlesic *et al.* (1998) provides a good reference. In addition to information regarding athletes' identification and context, it is important to clarify some aspects related to eating behaviours and body perception. Below, various strategies regarding the type of questions that should be posed to athletes, coaches and parents are analysed. Considering the objectives being pursued, this operation is based on a semi-structured interview model.

Weight-control methods   The eating behaviours athletes employ to control their body weight must be deciphered. As some of these conducts may be dependent on the sporting discipline, it is fundamental to analyse the following aspects:

- *Restricted eating or 'diets'*: specific information about the type and quantity of food being consumed should be requested (for example, athletes may be asked to detail everything they eat in a day). Likewise, the number of meals being consumed need to be established, studying whether any are being skipped (breakfast, lunch, afternoon snack and/or dinner). Nevertheless, this process must reflect the fact that some specialities require athletes to follow certain diets, making it more important than ever to fully understand the training and competitive structures of the sport in question (Dosil, 2002a, 2006). During the interview, athletes may be asked about the suitability of the diet they maintain, their reasons for developing certain eating habits and their future plans to improve their established practices (this should always be done from a technical perspective without showing any interest in detecting potential psychological problems). On the contrary, the focus with parents and coaches can be more clinical, leaving technical aspects aside. They may be asked more directly about the suitability of the methods being adopted by their athletes, whether they have collaborated in designing and/or supporting these habits, if they have applied any corrective strategies, or what they do if they observe irrational attitudes towards eating.

- *Compensatory behaviours*: athletes may be asked how they behave after having consumed so-called 'prohibited' foods. These conducts may include purgative/ compensatory behaviours, such as the habitual employment of self-induced vomiting, diuretics, laxatives or similar, or indeed any other form of non- purgative compensatory behaviour, such as fasting or excessive exercising. Once again, considering athletes as special individuals, the focus of the interview should be indirect and subtle. The sports psychologist should try to ascertain whether athletes feel bad about the eating strategies and habits they have developed, whether they think they need to be alert for any problems in the 'logical' development of their eating practices, or if they have observed any resistance from their coach or family, etc. Once again, coaches and parents may be asked more frankly about the existence of prolonged periods of absence after eating, whether they have observed behaviours which imply the athlete is hiding something, if they have noticed how the athlete 'disappears' to the bathroom following a mealtime, or if they detect certain irritability after eating, to give but a few examples.

Concerning purgative behaviours, sport psychologists should also consider certain methods that people consider as 'natural', such as infusions or other drinks provoking laxative effects. Similarly, some athletes may employ other forms of medication to counteract constipation after having consumed 'prohibited' foods.

Regarding excessive physical exercise, the assessment should start by establishing the daily exercise routine carried out by the athlete (communication with coaches is important at this stage). During the interview, athletes should be asked to state whether they consider their physical training programme as rational, giving their reasons. Parents and coaches should then be asked the same question, in order to identify potential incongruence. Third, this data must be contrasted against the opinion of an expert, who can objectively evaluate the suitability of the exercise regime. Where necessary, this specialist information may be used in second interviews to dismantle statements and reformulate questions surrounding the matter.

Over-consumption and/or binge eating should be carefully analysed, since many athletes exaggerate the amount of food they eat. Those taking up a sport, especially young athletes, often experience any alteration in their diet as over-consumption, despite only having increased their intake by a small and reasonable amount. There-fore, in this section, it is important to analyse the perceptions of excessive consump-tion, the motives driving over consumption, and whether binge eating is systematic or occasional. Once again, parents and coaches will be openly approached about the matter, whilst athletes will be questioned in a 'softened' manner to avoid creat-ing communicational barriers which could hinder the adequate development of the interview (for example: Do you think you sometimes overeat? Does this affect your sporting performance?).

Motivation to lose weight   Many athletes in high-risk sports (see Chapter 2) crave a lower body weight. In the majority of cases, they believe that losing weight is synonym of improved technique and/or performance. The social environment sur-rounding athletes and the pressures exerted by coaches further influence this factor (see Chapter 3). These attitudes may indicate the presence of an eating disorder and should be evaluated during the interview.

Likewise, sports psychologists should take into account the limits athletes estab-lish for losing weight, their obsession for doing so, and their planned or employed behaviours to achieve these objectives. When interviews reveal that eating behav-iour is severely altered, but the interviewee fails to regard the consequences as rele-vant, persisting in losing more weight, an eating pathology is at hand. In this situation, the interview strategy should work towards asking about the importance of losing weight to improve performance, relating low weight to enhanced results, and even linking weight loss to satisfaction and personal well-being as a way of life. From a technical perspective, coaches and parents may be asked to express whether it is reasonable for the athlete to lose more weight (something the interviewer him/ herself must also decide through the relevant assessment and consulting with experts); as well as whether they have evaluated the negative aspects of this weight loss, if they consider the athlete's attitude towards weight loss to be reasonable, or if they believe it is necessary to break the obsessive dynamic in which the athlete has entered.

Figure 4.3

Exercise amenorrhoea   In high-risk sports, interrupted menstruation or the delayed arrival of the first menstruation are common. Unlike the general population, where this indicator, along with other symptoms of anorexia nervosa, would confirm the diagnosis, in some sporting disciplines this symptom may be secondary, except when it coincides with severe weight loss. In certain sports, especially during competitive periods, amenorrhoea may occur naturally and does not necessarily constitute a reliable indicator of an eating disorder. Along these lines, Niñerola and Capdevila (2002) highlight the following abnormalities in the menstrual cycle:

- Oligomenarche: when an athlete has 3 to 6 menstrual periods a year, or when the difference between each menstruation is more than 38 days.

- Primary amenorrhoea: when an athlete aged 16 years has yet to have their first menstruation.

- Secondary amenorrhoea: when an athlete goes 3–6 months without any menstrual period.

Considering this indicator and having accessed the relevant information, interviews with coaches, parents and athletes should focus on the following aspects: whether they consider the existence of this organic problem as normal, whether they think it is important, and above all, whether they have taken any steps to solve it.

4.3.2   The assessment of body weight: anthropometrical indices

The DSM-IV-R criteria (American Psychiatric Association, 2000) for anorexia nervosa stipulate that an individual should be at least 15 per cent below their ideal weight. Nonetheless, given the characteristics of certain sporting disciplines, some athletes meet this criterion without suffering an eating pathology. Therefore, in order to adequately evaluate this aspect, sports psychologists must be careful to employ the appropriate anthropometrical indices for the sport and the body characteristics of the subject in question.

The anthropometrical diagnostic base is found through comparison. Its aim is to determine the characteristics of an attribute, that is to say, whether it can be considered as normal, or whether it deviates from the norm. In this sense, reference tables show the evolution and normal variability of a determined anthropometrical parameter according to sex and age. Nevertheless, on occasions, overall body measurements are not sufficiently explicit, making it necessary to enrich them by relating them to other measurements. These relationships are denominated *indices* and constitute the numerical expression of the proportional relationship between two or more measures (e.g. height and weight). These indices allow the quantification of differences or similarities, as well as constituting a reference point for the psychological evaluation being conducted.

The use of indices is important, as it contributes to understanding the organism in its totality and not as an aggregate of elements. In general, they are expressed in percentages and indicate tendencies. They have a functional character as parameters for estimating different variables, specifying their characteristics and recognising their meaning. In this sense, somatometric information acquires relevance when the anthropometrical measurements are integrated into a profile, selecting those characteristics with the greatest discriminative potential.

To gather somatometric data, it is necessary to create an anthropometrical index, orientated towards the aims of the study and the sporting discipline in question. Given that people suffering from eating disorders are usually resistant to any type of physical measurement (although many athletes are accustomed to bodily controls), the smallest number of anthropometrical indices possible should be considered, selecting those that provide the most information.

During interviews, athletes, coaches and parents should be asked about their perception of the results obtained from the anthropometrical indices: whether they consider them as normal or if they think they deviate more than is acceptable. More specifically, parents and coaches should be asked whether they consider the athlete needs help to solve any important digressions, or if they have already taken any corrective steps.

4.3.3 Body image perception: dissatisfaction and disturbance

Body image perception is an important factor in the diagnosis of eating disorders, and a sufferer's subjective perspective often dominates the objective reality. According to Thompson and Sherman (1993b), body image has three components:

- *The perceptual component*: how athletes evaluate their body or some body parts. This element does not assess how accurate this perception is compared to the reality; it simply describes the perceived perspective.

- *The subjective component (cognitive–emotional)*: the attitudes, feelings, cognitions and values athletes attribute to their body. Here, the rational and irrational ideas related to the body are extremely relevant.

- *The behavioural component*: the conducts related to body perception and the associated feelings. In this component, it is easy to appreciate certain behaviours commonly associated with eating disorders.

Two important dimensions to consider when studying this variable are: *body image disturbance* and *body dissatisfaction*. In agreement with the scientific literature, body dissatisfaction is considered a predictive factor for eating disorders, whilst body image disturbance is generally seen as displeasure with the body image.

The methods for evaluating body perception may be classified in two groups: methods of bodily estimation by parts and methods of overall body estimation. With the first method, subjects are asked to indicate the dimensions of certain parts of their body, such as the hips, thighs, glutei and breasts. With the latter method, subjects are placed in front of a video, photograph or mirror, which they are able to manipulate, making their body figure larger or smaller according to how they see themselves.

Along similar lines, certain aspects should form part of the interview with athletes, such as: Which parts of their body they like or dislike, and why? What feelings and emotions does their body image provoke? Are they satisfied or dissatisfied with their body? Again, parents and coaches should be asked more directly about general aspects, such as whether or not their athletes are satisfied with their body, how their athletes perceive their body image, how important this image is to them compared to other personal values, and whether they consider their athletes' body perception as rational.

4.3.4   The female athlete triad

Many investigations in sport have focused on the so-called female athlete triad (Beals *et al.*, 1999; Roth *et al.*, 2000; Sanborn *et al.*, 2000), which refers to the combination of amenorrhoea, osteoporosis and eating behaviour disorders. Although its prevalence is unknown, the female athlete triad is believed to affect many athletes at all ages and at all competitive levels (Sherman & Thompson, 2003). An interesting study by Torstveit and Sundgot-Borgen (2005), with 669 elite athletes and 607 non-athletes, gained some significant results to help understand the prevalence of the female athlete triad in the general and sports population: a higher percentage of non-athletes (69.2 per cent) than athletes (60.4 per cent) were shown to be at risk of the triad. These results, which may seem somewhat contradictory at first, become clearer if the elite athletes are divided into leanness sports competitors (70.1 per cent) and non-leanness sport competitors (55.3 per cent). Therefore, athletes competing in leanness sports and non-athletes are more at risk of the triad compared to athletes competing in non-leanness sports.

Currently, a more asserted effort is being made to prevent this problem, based on educating parents and coaches. However, several North American and Canadian studies have demonstrated that the majority of high school athletic programmes are not adequately screening girls for the components of the triad, and schools lack educational programmes targeting athletes and coaches (De la Torre & Snell, 2005; Rumball & Lebrun, 2005). As indicated by Niñerola and Capdevila (2002), there is a close relationship between each of the triad symptoms and any indication of one should unchain a prevention system for the others. Therefore, it is extremely important to take these symptoms into consideration during an interview with female athletes. If and when these problems arise, a multidisciplinary team (doctors, sport psychologists, and nutritionists) should move in to adequately solve them, since not only cognitive aspects are affected. Likewise, the diagnostic criteria for each symptom may be employed to assess the others. For example, the criteria for amenorrhoea may be included in interviews to assess the risks of osteoporosis.

Figure 4.4

In summary, considering all the relevant variables, sports psychologists can structure extensive interviews with athletes, coaches and parents, to help assess the existence of potential eating problems, the variables sustaining them, as well as discerning a determined psychopathological diagnosis. However, in addition to the aforementioned aspects, some other important characteristics help develop a more effective interview:

- *Comfort.* Interviews should be comfortable at all times for athletes. Whilst psychological comfort is created through the points described below, it is essentially vital that interviewees feel free to express whatever they deem suitable, without fear of being reproached. In this line of study, the principal objective of interviewers is for their subjects (athletes, coaches or family members) to perceive them as someone they can confide in without communicational barriers.

- *Absence of value judgements.* Regardless of the psychological problem being assessed, the interviewer should avoid any form of value judgements, since the contrary may cause subjects become defensive, impeding them from expressing anything that could be negatively judged (confrontational strategies of a defensive character). Eating disorders cause athletes to feel emotionally delicate at different phases of the disorder's development (anger, impotence, blame, shame . . .), and interviewers should approach interviews with equal delicacy, being careful not to emit judgements of any type, and in exceptional cases, only communicating those of a positive character.

- *Avoiding penalisation.* When interviewing athletes (or parents and coaches), psychologists must never allocate blame for what is happening. On the contrary, when it becomes necessary to confront the disorder, it should be done so by picking a line of argument from a posture of absolute respect for the subjects involved, providing practical guidance, never criticisms. Care should be taken not to blame or penalise athletes, since this would constitute emitting value judgements.

- *Being constructive.* The interviewer should display a positive and constructive attitude at all times. Subjects should perceive the psychologists' function as one of obtaining data for analysis, in order to form conclusions that will later form action guidelines to alleviate their psychological problems.

- *Sincerity.* The interviewer must remain sincere at all times, and the interviewees, especially athletes, should be able to appreciate this sincerity. Conducting an interview to the contrary can lead to athletes to feel betrayed by their psychologist, potentially provoking deterioration in their symptoms.

- *Knowledge of the sport.* Wherever possible, the sports psychologist who usually works with the athlete in question should conduct the interview, since he/she knows both the sport and the athlete's relationship with it in depth. In other words, the interviewer should understand the motives, values and attitudes involved during the practice of a specific sport. When this is not feasible, a sports psychologist, who complies with the greatest number or requirements, should carry out the interview.

- *Emotional control.* Finally, sports psychologists are reminded that interviews with athletes affected by eating problems are usually extremely frustrating. Amongst other behaviours, they tend to try to fool interviewers, dissimulate essentially important problems, refuse to confide, and continuously seek irrational justifications for their actions. This provokes a sensation of impotence and frustration which interviewers must know how to manage. Such emotional control is one of the essential characteristics required of sport psychologists conducting this type of interview.

4.3.5   *Observation*

The symptoms and indicators that point towards an eating disorder are frequently displayed through observable behaviours, although spotting them is usually extremely difficult. Therefore, observation becomes an essential technique in the process of psychological assessment.

In this particular context, a strategy of non-standardised observation is proposed. Unlike the observational registers used in the surveillance of disruptive classroom behaviour, for example, this strategy is structured to detect a series of indicators, which allow psychologists to regulate and focus further observation.

The same aspects considered for interviews may be applied for these indicators. Although it is not always possible to observe each and every one, the parameters to observe in the sports context include the following:

- *Dieting.* Psychologists should focus on the predominant food types being consumed at different mealtimes, how many meals are eaten a day, or the quantity of food being ingested. In high performance centres, where athletes tend to eat together, this process becomes simpler. On the other hand, psychologists must also look out for athletes displaying subtler behaviours, such as watching television programmes that deal with weight control, participating in internet forums or visiting web pages related to weight loss, opting to eat low-calorie products or so-called dietary foods, analysing the calorie contents of each food item in great depth, etc. Perhaps more importantly, psychologists should observe whether or not athletes frequently participate in conversations about weight control, and if this were the case, what aspects they cover in these discussions.

- *Compensatory behaviours.* Although difficult to observe, psychologists should be aware of certain behaviours: vomiting, the ingestion of diuretics, the use of enemas, etc. Moreover, psychologists must be aware of those behaviours which indirectly suggest the previously described conducts, such as absences immediately following mealtimes, taking medication and claiming it is for another ailment, etc.

• *Excessive exercise.* In theory, this indicator is relatively easy to observe. It involves observing two groups of very specific behaviours: on the one hand, psychologists need to verify whether athletes carry out more exercise than recommended by their coach, and whether the intensity of this exercise is rational according to the technical and physical objectives; and on the other hand, they may observe whether athletes illogically develop physical and/or sporting activities outside of their normal training sessions, without the approval of their coach.

• *Binge eating.* Once again, this aspect is relatively difficult to analyse, since it involves observing whether an athlete consumes food in an excessive manner. Given that binges are usually conducted alone, they are never easy to prove. Nevertheless, certain signs that give clues to the existence of this behaviour are observable: food going astray, an athlete spending an unexpected amount of money or eating in an accelerated manner during meals, etc.

• *Motivation for losing weight.* Psychologists must keep an eye out for this type of motivation, which athletes are unlikely to willingly express. Therefore, the aim is to observe conducts which provide this information, such as frequently talking to team mates or friends about weight loss and diet, frequently studying their body as if assessing whether or not they are thin, or looking in the mirror, seemingly evaluating their current physical state, etc.

• *Organic problems.* Any physical deterioration can be easily observed. However, psychologists must ascertain whether such bodily decline is in its initial stages or whether it is the result of a prolonged process. Along these lines, problems may include amenorrhoea, osteoporosis, hepatitis, or intestinal and stomach complications. Once confirmed by medical analysis, these symptoms must be treated, and psychologists may then proceed to observe other related behaviours to confirm their suspicions. Ideally, the aim is to treat specific behaviours to prevent the occurrence of further problems: can an athlete be seen taking any 'unexplained' substances? Are there any external changes to the skin condition or colour? Is there any other specific external deterioration? Does he/she seek information or hold conversations about certain physical problems?

• *Anthropometrical indices.* The majority of anthropometrical indices are observable just by looking, meaning psychologists simply need to test whether or not they are statistically 'normal', always taking into account the characteristics of the sporting discipline.

- *Body image.* The perception of one's body is a well-developed element in all human beings, helping to form personal identity. Nevertheless, concern for body image and fundamentally, dissatisfaction to the point of obsession escapes the realms of rationality. When individuals begin displaying certain repetitive conducts, they are revealing behaviours which contain a certain psychopathological component: thoroughly looking in the mirror, analysing each part of the body and measuring the skin folds, frequent weigh-ins, spending too much time analysing what type of diet will provide the right number of calories to meet weight loss objectives, etc.

- *General and sports psychological attitudes.* The psychological attitudes of athletes may be established through observing how much time they spend doing physical activity and/or sport, their willingness to do so and the satisfaction they feel afterwards. Similarly, how they speak about their sport and their emotional links to the sporting context further reveal their mind-set. However, such outlooks may also be reflected in other activities, such as the academic, professional or family panorama. If the attitudes displayed in all aspects are coherent with reasonable personal and sporting development, then there is no need to suppose an eating disorder. However, if attitudes become irrational to the point of obsessive, with excessive dedication to sport and the neglect of other activities, then there may be cause for suspecting an eating-related problem.

- *The emotional triangle.* Finally, a group of parameters should be observed in a more subjective manner. This involves verifying the type of relationships athletes maintain with their parents and coach. In an ideal scenario, all the variables in the emotional triangle are optimum: communication, establishing joint objectives, similar ways of understanding the athlete's dedication to the sport, assuming responsibilities, etc. However, if on the contrary, one or more of these variables is altered, the possibility of psychological problems increases. The probability that these problems are of an eating nature will depend on other associated factors such as personality variables or an athlete's natural predisposition. Therefore, observing this factor requires psychologists to ascertain the 'level of suitability of the emotional triangle'. In exceptional cases, when parents or coaches are observed encouraging athletes to develop irrational eating behaviours, the starting place of eating disorders may rest with these individuals, rather than the athlete.

The concern with food described in the previous section is frequent amongst anorexics: sufferers spend many hours a day thinking about food, collecting recipes or storing food items. Moreover, derived from the aforementioned factors, Swoap and Murphy (1995) indicate the following behavioural signs of eating disorders: weight loss, eating alone (avoidance of eating in public), obsessive concern for food, mood swings and distorted body image. Other anomalous behaviours include: eating excessively slowly, taking food out of the mouth and leaving it on the plate, examining food closely, spitting it out, etc. Similarly, Thompson and Sherman (1993b) associate eating disorders with depression, irritability and mood swings. Furthermore, the DSM-IV-R compares these conducts with the obsessive-compulsive disorder.

During behavioural observation, information from the family regarding eating habits and behaviour is important. Del Castillo (1998b) stresses a series of behaviours to consider when identifying athletes with anorexia and/or bulimia, highlighting that losing weight or being on a diet does not necessarily imply an eating disorder:

- insistent comments about being fat, despite being below the average normal weight;
- continued weight loss, even outside the sporting season, or extreme weight fluctuations;
- eating in secret;
- disappearing after mealtimes;
- apparent nervousness if unable to be alone following meals;
- red eyes after having been to the bathroom;
- mood swings;
- refusal to eat with the rest of the team.

On the other hand, a series of characteristic physical traits, which are visible at first sight, may also serve to detect eating problems: dry and cold skin, limp and fragile hair, weak nails with a tendency to deform and flake, lanugo (fine hair on face and arms), gum and tooth disease.

4.3.6 Questionnaires

Currently, the questionnaires used to detect eating disorders in athletes are usually the same as those used to diagnose the general population. Although classic instruments can provide suitable solutions for some athletes, it is necessary to adapt questionnaires to the characteristics of the sporting activity in question. Therefore, to attain increased reliability, the diagnostic criteria should be varied from one sporting discipline and another. Nevertheless, initiatives already exist to develop questionnaires for detecting these problems in specific sporting disciplines, which include items related to the risk factors described in Chapter 2.

Blasco *et al.* (1992) conducted an analysis of the data collection techniques used for the assessment of eating disorders in sport from 1980 to 1990. Although the studies carried out have multiplied in recent years, this data serves as a reference:

Table 4.3 Self-records used 1980–1990

EAT (Eating Attitudes Test) 18.60%
EDI (Eating Disorders Inventory) 18.60%
EAT-26 (Eating Attitudes Test-26) 9.3%
Obligatory Running Questionnaire 7%
MMPI (4.70%)
Many others appear in one article alone (Anorexia NI for self-rating –ANIS-, Offer Self Image
Q. Adolescents –OSIQ-, etc.)

54.43 per cent of the data collection instruments used in published empirical articles are self-records; 1.26 per cent are observational techniques and 44.3 per cent employ objective techniques consisting of physical and physiological variables (weight, size, hormonal levels, bone measurements, cardiovascular response, etc.).

Focusing on self-records, these authors describe the most frequently employed (Table 4.3).

In recent years the investigative panorama has changed, and although there are still many studies with athletes that use general questionnaires, more are beginning to employ more specific assessment instruments, closely linked to sport. The following sections describe some of the sport-specific questionnaires used for the evaluation of eating disorders in sport and physical activity (and related symptoms), as well as the general questionnaires that are still used in the sports setting.

Specific questionnaires for assessing eating disorders in athletes   One of the principal specific instruments for evaluating the so-called '*obligatory exerciser*' condition is the Obligatory Exercise Questionnaire (OEQ) by Pasman and Thompson (1988), modified from the Obligatory Running Questionnaire (Blumenthal *et al.*, 1984). Following this investigation, over the last 10 years, various attempts have been made to develop more specific assessment instruments, on the premise that sport and physical activity pose a series of unique elements which should not be disregarded at the evaluative stage. Along these lines, the following questionnaires, related to terms such as 'exercise dependence', 'excessive exercise' or 'obligatory exerciser', may be highlighted:

- The Exercise Dependence Questionnaire (EDQ) by Ogden *et al.* (1997): This Questionnaire assesses the motivation to exercise, aspirations for good health, need to control and modify appearance, and problematic exercise behaviours. It comprises 29 items, which are evaluated using a Likert scale, ranging from 1 (strongly disagree) to 7 (strongly agree), with a cut-off point of ≥116. The subscales are: withdrawal symptoms, exercise for weight control, positive rewards, stereotyped behaviour, interference with family/social life, positive rewards, insight into problems, and exercise for health reasons. This questionnaire has been employed in several investigations, including that of Bamber *et al.* (2000).

- The 'Exercise Orientation Questionnaire' (EOQ) by Yates *et al.* (2001): this instrument is composed of 27 items, which are evaluated using a five-point Likert Scale (ranging from 'agreement' to 'disagreement' with the statements). The EOQ covers six factors: self-control, exercise orientation, self-loathing, weight reduction, identity and competition. This instrument has been used in a diverse range of studies, such as those by Yates *et al.* (2003).

- The Exercise Dependence Scale (EDS) by Hausenblas and Symons (2002): This scale includes 21 items, which encompass questions related to exercise beliefs and behaviours that have occurred over the past 3 months. In total, 7 factors are measured (tolerance, withdrawal, intention effect, lack of control, time, reductions in other activities, and continuance) using a Likert scale, which goes from 1 (never) to 6 (always). Each factor is composed of three items. The obtained point scores serve to classify athletes in the dependence range (3 or more factors), the symptomatic range (3–4 range), or the asymptomatic range (1–2).

- The Exercise Addiction Inventory (EAI) by Terry *et al.* (2004): this instrument measures six addiction components (salience, conflict, mood modification, tolerance, withdrawal, and relapse), using a Likert scale ranging from 1 (strongly disagree) to 5 (strongly agree). The results of an investigation with 200 habitual exercisers demonstrated it to be an inventory with good psychometric properties, which serve to identify people affected by, or at risk of, exercise addiction (score above 24 points).

Without losing sight of the sports context, two initiatives that have focused on the development of sport-specific questionnaires may be highlighted. The objective of both these instruments is to evaluate athletes for eating disorders, employing specific items for the sports setting:

- The Athletic Milieu Direct Questionnaire (AMDQ) by Nagel *et al.* (2000): This questionnaire originally contained 119 items, which were formed following several investigations, and detect the diagnostic criteria for an eating disorder found in the DSM-III. The Athletic Milieu Direct Questionnaire items reflect psychosocial and athletic milieu behaviours relevant to weight management, diet, and exercise. The authors proposed three different versions of the AMDQ; each with 35, 19 and 9 items respectively; and employed it with the EDI-2 and the BULIT-R in order to compare the results and demonstrate the call for more sport-specific instruments for athletes. Nevertheless, few investigations have made use of the AMDQ since.

- The Eating Habits in Sport Questionnaire (*Cuestionario de Hábitos Alimentarios en el Deporte* – CHAD) by Dosil and Díaz (2006). This questionnaire consists of 34 items, measured using a Likert scale that ranges from 1 (totally disagree) to 6 (totally agree), grouped in five factors (fear of becoming fat, concern with body figure and image, weight and figure related irritability, satisfaction with weight and figure, and implementation of diets). The CHAD was applied together with the EAT, revealing some positive psychometric properties.

Now the principal assessment instruments used for detecting eating disorders in athletes have been described, the following section goes on to detail some questionnaires, developed for the general population, which are also applied in the sports setting:

Eating disorder symptoms   On an international scale, the most frequently used self-record for detecting the symptoms of eating disorders has been the Eating Attitudes Questionnaire (EAT-40), created by Garner and Garfinkel (1979). This test has been adapted and trialed in various countries (for example, on the Spanish population by Castro *et al.*, 1991), and has been used in multiple studies, including those conduced by Martin and Bellisle (1989), Furnham and Boughton (1995), Abraham (1996), Neumaerker *et al.* (1998), DeBate *et al.* (2002), Dosil and Díaz (2002), Hopkinson and Lock (2004), Okano *et al.* (2005), Toro *et al.* (2005), or Vardar *et al.* (2005), to give but a few examples.

Its objective is to identify the presence of symptoms and preoccupations, which are characteristic of eating disorders. Nevertheless, it should be highlighted that when this questionnaire was developed, bulimia nervosa was included in the diagnosis of anorexia nervosa, for which some studies have described it as too potent for the detection of anorexia nervosa alone.

It consists of 40 questions with six answer options. The international cut off point score is ≥ 30, indicating symptoms of an eating disorder. One easily applied version of this questionnaire is the EAT-26, which as its name suggests, reduces the number of items to 26 with a cut-off point score of ≥ 20. According to Garner *et al.* (1983), three factors should be noted:

- *Diet*: questions related to the avoidance of hyper-calorie products and concern for being thinner.

- *Bulimia and concern with food*: questions referring to thoughts or anxiety regarding food and components indicative of bulimia (overeating and/or compensatory behaviours).

- *Oral control*: questions connected to self-control, over eating and how the pressure of others to gain weight is perceived.

Another questionnaire that has been used broadly to evaluate eating disorders in sport is the Eating Disorder Examination Questionnaire (EDE-Q) by Fairburn and Beglin (1994), a semi-structured interview, specifically designed for detecting anorexia and bulimia. The EDE-Q uses a seven-point scale, in which the higher the point score, the more severe the eating disorder. The following scales are included in the questionnaire: restraint, shape concern, weight concern, and eating concern. This instrument has been used to determine the incidence of eating disorders in athletes in numerous investigations, including those by Bamber *et al.* (2000), Hulley and Hill (2001), Hopkinson and Lock (2004), Karlson *et al.* (2001) or Nichols *et al.* (2006), to name but a few.

Regarding the questionnaires used to specifically detect the symptoms of Bulimia Nervosa, one of the most commonly employed is the Bulimia Test (BULIT), created by Smith and Thelen (1984), and its revised version (BULIT-R), by Thelen *et al.* (1991). This questionnaire consists of 36 questions with five answer options. It is easily applied, taking just 10 minutes to fill-out, with point scores oscillating between 28 and 140 and a cut-off point of 104. Its objective is to identify the presence of symptoms and preoccupations characteristic of Bulimia. According to Smith and Thelen (1984), five factors are analysed:

- *Overeating*: the presence of overindulgence or binge-eating episodes (depending on their frequency).

- *Post binge-eating feelings*: the negative emotions, feelings of unease, anxiety or blame, which emerge following binge-eating episodes.

- *Vomiting*: the occurrence and frequency of self-induced vomiting.

- *Eating preferences during overeating episodes*: the tendency to consume high calorie foods during binge-eating episodes.

- *Weight fluctuations*: the presence of weight oscillations (indicating the magnitude).

Another questionnaire, frequently employed to evaluate bulimia symptoms, is the BITE (The Bulimic Investigatory Test Edinburgh) by Henderson and Freeman (1987), which consists of 33 items and comprises two scales: 'symptoms' and 'intensity-seriousness'. The first scale, 'symptoms', has four cut-off points, ranging from <10 (absence of compulsive behaviours towards food), to >20 (possible bulimia nervosa), and two intermediate cut-off points: 10–20 (patterns of abnormal eating behaviours) and 15–20 (possible subclinical bulimia nervosa). For the second scale, 'intensity-seriousness', the two cut-off points are 5–10 (significantly serious) and >10 (extremely serious).

Cognitive-behavioural factors   In addition to the EAT, the Eating Disorders Inventory (EDI) is another commonly used questionnaire on the international scene. EDI, created by Garner *et al.* (1983), endeavours to evaluate certain cognitive and behavioural characteristics related to anorexia nervosa and bulimia nervosa.

This inventory has been tested on a North American population (anorexics), as well as in other countries such as Spain (Guimerá & Torrubia, 1987) and Mexico (Alvarez *et al.*, 2000). More recently, it has been used in studies seeking analyse eating disorders and identify associated personality problems, such as the Millon Adolescent Clinical Inventory (Madison & Ruma, 2003). The analysis of this questionnaire, which does not produce a total point score, or an established cut off point, operates on the basis of eight subscales:

- *Drive for thinness*: excessive concern with diet and weight, an exaggerated desire to lose weight and an uncontrollable fear of gaining weight.

- Body *dissatisfaction*: unease with the overall physical aspect or some parts of the body.

- *Maturity fears*: the desire to remain within the security of the pre-adolescent years, apprehension towards the excessive demands of adulthood.

- *Bulimia*: the components or symptoms of bulimia nervosa, principally, over-eating, loss of control, binge eating and compensatory behaviours.

- *Lack of interoceptive awareness*: the incapacity to identify and differentiate between sensations of hunger and being full up.

- *Ineffectiveness*: feelings of inadequacy, insecurity, uselessness and lack of control over one's own life.

- *Perfectionism*: exaggerated expectations regarding personal achievements and an excessive emphasis on success.

- *Interpersonal distrust*: a generalised fear of establishing and maintaining lasting personal relationships, or expressing emotions to others.

The EDI has also been widely employed in the sports setting. Recently, Monsma and Malina (2004), and Taylor and Ste-Marie (2001), applied this instrument to evaluate eating behaviour disorders in ice-skaters. Likewise, Matheson and Crawford-Wright (2000) used the EDI with athletes and general exercisers. Equally, Hausenblas and McNally (2004) drew on the EDI-2, along with a questionnaire for diagnosing eating behaviour disorders in the general population, to examine the prevalence of eating behaviour disorders and their symptoms in secondary education pupils, comparing athletes with non. Similarly, some of the subscales are regularly used to analyse more specific aspects. Along these lines, Torstveit and Sundgot-Borgen (2005) adopted the Body Dissatisfaction and Drive for Thinness subscales to assess the female athlete triad.

Body image dysfunction On many occasions, athletes display a body image dysfunction. As previously indicated, two aspects of body image dysfunction may be highlighted: *body dissatisfaction* and *perceptual distortion*.

Body dissatisfaction is a predictive factor of eating disorders, and represents the degree to which athletes are content with the size and shape of their bodies. Amongst the instruments for measuring this construct, the Body Shape Questionnaire (BSQ), created by Cooper *et al.* (1987), and tested on a North American population (bulimics and control), has proved to be effective. This questionnaire consists of 34 questions with six answer options and an international cut off point of ≥105. No differential factors have been found (Cooper *et al.*, 1987). Its objective is to explore the self-perceptions of body image and more specifically, identify the presence of body dissatisfaction. When investigators wish to analyse body dissatisfaction, they frequently employ the corresponding subscale from the EDI, as mentioned beforehand.

On the other hand, *perceptual distortion* may be defined as the inability to accurately perceive one's body size. Generally, visual tasks are chosen to measure this aspect, such as the Body Image Assessment-Revised (BIA-R) by Beebe *et al.* (1999). This technique shows nine female figures on a sheet, from which athletes must indicate how they perceive their figure (real figure) and how they would like their figure to be (ideal figure). Similarly, the Figure Rating Scale (FRS) by Stunkard *et al.* (1983) evaluates the degree of satisfaction with body image in sport. The FRS has nine schematic female figures, ranging from underweight to overweight and displayed in a mixed order. In recent years, the FRS has been employed in several studies, including those by Duncan *et al.* (2005, 2006) or Fitzgibbon *et al.* (2000).

Finally, the development of several IT programmes over the last years, have served to improve the quality of the evaluative instruments for body image dysfunctions, for example, those created by Letosa-Porta *et al.* (2005) or Schlundt and Bell (1993).

The influence of aesthetic 'thin' models   Popular aesthetic models generally provide important input for explaining the high prevalence of physical dissatisfaction and eating disorders in the majority of countries, especially amongst the female population, and even more so in professions in which the body is considered the 'raw material', such as sport. Although few questionnaires have focused on this aspect, the Questionnaire of Influences over the Body Aesthetics Model (*Cuestionario de Influencia sobre el Modelo Estético Corporal*), or CIMEC, created by Toro *et al.* (1994), represents a good instrument for measuring this factor. Its purpose is to explore the internalisation of cultural influences on physical aesthetic models. Created in Spain, and tested on a Spanish population (anorexics and control), it consists of 40 questions with three answer options and has an international cut off point of ≥23–24. Its analysis contemplates five factors:

- *Unease with physical image*: the degree of anxiety in confronting situations that question the body or compare it with the predominating thin social models. This factor also includes the use of restrictive diets.

- *The influence of publicity*: the attention paid to publicity for weight loss products.

- *The influence of verbal messages*: the interest aroused by articles, reports, books and conversations related to weight loss.

- *The influence of social models*: the curiosity awoken by celebrities' bodies, such as actresses, publicity models, or even passers-by on the street.

- *The influence of social situations*: the perception of societal pressure in eating situations, and the social acceptance attributed to being thin.

4.4 Conclusions

This chapter has demonstrated the steps that should be taken to diagnose eating behaviour disorders in sport (through the development of an adequate psychological assessment system), taking into account the criteria used for the general population. The various sections developed here have covered the key concepts to consider when assessing potential eating behaviour disorders in athletes. The principal psychological disorders related to eating have been described (anorexia, bulimia and bigorexia), as well as the main strategies for psychologically assessing athletes: interviews, observation and questionnaires.

Here, the proposed objective is to guide professionals faced with eating problems in athletes. Similarly, coaches must be made more aware of the most frequently used assessment instruments and understand them as part of the process of psychological assessment with athletes.

Premature diagnosis, supported by a developed psychological evaluation, provides the best guarantee of successfully eradicating these illnesses. Consequently, coaches, parents and other individuals involved in sport must seek information if they suspect an athlete of displaying any of the symptoms detailed in this chapter. Information forms the basis of prevention.

5 Eating Disorders in Different Sports

Joaquín Dosil and Luis Casáis

5.1 Introduction

Eating disorders are an emerging problem in many aspects of today's society. Initially associated with girls from middle to high social-cultural classes, these illnesses have extended to other social groups.

Sport has become one of the contexts in which eating disorders emerge more frequently. Research into the risk factors affecting the development of these disorders reflects how their prevalence is higher in those social groups exposed to greater social-cultural influences, within which people carryout activities demanding thinness, such as certain sporting disciplines (Garner & Garfinkel, 1980).

The Spanish Federation of Sports Medicine, although unsure of the exact percentage, estimates that the prevalence of eating disorders in sportspeople lies between 4.2 and 39.2 per cent. Likewise, several studies show how a large proportion of athletes develop pathological weight-loss methods, such as fasting, without fully developing a diagnosable eating disorder. This explains the difficulty in accessing reliable data regarding the incidence of these disorders; a task made even more

Eating Disorders in Athletes   Joaquín Dosil
© 2008 John Wiley & Sons, Ltd

arduous considering the secrecy and denial often displayed by sufferers. Therefore, in order to establish more accurate statistics, Brownell and Rodin (1992) highlight the need for further research.

Chapter 2 described some 'high-risk' sports; in which participants are more likely to suffer an eating-related disorder. The characteristics of these specialities should be taken into account when studying eating disorders in sport. The following paragraphs detail the etiology of eating disorders, looking at the most relevant research studies in recent years, so to provide a broad but precise vision of the advances in this field. Likewise, an investigation carried out in Spain with several sporting disciplines is described.

5.2 The aetiology of eating disorders in sport

Research amongst the general population has concentrated principally on describing the factors that provoke certain eating disorders. Similarly, in the sports context, Swoap and Murphy (1995) distinguish five fundamental factors, which have been cited throughout this publication:

- *Weight restrictions*: diverse sporting disciplines demand weight limitations for competition (weight division sports). Nevertheless, continuous and uncontrolled weight loss leads to future eating problems.

- *The judges' criteria which stress thinness*: some sporting specialities use aesthetic criteria to evaluate sports performance, which can provoke the development of eating disorders.

- *The physical demands of sports that require extremely low body fat percentages*: certain sports demand a much thinner body than normal to perform at a high level. Such pressure to achieve the ideal low-in-fat body, in order to reach peak performance, can unchain eating disorders.

- *Pressures from the coach to lose weight*: coaches constitute a key figure in the sports environment. The influence they exert over athletes makes them an important factor to consider when assessing eating disorders. As will be seen in the following chapters, in the prevention and intervention stages, the coaching figure should always be consulted. Along these lines, the following studies prove interesting: Thompson and Sherman (1993a), on strategies for reducing the risks of eating disorders; Griffin and Harris (1996), on recommendations for the attitudes coaches should adopt with athletes who may be suffering from eating problems; Powers and Johnson (1996), on the perception of victory in preventative approaches to eating disorders; or Heffner *et al.* (2003), on advice for coaches to avoid the development of eating disorders. All of these aspects are more broadly dealt with in the following chapters, on the treatment and prevention of this group of psychological problems.

- *Pressure from team-mates to employ pathological weight loss techniques*: when referring to eating disorders, it is important to remember that the highest risk population are adolescents. During this period, the opinions of friends and teammates are of the utmost importance and feeling accepted in a group is a basic necessity for any youngster. One of the common causes of eating disorders amongst adolescents are team-mates suggesting a fellow athlete is overweight, or simply teasing and making comments regarding his/her physical aspect.

In addition to these predictive factors, sport psychologists should take into account the influence of athletes' personalities. In the general anorexic population some characteristic personality traits have been cited and are perfectly applicable to the sports context:

- *Competitiveness*: this characteristic goes beyond the normal competitiveness expected in sport, since it becomes a personality factor which obsessively drives an athlete towards victory, as well as the emotional 'downfall' of losing.

- *Tenacity*: this constitutes the capacity to insist on solving a problem, obstacle or circumstance, which impedes an athlete from obtaining greater performances, and in normal circumstances, is a positive characteristic. However, problems emerge when this tenacity brings about behaviours that are solely directed towards obtaining the established sporting objectives, abandoning other aspects of life, and even sacrificing physical health where necessary.

- *Perfectionism*: this is a pathological need to do everything flawlessly, to the extent that any variation from the 'plan' provokes noticeable emotional alterations.

- *Body dissatisfaction*: although this cannot be considered a personality characteristic in strict terms, it is evident that many athletes form a pattern of behaviours based around their pathological body dissatisfaction, taking steps towards solving this discontentment, even if it means going against their own organism.

Likewise, the cognitive distortion, that causes athletes to interpret information in an erroneous manner, may also be considered a characteristic. This distortion usually consists of altered thoughts related to food, weight and body shape. Chapter 6 of this book expands further on this matter. Likewise, the revision study and recommendations for eating disorders in athletes, created by Garner *et al.* (1998), analyse the aspects related to the personality characteristics associated with eating disorders.

5.3   Research into eating disorders in 'high-risk' sports

Research investigations directed towards the study of eating disorders in sport have received an important boost over the last decade. Caballero *et al.* (2001) carried out an exhaustive bibliographical analysis of the research conducted throughout the nineties, observing that an average of 21 articles were published in this field each year. Amongst the conclusions formed from this study, the following three may be highlighted: age and gender are considered as risk factors; the investigations focus principally on anorexia and bulimia; and the most frequently cited subjects are: the female athlete 'triad', body image perception and weight control/eating habits in determined sports.

In light of the 'high-risk' sports classification, presented in Chapter 2, some studies have been reviewed. In general terms, these are based on the idea that eating disorders are more common in certain sporting disciplines than in others, and in females than in males. Therefore, the most significant sports from each 'high-risk' group of sports are discussed.

5.3.1   Aesthetic sports: gymnastics, figure/ice-skating and ballet dancing

The prevalence of eating disorders in aesthetic sports is usually higher than in other disciplines. Garner *et al.* (1998) indicate that sports emphasizing leanness to enhance performance or appearance are at greater risk of eating disorders, giving the examples of gymnastics, wrestling, figure skating, diving and ballet. Along these lines, Sundgot-Borgen and Torsveit (2004) highlight the fact that the incidence of eating disorders in so-called aesthetic sports lies at 42 per cent, whilst in other disciplines, such as endurance (24 per cent), technical (17 per cent), and ball game sports (16 per cent), the percentages are much lower.

Amongst so-called 'aesthetic' sports, *rhythmic gymnastics, artistic ice-skating, dance* and *synchronised swimming* constitute the four most cited disciplines in eating disorder literature. Smolak *et al.* (2000) studied the relationship between female athletes and eating disorders, employing some 34 articles, referring to specific sports, elite sport and the age variable. Compared with non-athletes, they discovered that participants of dance and gymnastics are at much greater risk of suffering an eating disorder, emphasising the desire to be thin. Garner *et al.* (1998) consider that there are greater possibilities of suffering an eating disorder in sports requiring a thin physique in order to increase performance or physical appearance, as is the case of rhythmic gymnastics or artistic ice-skating. Furthermore, they indicate that the training of coaches in these sporting disciplines should include greater knowledge of eating related problems (physical, psychological and behavioural symptoms), so to assist in their prevention.

Figure 5.1

The prevalence of these illnesses in elite *gymnasts* is well documented, reflecting a relatively elevated incidence. For example, Sundgot-Borgen (1996) carried out an investigation with 12 gymnasts from the Norwegian national team, in which the prevalence of anorexia nervosa and athletic anorexia was examined. The results obtained confirmed the presence of anorexia nervosa (two gymnasts) and athletic anorexia (two gymnasts). That is to say, 33 per cent of the gymnasts suffered from an eating disorder. Similarly, Matejek *et al.* (1999) compared gymnasts suffering from athletic anorexia with non-sporting patients suffering from anorexia nervosa, discovering certain parallels between the two groups, implying that elite gymnasts who maintain excessively restrictive eating habits may go on to develop anorexia nervosa. Nevertheless, it is important to highlight that within each sporting discipline, there are marked differences in the eating disorder prevalence rates between different countries, and even different training groups. Okano *et al.* (2005) employed the EAT-26 to evaluate the symptoms of eating disorders in a sample of rhythmic gymnasts from Japan and China. The results indicated that whilst 19 per cent of the Japanese gymnasts presented eating disorder symptoms, only 2 per cent of the Chinese rhythmic gymnasts obtained elevated point scores on this questionnaire. The authors blamed these results on socio-cultural and socio-economic differences, affecting the imposed desire to be thin and to go on diets.

The extensive media coverage relating rhythmic gymnasts to eating problems and unhealthy eating habits has created a social perception that all gymnasts are likely to suffer from an eating disorder at some point. Without a doubt, the demands and pressures of this sport mean that information and prevention should form part of its structure. Amongst the common characteristics of gymnasts, cited by Toro (1995), the following may be highlighted: delay in pubertal, physical and neurological–hormonal development; and significant delays in the start of menstruation. Consequently, gymnasts maintain a childlike body for longer than normal.

In gymnastics, there is an obvious concern for weight, food and extreme thinness, displayed by coaches and gymnasts alike. It is important to remember that one of the criteria for scoring points in competitions is aesthetics. On the other hand, being an anaerobic sport, there is less calorie consumption compared to aerobic disciplines, implying that gymnasts frequently resort to restricted eating or other weight loss methods. Tragically, some extreme cases can emerge, such as the death of the gymnast Christy Henrich in 1994 from anorexia, aged just 22 years and weighing a meagre 29 kilos (documented by Noden, 1994, in the article 'Dying to win: for many women athletes, the toughest foe is anorexia. Gymnast Christy Henrich lost her battle').

Toro (1995) has compiled some studies which were carried out in the 1980s, in which the importance of weight may be perceived as a factor of performance and physical well-being: an investigation by Rosen et al. (1986) indicates how some three-quarters of all college university gymnasts develop pathological eating behaviours in order to control their weight (vomiting, laxatives, diuretics, tablets, fasting); likewise, Rosen and Hough (1988) obtained similar results from a later study, in which all gymnasts employed diets, whether to improve performance or to enhance their physical aspect (75 per cent used pathogenic weight loss methods).

Nevertheless, some studies fail to demonstrate a direct relationship between eating behaviour disorders and gymnastics. For example, O'Connor et al. (1995) employed the EDI with a sample of 25 gymnasts in order to demonstrate the existence of eating disorder symptoms. These authors observed that, compared with the control group, the gymnasts did not differ significantly on any of EDI subscales. The only exception were the point scores obtained in the subscale, 'motivation to lose weight', in which gymnasts attained notably higher scores, meaning this subscale constitutes a useful indicator for measuring risk in gymnasts. Moreover, 61 per cent of the gymnasts had suffered interruptions in their menstrual cycle of 3 months or more. In another study with 20 gymnasts, Bale et al. (1996) failed to find a direct association between anorexia and athletic performance (although some of the gymnasts displayed typical characteristics of individuals suffering from an eating disorder). The controversy surrounding these results may be explained by the samples employed. Along these lines, Kerr et al. (2006) confirmed that retired gymnasts reported more eating disorders and negative views of their experience in this sport than current gymnasts. Perhaps when it comes to answering questions, 'social desirability' can lead to distorted responses.

The problem of eating disorders has also been verified in other sports such as artistic ice-skating or figure skating. Taylor and Ste-Marie (2001) conducted research into the prevalence of eating disorders amongst female ice-skaters, whilst Monsma and Malina (2004) carried out a similar investigation with competitive female figure skaters. Applying the EDI, they obtained elevated point scores in various subscales, stating that the majority of skaters had attempted to lose weight at some point, and in some cases, presented eating disorder symptoms. Likewise, Taylor and Ste-Marie (2001) discovered that 92.7 per cent of participants felt under pressure to lose weight, given the characteristics of the sporting discipline. These results correspond with those obtained by Jonnalagadda *et al.* (2004), who examined body image perceptions and dieting behaviours of 49 figure skaters, finding that 30 per cent of the female skaters considered themselves overweight and indicated a preference for a thinner body contour. In a posterior study with 123 skaters, Ziegler *et al.* (2005) found clear differences between the perceived ideal and current body shapes, which suggest that in this discipline it is important to examine the psychosocial and emotional correlates related to body image and weight concerns.

Therefore, it becomes clear that the aforementioned sporting disciplines display certain characteristics that make them high-risk specialities, in terms of eating disorders (see Monsma and Feltz, 2006 for a description), in which the criteria applied to evaluate competition performance take into account the aesthetic aspect of the exercise.

However, adequate guidance for coaches, parents and athletes could prove sufficient to eradicate the majority of eating disorders amongst gymnasts and ice/figure-skaters. Along these lines, a study carried out by Benardot and Retton (1994) describes the action taken by the United States gymnastics team, in which the gymnasts are taught appropriate nutrition and diet, as well as correct eating habits.

Although other disciplines, such as synchronised swimming, have broadly been dealt with by scientific literature related to eating disorders (Ferrand *et al.*, 2005; Smithies, 1991), ballet dancers have received more attention from studies related to aesthetic sports and eating disorders.

In the 1980s numerous studies referred to the high prevalence of eating disorders amongst dancers. For example, in a study with 55 adult dancers, Brooks-Gunn *et al.* (1987) related eating problems and amenorrhoea, discovering that 50 per cent of those suffering amenorrhoea reported anorexia nervosa, while only 13 per cent of the normal population did so. Some years later, Abraham (1996) studied the characteristics of anorexia and bulimia in ballet dancers, finding higher scores on the EAT. This study concluded that dancers are at risk from developing eating disorders because they are under pressure to maintain a low body weight. Nevertheless, this author highlighted that in those sports in which there is great pressure to diet, low body weight and amenorrhoea alone are not sufficient criteria to diagnose anorexia nervosa.

Following the abundance of studies developed throughout the 1980s and 1990s with ballet dancers, in recent years, several investigations have tried to assess whether dancing should still be considered a high-risk sport in terms of eating disorders. Therefore, in a study with 29 female ballet dancers, employing the EDI, Ringham *et al.* (2006) found that 83 per cent of dancers met lifetime criteria for anorexia (6.9 per cent), bulimia (10.3 per cent), anorexia+bulimia (10.3 per cent), or EDNOS (55.0 per cent), concluding that dancers frequently engage in binge eating and purging behaviours.

Current investigations with this discipline have tended towards comparing the results obtained from general eating disorder evaluative instruments between elite and non-elite ballet dancers, or dancers of different ages and genders. Some of the most significant studies are detailed below:

- Ravaldi *et al.* (2003) carried out an interesting study with female non-elite ballet dancers, female gymnasium users, and other sportspeople, finding that non-elite ballet dancers reported the highest prevalence of eating disorders (anorexia nervosa 1.8 per cent; bulimia nervosa 2.7 per cent; eating disorders not otherwise specified 22.1 per cent), followed by gymnasium users (anorexia nervosa 2.6 per cent; eating disorders not otherwise specified 18 per cent).

- Thomas *et al.* (2005) employed the EDI to conduct research into the prevalence of eating disorders with a sample of 239 female ballet students, producing elevated point scores, especially on the subscales Drive for Thinness and Perfectionism.

- Neumarker *et al.* (2000) also used the EDI to compare the differences between ballet dancers and a control group, taking age and gender into account. The female dancers produced higher point scores than the controls in five subscales of the EDI and the most conflictive group were those aged 16 years. Regarding the male subjects, the dancers produced similar point scores to the control group (higher scores only in the subscale Ineffectiveness).

Nevertheless, not all research investigations have demonstrated that dancers are more likely to suffer an eating disorder. Along these lines, Bachner-Melman *et al.* (2006) compared the symptoms, personality variables typical of anorexia nervosa, and lifetime eating disorder prevalence rates, across four groups of Israeli women (anorexics, dancers, non-aesthetic athletes, and controls), finding that the scores of the anorexic subjects differed from those of the three other groups. The greatest difference was found in the diagnosis of EDNOS, where the dancers obtained higher percentages (11.7 per cent compared to 5.8 per cent of non-aesthetic athletes, and 4.4 per cent controls). However, as previously noted in other sections of this publication, cultural differences can also determine the results of investigations.

5.3.2 Weight division sports: judo, wrestling and rowing

The existence of weight categories in certain sports can potentially produce problems when athletes' desires to win lead them to compete in a lower category than their natural weight, provoking the use of pathogenic weight loss methods.

In judo athletes must possess great physical form, flexibility, speed and agility, as well as being capable of anticipating their opponents' movements, using their force in the opposite direction in order to throw them off balance. The competition structure includes various weight divisions. Male judo is divided into 10 levels, ranging from under 60 kg to over 95 kg, whilst female judo has just seven levels, ranging from under 48 kg to over 72 kg. It is difficult for judokas to know with certainty in which category they will perform best, and objective evaluations often lose out to subjective judgements. Along these lines, Ren *et al.* (2000) investigated the ideal morphological characteristics for judo. First, they analysed 61 female judokas, concluding that the necessary physical characteristics vary between categories (under 48 kg to over 72 kg). Therefore, it is apparent that the ideal body for peak performance differs from one competitor to the next. Bearing in mind the previously mentioned subjectivity, certain athletes consider moving down to a lower weight category, resorting to so-called 'express diets'. The repercussions of such hasty slimming have been the object of discussion on more than one occasion. Coksevim *et al.* (1997) studied the effects of rapid weight loss on judokas' performance. The sample consisted of 16 competitors who were monitored before and after a 5 per cent weight loss. The results demonstrated a reduction in energy, vitality, strength, resistance, flexibility and agility, concluding that rapid weight loss produces adverse effects on athletes. Similarly, Filaire *et al.* (2001) carried out research with 11 judokas, focusing on eating restrictions, psychological state, and their relation to performance, observing notable negative effects in the physical–psychological sphere, diminishing general performance. Moreover, Kowatari *et al.* (2001) studied the effects of weight loss produced through increased training and restricted eating in 18 male judokas, highlighting how it is more appropriate to increase training than reduce food intake (a practice widely used by the majority of judokas prior to a competition). More recently, with a sample of 20 male judokas, Degoutte *et al.* (2006) found that the combination of energy restriction and intense exercise training, which causes weight reduction before a competition, adversely affects the physiology and psychology of judo athletes and impairs physical performance before the competition. Yoshioka *et al.* (2006) produced similar findings. These authors applied the Mood State Profile to a sample of 22 male judokas and 8 female judokas, who required weight reductions before a competition, in order to identify differences prior to and following the weigh-in. The TMD (Total Mood Disturbance) score in the POMS (Profile of Moods States Questionnaire) significantly increased after weight reduction only in WR group males. In the female WR group, the anger and depression scores decreased after weight reduction, and the pre-value of the TMD score in this group was relatively high. In female judokas, psychological stress may be caused by anxiety prompted by the overall concept of weight reduction before any actual weight reduction has taken place, whereas in male judokas, it may be caused by the actual weight reduction.

Figure 5.2

The NCAA (National Collegiate Athletic Association) did not delay in finding a solution to this type of behaviour, created a Weight Certifying Programme for judokas (Davis *et al.*, 2002). This programme achieved some noticeable results within its first year, with judokas increasing their weight from the previous seasons' competitions and avoiding weight fluctuations throughout the season.

As a weight division sport, wrestling constitutes another 'high risk' discipline. In recent years, research into the weight loss methods used by wrestlers and their subsequent effects on health/performance has been rife. Pate *et al.* (2003) indicate that wrestlers are at particular risk of inadequate eating behaviours, since they regularly engage in rapid weight-loss routines to compete in specific weight categories. In 1997, the death of three wrestlers after having participated in a rapid weight loss programme, based on strenuous exercise in excessive clothing, diet and sauna, shocked the world of wrestling (Utter, 2002). Another case is that of Jeff Reese, who passed out when getting on the scales prior to a competition. His main objective was to lose 8 kg to compete in the 150lb (68 kg) category (Romo, 1998). In a case study, which reinforces these incidents, Myers *et al.* (1999) describes the pathological weight loss methods used by wrestlers: laxatives, diuretics, dehydration, stimulants, etc., emphasizing the dangers of this type of practice amongst athletes, and urging coaches to be more aware of their existence.

Dale and Landers (1999) proved there is a direct relationship between eating disorders and wrestling. Comparing the EDI scores of 85 wrestlers and 75 non-wrestlers, they observed significant differences on the scale 'motivation for losing weight' during the season. Similarly, Dick (1991) highlighted how 7 per cent of wrestlers manifested eating disorder behaviours. Many other investigations have focused on the consequences of 'express diets'. For example, Choma et al. (1998) studied the consequences of rapid weight loss on 14 wrestlers, finding potential negative impacts on cognitive functions. Nonetheless, years later, Landers et al. (2001) concluded that wrestlers submitted to rapid weight loss prior to competitions displayed affective type alterations, not cognitive variations as previously hypothesised. Along these lines, a study conducted by Kraemer et al. (2001), with 20 wrestlers, indicated that the skills related to physical performance were maintained throughout the competition, even if the athlete had employed rapid weight loss methods the week beforehand. Similarly, Yan et al. (2000) carried out a study with 34 wrestlers, finding that rapid weight loss preceding a competition can produce vitamin deficiencies, which can in turn affect the athlete's health.

These studies demonstrate the importance of taking steps to controlling the weight-loss methods used by athletes prior to competitions. Along these lines, and in light of the tragic deaths of the wrestlers we have mentioned, several governmental programmes have been proposed to eradicate these extreme practices. For example, the National Collegiate Associaton (NCAA) Wrestling Committee and Safeguards and Medical Aspects of Sports Committee adopted significant rule changes in 1998 to address weight-loss issues in wrestling (Ransone & Hughes, 2004). Six rule changes were enacted to address this issue: each existing weight division was increased by 3.18 kg; permanent weight divisions were established for each wrestler from the first week of December; official weigh-ins 1 h before the start of each match and for each day of a multiple-day tournament were introduced; the use of saunas, steam rooms, and impermeable suits was banned; and all wrestling coaches were required to undergo cardiopulmonary resuscitation and first-aid training (NCAA, 1998). Following the introduction of these new regulations, several studies have analysed their effectiveness (Oppliger et al., 2003, 2006), confirming that those wrestlers competing under the new set-up improved in the desired aspects, reducing unhealthy weight cutting behaviours and promoting competitive equity. Nevertheless, more resent investigations, such as that by Alderman et al. (2004) with 2638 wrestlers, found that rapid weight-loss methods (principally excessive running, saunas, and vapour-impermeable suits) continue being used during competitions. The results of a study carried out by Ransone and Hughes (2004) with 78 wrestlers, further support this theory, finding that most lost significant amounts of weight before and gained significant amounts of weight after competition.

The world of rowing has also been stained by cases of eating disorders. One of the most recently documented cases is that of Caroline Ingham, considered one of the best rowers in the USA, who described her fight to overcome the eating disorders she had suffered (Johnson, 2002). At first sight, the characteristics of rowing do not seem indicative of eating disorders. Nevertheless, the battle to reach peak performance and the weight limits dividing competitive categories can prove a dangerous combination if confronted without control. The existence of weight divisions within the sporting structure means rowers try to compete within the 'lightweight' categories (for men, less than 72 kg; for women, less than 59 kg), in order to avoid the heavyweight divisions in which they might confront stronger and more resistant rivals.

Figure 5.3

Sykora *et al.* (1993) carried out one of the first investigations in this sport, studying the alterations in food intake, weight and diet of 162 male and female rowers competing in both 'lightweight' and 'heavyweight' categories. On the contrary to the expected results, the conclusions failed to demonstrate significant differences between the two categories, although they did show a high incidence of inadequate weight loss behaviours, both amongst males and females. A later study, conducted by Terry and Waite (1996), employing the EAT and the BSQ with 124 participants in the Great Britain Championships, found that 16.2 per cent of the subjects produced scores above the established cut-off point, indicating 'eating disorder symptoms'. The same investigation concluded that the risk of suffering from eating disorders in rowers might be related to age, sex and division (lightweight or heavyweight). Years later, Terry *et al.* (1999) went on to conduct a study with 103 elite rowers, who completed the EAT, the BSQ and the POMS-C. The sample was divided into competitive categories and gender. The results demonstrated that 12 per cent of the 'lightweight' rowers generated high scores in the EAT, indicating eating disorder symptoms. More recently, Slater *et al.* (2005) examined the body-mass management practices of lightweight rowers prior to competitions, comparing these with current guidelines of the International Federation of Rowing Association (FISA). The conclusions reflected how, given their natural weight and constitution, few rowers should really be in the lightweight division, meaning they must employ different weight-loss methods to do so (gradual dieting, fluid restriction, and increased training). A later study by Slater *et al.* (2006) studied the effects of these weight-loss practices on performance, concluding that acute weight loss of up to 4 per cent over 24 h, when combined with aggressive nutritional recovery strategies, can be undertaken with minimal impact on on-water rowing performance, at least in cool conditions.

5.3.3 Gym sports: aerobics and bodybuilding

Gyms have become a fashionable place to be. The multitude of activities offered and the broad range of users have made them the most prosperous sporting facilities in any city. Aerobics, keep fit, spinning, step, weights, are just a few of the possibilities to choose from, on many occasions, without any form of time limit or personalised control. The existence of 'activity anorexia' regularly enters into discussion when referring to the gym setting, since it is recognised as an ideal location for its development.

Regarding aerobics, Dosil and Diaz (2002) studied the eating behaviour of 123 aerobics participants, applying the EAT questionnaire. The results verified that 9.2 per cent of the subjects obtained point scores higher than 30 (indicative of 'eating disorder symptoms'). Similarly, applying the EDI, Olson *et al.* (1996) examined the potential eating disorders in 30 fitness instructors. The results revealed a previous history of bulimia in 23 per cent of the instructors and anorexia in 17 per cent, as well as exposing behaviours and attitudes comparable with athletes from sporting disciplines characterised for having thin participants.

Within the gym context, weights rooms are another significant area in terms of eating disorders. Bodybuilders often work out on a daily basis, with the principal objective of developing a fibrous body and reducing any fat accumulated around the muscular fibres, so their muscles stand out for the judges during competitions (see Smith, 2006 for a review of the psychological characteristics of this sport).

Today's 'body-cult' society is more than evident. The ever-increasing offer of products and services related to beauty, diet, or muscular development, only serves to feed the idea that having the 'perfect body' is a social 'requirement'. The continuous publicity of these products has become a form of pressure, under which many individuals become 'trapped' without realising it. Marzano (2001) confirmed these suspicions, comparing bodybuilders with exercise addicts and eating disorder sufferers. This author considers these individuals as victims of their own extreme control over their bodies, products of societal pressure.

Going back to gym sports and their relationship with eating disorders, it is important to highlight the use of the sauna. Bodybuilders frequently attend sauna sessions, since it reduces the water contents in the skin, accentuating the vein structure so highly valued by judges (Yates, 1991). To help achieve this objective, in addition to the sauna, bodybuilders tend to stick to a strict diet, high in proteins, low in fat and without any sugar (Toro, 1995). The publicity offering products that claim to help this mission is innumerable. From the great 'database' that is the Internet, to specialised press, there is an enormous range of protein preparations and eating supplements on offer, promising increased muscular growth. These substances, and their corresponding publicity, are characteristic of bodybuilding. This use of supplements is not so common in other sports, and constitutes a conditioner that must be considered in bodybuilding, since their use can become obsessive.

Figure 5.4

Various authors have studied the relationship between eating disorders and bodybuilding (Couchman & Bayly, 1992; Pope *et al.*, 1993; or Siff, 1992), concluding that anorexic behaviours exist amongst participants. Walberg and Johnston (1991) observed how 103 bodybuilders obtained higher point scores than the control group in every scale of the EDI, as well as in the weight loss methods used (female bodybuilders displayed a greater fear of becoming fat, obsession with food, and use of laxatives to lose weight, as well as a higher incidence of eating disorders). Goldfield *et al.* (2006) studied competitive and recreational male bodybuilders, who produced high rates of weight and shape preoccupation, extreme body modification practices, binge eating, and bulimia nervosa (principally amongst competitors). Nevertheless, not all the people who exercise using weights are at risk of pathological body image or eating disorders (Blouin & Goldfield, 1995). Along these lines, Guthie *et al.* (1994) conducted research with 13 female bodybuilders competing at championship level, finding they had a greater positive image of their bodies, and none of them displayed signs of anorexia or bulimia nervosa. Nevertheless, the subjects did exhibit an excessive concern for nutrition and specific behaviours related to self-perception. In a more recent study, Pickett *et al.* (2005) studied the levels of 'muscle dysmorphia' between competitive bodybuilders and either non-competitive weight trainers or physically active men who do not train with weights, without finding any significant differences. Moreover, some investigations have stated the psychological benefits of practising bodybuilding. For example, Finkenberg and Teper (1991) found that competitive bodybuilders had higher scores than non-bodybuilders in personal, social, and self-concept, as well as lower scores in self-criticism. Likewise, Martin and Lichtenberger (2002) highlighted the fact that gym-goers who do weights tend to improve their body image.

Finally, the Body Building Dependence Scale (BDS), by Smith and Hale (2004), is a specific instrument that can be used to measure the degree of exercise reliance in bodybuilders. It comprises a nine-item measure, incorporating three subscales: social dependence, training dependence, and mastery dependence. The BDS has been tested with a sample of 285 bodybuilders, producing some positive psychometric properties. As noted in the previous chapter, the future of research into eating disorders and related pathologies in sport tends towards the creation of more specific instruments, which take into account the definite characteristics of each discipline.

5.3.4 Endurance sports and disciplines requiring low weight for high performance: athletics, swimming, and horse racing

Athletics, in terms of middle-distance and long-distance events, is one of the most widely practised sports given its accessibility for all social classes. Being thin, fibrous and fat free ('being lean' in athletic jargon) constitute the main physical aspects enhancing performance.

Some athletes resort to strict diets, believing that losing body fat is directly related to improving their times. In a study with 17 long-distance athletes, Rosen *et al.* (1986) found that 50 per cent used some pathogenic weight loss method. The problem with these methods is that in addition to reducing body fat, lean body mass is also lost, which is not maintained when the weight loss is very hasty. This reduction in body mass can prove counteractive for athletes immersed in intensive training programmes.

Various research studies have demonstrated the relationship between eating disorders and runners. For example, Weight and Noakes (1987), in an investigation with 125 long-distance athletes, found that 14 per cent displayed symptoms of an eating disorder (the instruments applied were the EAT and the EDI). Likewise, Estok and Rudy (1996) established that 25 per cent of women who ran more than 30 miles per week displayed eating disorder symptoms, given the high point scores produced in the EAT. Also, Hulley and Hill (2001) applied the EDE-Q to a sample of 181 middle-distance and long-distance athletes, discovering that 16 per cent had an eating disorder at the time of the study (7 anorexia, 2 bulimia, and 20 EDNOS). More recently, employing the EAT-26 with a sample of Japanese and Chinese female runners, Okano *et al.* (2005) found that the prevalence of disordered eating was 21 per cent in Japanese and 4 per cent in Chinese athletes. However, despite these studies, there is an abundant bibliography documenting the *negative* relationship between eating behaviour disorders and athletes (Garner *et al.*, 1998). Along these lines, Marti (1991) studied a group of amateur and professional long-distance runners, observing how the prevalence of anorexia nervosa in these groups is no higher than in the normal population. Similarly, other investigations, such as that conducted by Parker *et al.* (1994), indicate that the implications of eating disorders in athletics are debatable. What is more, Karlson (2001), in analysing the prevalence of eating behaviour disorders in 'lightweight' rowers and long-distance runners, further supported these conclusions, finding in neither case a direct association with eating behaviour disorders.

Figure 5.5

In light of this apparent contradiction, it is important to analyse the results of research with runners with caution, employing them to reinforce the idea that the characteristics of this particular sporting discipline can favour the development of eating disorders.

Much research has also related swimmers to eating disorders (Jones *et al.*, 2005; Rosenvinge & Vig, 1993). Nevertheless, other studies, such as those by Taub and Benson (1992), failed to find a direct relationship. These authors studied concern for weight, weight control techniques and eating disorders, in a sample of 85 adolescent competitors. The conclusions showed that none of the male or female subjects were particularly susceptible to eating disorders or using pathological weight loss methods.

In contrast to these results, a year later, the same authors (Benson & Taub, 1993) employed a sample of 298 elite female swimmers to study why swimming is considered as a 'high-risk' sport in terms of eating disorders. The point scores obtained in motivation to lose weight, body dissatisfaction, and excessive weight control constitute the factors that pressurise swimmers into employing unhealthy weight loss methods. In a previous study, Benson et al. (1990) had demonstrated how, on the EDI scale related to bodily dissatisfaction, female swimmers (38 per cent) scored higher than both gymnasts and the control group (similar results were found with other scales). Correspondingly, a study developed by Drummer et al. (1987) with 955 competitive swimmers aged between 9 and 18 years, demonstrated how they tended to perceive themselves as overweight. Forty per cent of the subjects confessed to being frequently or permanently concerned about their weight and 15 per cent employed pathological weight loss methods. Popovich effected an important investigation in 1998, using a sample of 148 elite female swimmers, and applying the EAT-26, the ED12 and the BDS. The author obtained point scores signifying that a high proportion of the subjects presented eating disorder symptoms. Curiously, the control group (comprising 50 university females) also obtained high scores in some of the scales.

Figure 5.6

These studies have urged the scientific community to develop programmes for the prevention of eating disorders, based on training coaches and providing information to swimmers. Along these lines, Franseen (2000) highlights the importance of preventing eating disorders and describes how these illnesses influence swimmers, principally in synchronised swimming, given its clear aesthetic component.

Finally, a mention must be made of jockeys. The bibliography on these sportspeople focuses on the fact that they are required to maintain a low body weight throughout the competitive period. The pressure from their representatives, the media and the obvious physical advantages of weighing little, convert jockeys into a 'high risk' population. Moore *et al.* (2002) studied the weight management programmes and weight loss strategies of 116 jockeys throughout a competitive season. They observed how an elevated proportion (81 per cent) employed weight loss techniques based on restricted eating 24 hours prior to a competition, along with complementary methods such as sauna, techniques inducing perspiration (29 per cent), and diuretics (22 per cent).

5.4   Eating disorder symptoms: the sporting discipline and gender

The investigations described in the third section of this chapter serve to conceptualise the current state of research into eating disorders in different sports. A research study was conducted in order to verify whether the results of these studies correspond with the Spanish sporting population. This investigation compares some so-called 'high-risk' sports to other disciplines, which are not initially recognised as 'high risk' in terms of eating disorders. The chosen sample comprised 420 athletes (260 males and 160 females) from various sporting disciplines. The selection criteria dictated that all subjects should compete at a high level, being professional or semi-professional in their respective sport. However, this criterion was slackened in the case of aerobics, an activity that most participants choose as a 'hobby' or a way to 'keep fit' (Dosil, 2002b). Table 5.1 details the specific composition of the sample in terms of gender and sporting discipline.

As may be observed from Table 5.1, the subjects are distributed across various sporting disciplines, accordingly divided into two main groups:

- Group 1 (183 subjects): 'Low-risk' sports, in which weight does not directly influence performance: football, indoor football, basketball, handball, volleyball and rowing/canoeing.

- Group 2 (237 subjects): 'High-risk' sports, in which weight constitutes an important factor affecting competition and training performance: swimming, judo/wrestling, bodybuilding, aerobics, athletics (middle-distance and long-distance) and rhythmic gymnastics.

The EAT-40 was employed to assess the prevalence of eating disorder symptoms. To analyse the results, the international cut-off point was established accordingly:

Table 5.1 Size and composition of the sample used in Dosil (2002b)

	Sport	Males	Females	Total
Group 1, 'low risk' sports	Football	61	2	63
	Indoor football	12	1	13
	Volleyball	4	9	13
	Basketball	26	44	70
	Handball	5	3	8
	Rowing/ canoeing	12	4	16
Total group 1		120	63	183
Group 2, 'high risk' sports	Swimming	5	8	13
	Judo/ Wrestling	56	13	69
	Aerobics	1	21	22
	Athletics	60	31	91
	Rhythmic gymnastics	0	24	24
	Bodybuilding	18	0	18
Total group 2		140	97	237
Total		260	160	420

scores equal to or higher than 30. However, a cut-off point score of 21 was also taken into account, constituting a widely used criterion by numerous investigations (Raich, 1997). The hypothesis is the following: 'There is a greater prevalence of eating disorders in high-risk sports and amongst female athletes'.

Below, the results are analysed in terms of the group ('low-risk' or 'high-risk') and the gender variable.

5.4.1 The influence of the sporting discipline

The EAT-40 questionnaire was applied to the different sporting disciplines. Tables 5.2 and 5.3 present the point scores in the 'low risk' and 'high risk' groups respectively.

Applying a cut-off point of 30, it may be observed how 4.37 per cent of the 'low risk' (Table 5.2) sample equals or surpasses this score, whilst this proportion reaches 10.97 per cent amongst the 'high risk' subjects (Table 5.3). If the *cut-off point* is lowered to 21, similar findings are produced, with a higher proportion of the 'high-risk' subjects (19.40 per cent, Table 5.3) reaching this mark, compared to the 'low risk' group (10.38 per cent, Table 5.2). These results confirm the hypothesis that certain sports pose higher risks of developing eating disorders.

Focusing on the specific sports covered in this study, the highest point scores (with both cut-off points – 30 and 21 respectively) are produced by athletes from 'high-risk' disciplines (Table 5.3): judokas/wrestlers (13.04 per cent and 23.19 per cent), aerobics participants (13.64 per cent and 27.27 per cent), gymnasts (12.5 per

Table 5.2   Point scores >30 and >21 in 'low-risk' sports

	Cut-off point EAT > 30	Cut-off point EAT > 21
Sport	Proportion of subjects	Proportion of subjects
Football	0%	6.35%
Indoor football	23.08%	23.08%
Volleyball	7.69%	15.38%
Basketball	4.29%	11.43%
Handball	0%	0%
Rowing/canoeing	6.25%	12.5%
Total	4.37%	10.38%

Table 5.3   Point scores >30 and >21 in 'high-risk' sports

	Cut-off point EAT > 30	Cut-off point EAT > 21
Sport	Proportion of subjects	Proportion of subjects
Swimming	7.69%	15.38%
Judo/wrestling	13.04%	23.19%
Aerobics	13.64%	27.27%
Athletics	7.69%	13.19%
Rhythmic gymnastics	12.5%	29.17%
Bodybuilding	16.7%	16.7%
Total	10.97%	19.40%

cent and 29.17 per cent), bodybuilders (16.7 per cent with both cut-off points), swimmers (7.69 per cent and 15.38 per cent) and athletes (7.69 per cent and 13.19 per cent). Applying a cut-off point of 30, these percentages may be considered *elevated*, and *extremely elevated* if the cut-off point is lowered to 21, indicating the eminent influence of eating behaviour disorders in these sporting disciplines.

In the 'low-risk' group of sports, the general point scores are much lower. Nevertheless, a more detailed examination of each sporting discipline reveals a certain degree of incongruence (Table 5.2): in volleyball the point scores are elevated (7.69 per cent and 15.38 per cent), although this is putdown to the sample employed and the gender variable (see section 5.3.2). The same explanation is applicable to basketball (4.29 per cent and 11.43 per cent) and rowing/canoeing (6.25 per cent and 12.5 per cent), where the percentages obtained convert them into 'high-risk' disciplines. However, the percentage produced in indoor football is inexplicable (23.08 per cent), although the sample may be limiting reliable results in a sport that is not initially known for excessive concern for weight or food. In football, there only exist a small number of cases where the cut-off point is lowered to 21 (6.35 per cent). Finally, handball is the only sport in which no point scores surpass either of the established cut-off points.

In general terms, subjects from so-called 'high-risk' sports obtain higher point scores in the EAT-40. However, it should be noted that in some of the sports, the sample employed is not sufficiently ample to form solid conclusions, although they can serve to suggest possible tendencies.

5.4.2 The influence of gender

The influence of gender in the development of eating disorders has been proved as one of the most significant risk factors. The majority of investigations confirm women as more susceptible to suffering eating disorders, although in recent years, an increasing number of men also undergo these problems (Baum, 2006; Pate *et al.*, 2003). In terms of gender, this particular study produces a diversity of point scores. As Table 5.4 demonstrates, a broad range of the sports produced point scores higher than the 30 cut-off point, and they are not exclusively generated by female subjects. Along these lines, male indoor football players produced the highest proportion of point scores equalling or exceeding both cut-off points (25 per cent). Although the sample employed for this particular discipline was small, it can still be considered a significant result. Similarly, in judo/wrestling, 14.28 per cent of males and 7.69 per cent of females equalled or exceeded the 30 cut-off point in the EAT-40.

Football, as a 'low-risk' sport, produced by far the lowest point scores, with none of the 63 subjects equalling or exceeding the established cut-off point of 30. Likewise, none of the handball subjects produced the elevated point scores indicative of eating disorder symptoms. Interestingly, in basketball, the only cases correspond to female players (6.81 per cent), as with swimming, in which the only point scores

Table 5.4 Results in the EAT-40 using a cut-off point of 30

	Point scores in the EAT-40 (n = 420)			
	Proportion of cases exceeding the cut-off point eat > 30		Proportion of cases not exceeding the cut-off point eat < 30	
Sport	Males	Females	Males	Females
Football	0%	0%	100%	100%
Swimming	0%	12.50%	100%	87.50%
Judo/Wrestling	14.28%	7.69%	85.70%	92.30%
Indoor football	25%	0%	75%	100%
Aerobics	0%	14.28%	100%	85.70%
Volleyball	0%	11.11%	100%	88.88%
Athletics	8.33%	6.45%	91.65%	93.54%
Basketball	0%	6.81%	100%	88.45%
Rythmic gymnastics		12.50%		87.50%
Bodybuilding	16.66%		83.34%	
Handball	0%	0%	100%	100%
Rowing/ caoeing	0%	25%	100%	75%

equalling or exceeding the established cut-off point of 30 were produced by female swimmers (12.50 per cent). Likewise, in volleyball, all of the cases produced belonged to women. In rowing/canoeing there is 'only' one case, corresponding to a female subject who constitutes 25 per cent of the sample. On the other hand, in athletics, elevated point scores were identified both in male and female athletes (8.33 per cent and 6.45 per cent, respectively). In aerobics, three female participants produced elevated point scores (14.28 per cent of the sample). Moreover, in rhythmic gymnastics, a 'high-risk' sport according to previous statistics, only three gymnasts (12.50 per cent) produced a point score equal to or higher than 30. Finally, in bodybuilding, three cases emerged, representing 16.6 per cent of the sample.

Going back to the hypothesis established at the beginning of this study, referring to a greater prevalence of eating disorder symptoms in females, it is difficult to confirm this premise, given the fact that the samples used for the majority of sports comprise a greater male participation. In sporting disciplines such as basketball, where a broader female sample has been formed, it becomes easier to appreciate the gender differences.

If we establish the criteria for the scores produced by the EAT as being equal to or higher than 21, there are clearer differences compared to the 30 cut-off point (Table 5.5). As with the previous case, indoor football, with 25 per cent, followed by judo/wrestling with 13 men (23.21 per cent) and 3 women (23.07 per cent), are the sporting disciplines displaying the most marked differences. In athletics, there are eight males (13.33 per cent) and four females (12.90 per cent) producing elevated point scores. In basketball, eight females (13.33 per cent) produced a point

Table 5.5 Results of the EAT-40, applying 21 as the cut-off point

	Point scores in the EAT-40 (n = 420)			
	Proportion of cases exceeding the cut-off point eat > 21		Proportion of cases not exceeding the cut-off point eat < 21	
Sport	Males	Females	Males	Females
Football	7%	0%	93%	100%
Swimming	0%	25%	100%	75%
Judo/Wrestling	23.21%	23.07%	76.79%	76.93%
Indoor football	25%	0%	75%	100%
Aerobics	0%	28.57%	100%	71.43%
Volleyball	0%	22.22%	100%	77.78%
Athletics	13.33%	12.90%	86.67%	87.10%
Basketball	0%	18.18%	100%	81.82%
Rhythmic gymnastics		29.16%		70.84%
Bodybuilding	16.66%		83.34%	
Handball	0%	0%	100%	100%
Rowing/canoeing	8%	25%	92%	75%

score equal to or exceeding the established cut-off point, representing the only sport in which only the female athletes present eating disorder symptoms. In aerobics, the sample produced 6 cases (28.57 per cent), gymnastics generated seven cases (29.1 per cent), and football produced four male cases (7 per cent). Handball is the only sport not producing any point scores equal to or higher than the established cut-off point. On the other hand, sports such as swimming, rowing/canoeing or volleyball, hardly present any eating disorder symptoms, perhaps due to the small size of their respective samples.

In light of the results gained from this study, although it is not possible to generalise, some conclusions may be drawn, which relate eating disorders to the sporting discipline and gender:

- Compared to 'low-risk' sports, 'high-risk' disciplines produce a higher proportion of subjects equalling or surpassing both cut-off points.

- Basketball provides the best case for illustrating gender differences, given that the only subjects producing elevated point scores were female players.

- The prevalence of eating disorders in rhythmic gymnastics does not appear as high as in previous studies. However, it must be highlighted that the gymnasts comprising this study come from the same team.

- Handball is the only sport in which no cases of eating disorders were identified, regardless of the cut-off point employed.

- Sports in which an athletes' weight determines their competitive category, suppose higher risks of developing inadequate eating behaviours. Such sports include judo and wrestling.

- Women do less sport than men. Moreover, the average age of females engaging in sporting activity is lower than men, perhaps given their changing role with age.

- Bodybuilding, whilst representing the sport in which participants most look after their eating habits, also reflects higher risks of developing eating disorder symptoms.

5.5   Conclusions

The prevalence of eating disorders in different sporting disciplines is a proven fact. Throughout this chapter, it has been possible to see the most recent investigations into eating disorders in athletes from different sports, as well as the results of an investigation conducted within the Spanish national panorama. The data confirm the proposed hypotheses, implying there is a greater probability of developing eating disorders in certain sporting disciplines than in others, and it is more likely that female athletes develop an eating disorder than their male counterparts. Nevertheless, the results produced some unexpected statistics, in which seemingly 'low-risk' sports generated elevated point-scores, urging the need to develop future investigations in these areas. Without a doubt, the most significant advance would be the development of specific assessment systems for each sport, constituting a step forwards in consolidating a thorough and prolific line of investigation.

Diversifying the research with each of the sports on a more individual basis is a pending matter. The majority of research investigations focus on a limited number of sporting disciplines, which only serves to restrict the field of action and overlook the fact that eating disorders can emerge in 'unlikely' sports. The general emphasis acquired by eating disorders in recent times allows us to consider sport as a global institution, in which some of its entities may be considered as 'high-risk' areas.

Without a doubt, preventing eating disorders will prove a more arduous task in some specialities than others, given that the intrinsic characteristics of each modality are what mark their functioning as a sport. Hence, it becomes vitally important to train coaches and parents to transmit appropriate eating behaviours to young athletes, enabling them to objectively evaluate which behaviours will prove beneficial or damaging to their sporting performance, as well as their physical and mental health.

6 Treating Eating Disorders in Sport

Joaquín Dosil and Olaia González

6.1 Introduction

This chapter describes various aspects to consider in the treatment of eating disorders in athletes. Sports psychologists must be aware of the numerous treatment alternatives, allowing the characteristics of each individual case to sway the decision between one option and another. Indeed, sport psychology professionals should work on the basis that no one treatment is commonly accepted, nor 100 per cent effective. Nonetheless, the majority of specialists agree that the best 'treatment' is prevention, and once an eating disorder has developed, the intervention should be personalised according to the characteristics of each patient. Therefore, a multi-component treatment, using diverse strategies, appears to be the most effective alternative.

In sport, as in other contexts, prevention is the best form of treating eating disorders. The advice detailed in Chapter 3 serves to increase awareness about this type of illness, highlighting how everyone implicated in the sporting context can commit to the prevention of these disorders. Undoubtedly, the introduction of specialist sports psychologists into sports clubs and institutions, and guidance from team doctors and nutritionists, guarantees a greater detection and prevention of eating-related problems. Initially, a combined intervention involving coaches and parents may prove sufficient to prevent the development of a problem; however, once an

Eating Disorders in Athletes   Joaquín Dosil
© 2008 John Wiley & Sons, Ltd

eating disorder has already taken hold, collaborating with a broader spectrum of individuals involved in the sports context may facilitate eradicating the problem.

This chapter is structured into three main sections. The first refers to the treatment regime, the second deals with the elements to consider when confronted with an eating disorder in an athlete (the objectives, techniques and instruments to be employed), and the third discusses the different treatment alternatives.

6.2   The treatment regime

Once an accurate diagnosis has been made, and prior to commencing any form of intervention, the therapist must decide under what regime the treatment will be conducted: within a specialised hospital unit (fully or partially admitted) or under a clinical regime. The decision to admit a patient to a specialised hospital will depend on a series of aspects, which must be carefully considered and evaluated:

- Weight loss: when there is serious malnutrition, accompanied by extreme weight loss (between 25 and 30 per cent), according to age and stature; or below 25%, but in a short space of time.

- Physical complications: in any case where there is significant organic deterioration that could put the athlete's life in danger (electrolytic disequilibria, serious alterations in the metabolism or vital signs, physical complications or serious infections).

- Psychological complications that produce suicidal thoughts.

- Crises in family relations: when the family or social situation surrounding a patient has seriously deteriorated.

- Poor response to clinical treatments: provoked by patients' non-compliance with agreed treatments, lack of motivation to change, or any cause impeding them from getting better.

In some cases, when clinical treatment becomes practically unfeasible, hospitalisation is the best option. Nevertheless, it should always be seen as the last resort, since despite its many advantages, treatment outside an athlete's natural environment has many drawbacks. Therefore, wherever viable, the possibility of admitting patients under a partial rather than full regime should be considered. Similarly, it is important to take into account the nature of the sport in question, since some physical alterations, such as weight loss or electrolytic disequilibria, may be partly due to the sporting activity itself, rather than the onset of an eating disorder. In other words, sports psychologists need to adjust the parameters to the sporting discipline at hand (e.g. a female long distance runner who is not suffering from an eating problem usually weighs much less compared to the average woman of the same age and stature). For this reason, it is recommendable to conduct a preliminary study into the training and competition regime of a patient so that sports psychology professionals can ensure they provide the most adequate treatment for each specific case, allowing them to decipher the exact degree to which the illness has developed.

Before going into the fundamental aspects of treatment, it is important to clarify that this description focuses on the clinical treatment of females, since studies with athletes reveal a higher prevalence of eating disorders in this gender (Pate *et al.*, 2003).

6.3   The treatment steps

6.3.1   *Developing the motivation to change*

Once the decision has been made regarding the regime under which an athlete is to be treated, the first step is to motivate the individual to change. In order to appreciate just how difficult this is for an athlete, the following questions may be considered: How would we feel if everything we have fought for all of our lives was taken away from us? What if somebody discovered, and tried to control our best-kept secret? Nonetheless, it is hard to imagine exactly how difficult it is for people suffering from anorexia, bulimia, bigorexia, orthorexia or an EDNOS to modify their behaviour. For these individuals, eating disorders constitute a way of seeking perfection and control, and in their eyes, just when they were beginning to make progress somebody tries to interfere in the process. Therefore, once treatment has commenced, it is common to for patients to display feelings of lack of control.

Initially, athletes suffering from an eating disorder tend to deny they have a problem, often using the characteristics of their sport to mask the fact. Moreover, the pressure of the sporting context may be such that athletes consider pathological weight loss methods and inappropriate eating behaviours as something necessary and even normal. What is more, although on the inside these athletes may feel somewhat 'different' to their team-mates, they frequently believe the situation is under control. Comments such as: 'I know exactly what I'm doing', 'it's just for this part of the season', or 'I'm not sick', are common in these cases. Patients' failure to recognise their illness is what produces such great resistance to change. Consequently, it becomes the principal objective of sport psychologists to earn athletes' cooperation, since counting on their willingness to collaborate constitutes the most important base for successful treatment. Therefore, without pressurising athletes, sports psychologists should approach the problem in a realistic manner, warning them about the serious dangers their situation poses. Sadly, in extreme cases, some patients would rather die than change. In these circumstances, it is important to make patients see everything they are missing out on, the things they used to do when they were 'healthy' (often, training and competing may help re-establish an athlete's motivation to change). In sport, eating disorders often emerge as the result of an athlete's search for perfection. Consequently, during this initial stage of treatment, athletes should be made to understand that there are other ways of 'being the best' in their sport, and that other alternatives are healthier than the option they have chosen up until now.

Moreover, at this stage of the treatment, the sports psychologist's attitude proves crucial. Particularly during the initial period, the therapist should subtly manage the athlete's perception and cognitions regarding body image (focused on the need to be thin and the desire to continue losing weight). Considering that the majority of patients' worries revolve around this matter, to begin with, it is not advisable to focus exclusively on distorted thoughts. It is more beneficial to postpone these aspects until later treatment stages and focus on other matters that may help establish a solid therapist-athlete relationship, so important to the treatment process. According to Clinton (1996) the high proportion of patients who drop out of treatment is due to differing therapist and patient expectations. In this sense, both therapist and athlete should take an active role in decision-making. What is more, the sports psychologist should reinforce any progress the athlete makes, however small it may appear, providing encouragement and the adequate amount of pressure as and when necessary. Below is an extract from an athlete – psychologist conversation, which reflects some of the previously described elements.

Sports Psychologist:SP
Athlete:A

SP   How are you?

A   Pretty bad, I hate not being able to train . . . all my mates are training right now . . .

SP   Yea, it's a shame . . . I can see you are making real progress and you have the right qualities to go far in this sport.

A   Yea, but stopping training isn't helping me . . . the opposite, I should be training more . . . if I carry on like this, I'm going to be totally out of shape in no time . . .

SP   It's logical if you look at it that way, but before you go back to training, we should solve the problem that has brought us here.

A   Yea, but all this is really getting me down.

SP   I know it's a complicated situation for you. You've gone from doing what you like best and what you spend most of your time doing, to not doing it at all . . . it's a big change for you.

A   That's what's got to me the most.

SP   The most important thing at the moment is to focus on creating the base that is going to allow you to return to training, stronger than before.

A   Do you think we will get to that point soon? I'm not so sure . . . it seems to be taking forever.

SP   If we continue working well, I'm sure you'll be training and competing again soon . . . but first, you need get involved 100% . . .

As may be appreciated from this text, it is important to create a strong athlete-psychologist relationship, seeking an adequate and pleasant treatment environment. Nevertheless, on occasions, therapists lack the motivation to work with certain cases or athletes (perhaps because of the athlete's personality, or the type of a case), which can seriously damage the quality of the professional relationship. Burke and Schramm (1995) confirmed this in a study with 90 therapists, finding that 31 per cent desired not to treat such patients. The sport psychologist should make sure the athlete always feels comfortable, allowing them to regard treatment sessions as something beneficial and a necessary step towards change. Therefore, introducing aspects related to a patient's sporting activity can help increase motivation, especially if these aspects help the patient identify a set of advantages in fighting to get better. Along these lines, Vitousek *et al.* (1998) highlight that in order to increase the motivation to change in treatment-resistant eating disorders, four themes are crucial: the provision of psycho-educational material, an examination of the advantages and disadvantages of symptoms, the explicit use of experimental strategies, and an exploration of personal values. Other studies have focussed on how the therapist can affect treatment success, concluding that not only are excellent professional and personal skills necessary (Dosil & Garcés de Los Fayos, 2007), but that female patients often prefer a female therapist (Waller & Katzman, 1998).

Figure 6.1

6.3.2 Treatment objectives

Once an eating disorder has been diagnosed, it is fundamental to commence treatment promptly. The longer it is left, the tougher the battle will be, and the more ground the illness will have gained. Initially, treatment is intense, commencing with a frequent appointment regime (various times a week, according to the athlete's 'deterioration'), becoming less recurrent over time, depending on the improvement displayed.

The first treatment objective is related to the physical component. If the athlete presents excessive weight loss, treatment commences by establishing weight increase goals (at least until weight recovers to within the acceptable limits). This step is not just a question of priorities, but is also necessary for working on other key treatment facets. The aspects to consider in this process are described below:

Progressive weight gain, until an adequate weight has been achieved, according to sex, stature, age and sporting discipline   The athlete and sports psychologist should agree on the weekly weight gain, creating a form of flexible contract. To assess whether the proposed weight is gained, the patient is weighed in the clinic. The athlete needs to be aware of their progress, but must be advised not to weigh him/herself at home, so to avoid the anxiety that so frequently accompanies weight gain. Sometimes the advances may be small, and in some cases, patients may even suffer relapses, but it remains important to continue motivating and encouraging any improvement made, no matter how small it may seem, without basing the analysis solely on the readings from the scales (in some sports, the scales represent a form of pressure for athletes, often associated with performance). For example, an athlete who has failed to gain weight, but has managed to eat a small slice of toast every morning for a week, all on their own, should still be rewarded for their progress. What would be achieved by negatively commenting a patient's lack of improvement? The patient would leave the clinic with a long list of negative thoughts, feeling their efforts have gone unnoticed and the only thing that is valued are the numbers on the scales. Regarding these weight checks, when faced with the fear of not having reached the agreed weight target, some patients resort to drinking large quantities of water (amongst other tricks . . .) prior to getting on the scales. Consequently, without giving the patient ideas, therapists can subtly discuss the temptation to use such techniques, making it clear that they are aware of their existence. Being weighed is difficult for athletes with eating-related problems; nevertheless, sports psychologists can help reduce this ordeal, normalising the task and making the most of the circumstances to work on adapting the negative thoughts related to getting on the scales. Removing athletes' fears of being weighed is extremely important, especially in sports in which weigh-ins and physical checks are commonplace (e.g. in weight division sports).

Although monitoring a patient's weight is a necessary part of the treatment process, therapists should avoid treating it as the principal objective of the therapy; the lives of these individuals revolve around weight, food and figure, and the aim of the therapy is to change these life 'objectives'. Therefore, it is not advisable to talk about 'ideal' weights, or make comments such as 'you need to reach 53 kg', 'your ideal weight is 70 kg'. Patients suffering from these pathologies are usually obsessed with the readings on the scales, and putting too much emphasis on the importance of their weight progress runs the risk of worsening their obsession.

Normalising food   The ultimate aim is to teach athletes that eating a healthy and balanced diet is something normal. Therapists should teach them to eat a variety of foods, since their diets tend to be especially repetitive as a result of their long list of 'prohibited' foods.

Depending on the degree to which an athlete's diet has been altered, therapists should focus initially on one of the daily meals (e.g. breakfast). Gradually, the entire daily food intake may be dealt with. 'Prohibited' foods should be incorporated very gradually. Herrin (2003) discusses how to conduct nutritional counselling in the treatment of eating disorders, and although directed towards the general populations, his approach towards interventions may prove beneficial to the sports context.

One thought which frequently plagues eating disorder sufferers is the fear of losing control over their body and what they eat: 'If I start to eat I won't be able to stop', 'everything I eat makes me fat'. Therefore, it becomes essential to deal with nutritional aspects such as: the functioning of the digestive system, calorie intake and calories burned, stabilizing the ideal weight once it is achieved. . . In other words, arming patients with the relevant knowledge endows them the capacity to feel in control, helping them understand why they need to do what they are doing, not just blindly following the therapist's advice.

A commonly used method to help normalise eating is the use of weekly records, in which patients note down their consumption at each mealtime. In some cases, these records are prepared beforehand with the collaboration of a nutritionist, whilst in others, the patients themselves note down what they have eaten afterwards, granting them a certain degree of trust. Nevertheless, on occasions, the use of such records is not always recommended, since it impedes the athlete from escaping the subject of food.

Giving up laxatives, diuretics and other pathogenic weight-loss methods   Whether this is done drastically or gradually, all inadequate weight-loss behaviours should be eradicated. Different techniques can be used for this, depending on the degree of the patient's dependence. Amongst others, relaxation techniques prove useful to help with the digestive process and the completion of self-records. In the sports context, many of these weight-loss methods have come to be considered as 'normal' and many athletes employ a wide variety of them as part of their routine. Therefore, providing information about the negative effects on health and sporting per-formance can help persuade athletes to give up any inappropriate weight-loss methods.

Detecting and modifying distorted thoughts regarding food, weight and figure   The use of cognitive techniques is highly important in the treatment of eating disorders. Distorted thoughts should be worked on from the beginning of the therapy, select-ing those that become relevant to debate at each stage, without putting excessive pressure on the patient.

The restrictive diet of an athlete with anorexia is not an isolated fact, it is closely linked to a large quantity of characteristic thoughts that provoke, in turn, behav-ioural alterations. These distorted thoughts, which end up invading and totally controlling the athlete's mind, do not only constitute predictive factors and a great source of anxiety, but also the principal factor holding together the athlete's overall condition. Toro and Vilardell (1989) point out the principal cognitive alterations that characterise these patients:

- *Selective abstraction*: forming conclusions from isolated details, ignoring any evidence to the contrary (e.g. 'I'll only be happy if I'm thin').

- *Arbitral inference*: arriving at a conclusion without evidence that supports it, or with evidence to the contrary (e.g. 'everyone looks at me when I go past, they must be thinking how fat I am').

- *Overgeneralisation*: forming a conclusion on the basis of isolated events and applying them to different situations (e.g. 'when I ate everything I was fat, if I want to be thin I can' eat at all', 'apples don't make you fat, so I'll just eat apples').

- *Magnification*: exaggerating undesirable consequences of certain events (e.g. 'If I put on a kilo I'll be really fat and I'll compete badly', 'I've put on two kilos, I won't be able to wear shorts anymore').

- *Dichotomy*: thinking in extreme terms (all or nothing, black or white) (e.g. 'if I can't control my weight, I'll lose control of my life', 'If I put on a kilo, I'll end up weighing 100 kilos').

- *Personalisation and self-referencing*: egocentric interpretations of impersonal events, or over interpretation of relative events (e.g. 'I feel uncomfortable when other people see me eating', 'when I eat in the cafeteria, everyone looks at me').

- *Superstitious thoughts and catastrophic visions*: creating a cause-effect relationship between non-contingent events (e.g. 'If I eat potatoes, I'll put on a kilo', 'If I eat fatty foods, I'll end up as big as a whale and my life will be ruined').

Figure 6.2

Attention to feelings of blame and loss of control   These two aspects characterise the majority of patients. As if it were a doctrine, patients being treated for eating disorders feel as if their world is caving in under the pressure of an imminent enemy ('the changes treatment implies in their way of life'), which they experience as a total loss of control. Therefore, it is important to help them find new alternatives and objectives, transmitting security and confidence at the same time, proposing a new and positive way living. Sports objectives usually have a positive effect, always when they are introduced at the right moment and adapted to the needs of the athlete.

Moreover, the great anxiety and mental torment which eating produces often lead to feelings of immense blame following mealtimes ('I feel so guilty when I eat more than planned'), after all, patients' lives revolve exclusively around their body and obsessive thoughts. Many athletes with eating disorders express this experience in symbolic terms, speaking of two characters in their heads: a giant and a dwarf. The 'dwarf' advises them to eat, telling them they cannot carry on this way, whilst the 'giant' torments them constantly when they eat anything or 'don't look after themselves'. The aim of treatment is to gradually give the 'dwarf' more power and eradicate the 'giant', allowing patients to feel proud. In this sense, mental control is the key to treatment and it is important to relate it to competitive capabilities, using sporting situations to help patients understand and perceive exactly how therapy can alleviate their current problem and help with future training/ competitions.

Attention to non-specific symptoms   This section refers to problems such as low self-esteem, phobias, depression, insomnia, deteriorated social or family relationships, and any other aspects the patient considers problematic. In many cases, these problems get better as treatment advances and the patient gains weight, but on other occasions, they require a more specific treatment. Non-specific symptoms are highly important during the final stages of treatment, when it becomes necessary to crate a context of maximum security to support the progression made. Once again, the use of sport as a bridge between the patient and 'other problems' can prove very effective.

Preventing relapses   Undoubtedly, any individual who has already suffered an illness is susceptible to relapses, especially when emerging from treatment. Eating disorders are no exception and any recently recovered patient must be aware of this. Moreover, it is more than likely that, as well as being especially sensitive to certain subjects related to their illness, patients will encounter difficult circumstances they have yet to overcome. Therefore, although relapses should not be regarded as something acceptable, patients need to be prepared for this eventuality. Treatment brings change, but the true achievement is maintaining this new way of life, and improving it over time, something that implies a great deal of effort and dedication. In sport, athletes will continue to come across the intrinsic pressures of their discipline, making their return to sporting activity a key issue in the prevention of relapses.

Fairburn and Wilson (1993) number a series of concerns to consider in the prevention of relapses, including the following:

- Apply the most effective therapeutic techniques for the situation at hand.

- Do not skip any meals.

- Adequate time planning.

- Seek activities that are incompatible with binge eating, scheduling them at times when there is a greater risk of this occurring.

- Avoid weighing oneself too often.

- Confide in someone when necessary.

- Set realistic goals, praising oneself for each and every achievement, no matter how small.

6.3.3 Techniques and methods used in the treatment of eating disorders

Numerous techniques and methods may be used to treat eating disorders. The methods chosen should adapt to the demands of each specific case and the characteristics of the individual athlete. The techniques that may prove appropriate for one athlete may be counterproductive for another.

A summary of techniques and instruments that may prove valuable in the treatment of eating disorders are described below. The explanation of each is kept brief, since numerous handbooks already provide a more detailed analysis (see, for example, Garner & Garfinkel, 1997):

Weight cards: Athletes record their weight on cards throughout the treatment process. By collecting the cards completed over various months, it is possible to observe the athlete's progress, as well as deciphering whether or not the treatment has been successful.

- *Self-records*: This is a frequently used technique in the treatment of eating disorders. Various types may be employed, depending on the aspects being treated, recording information such as: meals eaten, physical exercise carried out, thoughts, relaxation exercises used, use of social skills . . .

- *Administration of rewards*: One of the strategies most applied by therapists is rewarding patients. It is important to reinforce small achievements and acquire motivation for change based on internal and external reinforcements. These will prove key to successful treatment.

- *Systematic sensitivity reduction*: This is one of the most commonly used techniques in clinical psychology. With eating disorders, it is employed in specific aspects of treatment: difficult situations related to food, weight and figure . . . Moreover, it is frequently used to approach so-called 'prohibited' foods or other situations that incite elevated states of anxiety.

• *Relaxation*: Used for learning to control moments of increased arousal and tension. Patients suffering from eating disorders face numerous situations that provoke anxiety (principally, having to put on weight), which they confront more or less successfully, depending on the strategies/skills they have learned. Relaxation can play an important role in controlling these situations.

• *Exposure techniques*: Used to confront evasive behaviours and frequently used in cases where patients are hospitalised with advanced eating disorders. This form of treatment is usually accompanied by the application of reinforcements, depending on how the patient responds.

• *Models to acquire or inhibit behaviours through observational learning*: Using videos and dramatisations, patients can be taught adequate behaviours for the numerous situations that may prove problematic for them in the future. Training this type of skills is essential for successfully confronting the sports context.

• *Skills therapy for confronting and managing situations*: As with the previous example, this allows patients to confront a diversity of situations they are likely to come across. This type of therapy combines the learning of new skills: self-talk, thought stoppage, relaxation, etc.

• *Problem-solving techniques for approaching difficult situations that may arise during the treatment process*: For example, decision-making skills, which are fundamental for athletes, who must make quick decisions in stressful situations.

• *Role-playing*: This technique proves useful for social situations that may emerge during and after the treatment process (such as how to act in front of individuals who continually ask about their physical aspect, what reply to give . . .). Role-playing gives patients more confidence in themselves, making treatment more consistent.

• *Training social skills*: Learning how to be less dependent on what others say or do, being more assertive and less passive.

• *Rational and cognitive restriction therapies*: These are widely used in clinical psychology and are effective in the treatment of eating disorders. For example, self-talk allows patients to confront certain situations, supporting other strategies; whilst cognitive therapy, developed by Beck, allows patients to identify and modify altered cognitive processes.

- *Control and cognitive distraction*: This consists of changing thoughts, focussing the attention on other things (for example, an image), and maintaining it until the feelings of unease reside.

- *The 'inoculation of stress' technique*: A multifaceted technique using a combination of relaxation, self-talk, and social skills, etc., requiring a previous knowledge of the other aforementioned skills.

6.3.4   Sequencing treatment

When treating eating disorders in athletes, it is essential to have a clear and personalised action plan for each individual athlete. Villapiano (2001) highlights some of the elements to consider for successfully treating athletes suffering eating related problems, discussing some aspects, which despite often going unnoticed, are enormously important when it comes to the intervention (from the decoration of the waiting room, the setting of the initial meeting, to the therapist's personal skills). The sequencing of treatment will vary from one patient to another, for which this section indicates some general aspects to take into account (based on a female patient being treated under a clinical regime).

Initially, sessions should be held on a weekly basis, gradually becoming less frequent as and when the patient recovers weight. Moreover, the control exerted by the therapist should reduce over time, according to how the patient improves, giving the individual more capacity to make his or her own decisions. Another important aspect throughout the treatment process is family involvement. Family conflicts provoked by an eating disorder should be dealt with from the beginning of treatment. If the clinical facility allows, a 'parallel treatment' may be applied, meaning that whilst one therapist focuses on the patient (clinical and sport psychology specialist) another attends the family (specialist in family assessment and guidance). Nevertheless, this model is expensive and treatment tends to be provided by one therapist alone (assessing both the patient and family).

Treating physical complications (constipation, diarrhoea, amenorrhoea), with the help of specialist doctors, is another resource to be considered, although the majority of physical problems deriving from an eating disorder (principally in less serious cases), disappear as the patient gets better. As with physical complications, other pathologies associated with eating disorders (depression, anxiety, insomnia . . .), generally clear up as the individual recovers, although it remains advisable to assess whether some of these symptoms linger, treating them accordingly.

Another relevant aspect, which should be covered during treatment, is social pressure. It is important to provide the patient and family with strategies to increase their confidence, allowing them to respond more adequately to the diversity of situations they will confront. Families and patients claim that one of the greatest problems they face is the 'lack of understanding' and 'harm' done by those around them. Along these lines, it is necessary to appreciate that the majority of the general popu-

lation lack adequate information about these illnesses and, above all, the psychological strategies that would allow them to 'help'. This 'lack of understanding' and
the 'harm' done by others, usually results from the culture surrounding these disorders. In the sports context, this factor becomes even more important, since training colleagues and other athletes will become curious about the athlete's absence
from the sport. Therefore, the patient should be prepared to respond to questions
such as: 'what happened to you?', 'Have you been injured?', etc., or simply, 'I
haven't seen you in ages, you look so different, you've put on weight!'. If the athlete
fails to successfully confront this type of inquisition, it could complicate the treatment and provoke relapses when things seem to be going well.

With regards to exercise, it should be employed as a form of reinforcement, so
the athlete perceives it as a reward rather than a form of losing weight. Rationalising
the amount of time the athlete dedicates to this activity is fundamental. Along these
lines, Sundgot-Borgen *et al.* (2002) carried out a study, in order to compare the
effectiveness of exercise, cognitive therapy and nutritional assessment amongst a
group of bulimics. The results showed that exercise is more effective than cognitive
therapies in some important areas such as 'seeking thinness, changes in body composition, frequency of vomiting, abuse of laxatives . . .', making it a potentially
useful technique with certain cases. As emphasised throughout this chapter, with
patients from the sports context, the possibility of returning to partial training
should always be considered, and would be regarded as a sign of progress in the
treatment process.

An example of a two-staged treatment process is detailed below, in which the
previously described techniques and instruments, as well as the principal objectives
detailed throughout the chapter, are covered.

Stage one   At this initial stage, two objectives are sought, through four sessions.

Objective 1: Change food intake

(a) Introduce four daily meals: breakfast, lunch, an afternoon snack and dinner
    (the sessions gradually introduce these mealtimes until each one has been
    normalised).

(b) Increase the flexibility of these meals and progressively introduce 'prohibited'
    foods into the diet.

Objective 2: Progressive weight-increase

(a) Weigh the patient on a weekly basis (weight cards).

(b) Establish how much weight the patient is to increase each week.

Session 1

1. Initial contact with the athlete (patient) and family.

2. Information about the problem is gathered (clinical history), from the patient's, the family's and the coach's points of view. The exact nature of the illness should be assessed from these three perspectives, as well as the following:
   - eating habits;
   - weight control methods used;
   - attitudes towards weight and figure;
   - general psychopathology;
   - social and family circumstances;
   - physical health;
   - clear information about the disorder;
   - sporting context.

Session 2

1. The athlete is weighed and her weight is noted down on their weight card.

2. Brief explanation of how the treatment will be conducted.

3. Presentation and justification of the eating and physical exercise records.

4. The treatment contract is presented, in which a series of conditions are established. These conditions form the base of the treatment process (attendance, following the instructions given in each session, carrying out the inter.-session tasks . . .) and non-compliance means 'breaking' the contract and the hence, the termination of the treatment process.

5. Direct family guidance

Session 3

1. The athlete is weighed and the weight is noted down on their weight card.

2. The weekly weight gain is established, advising the patient not to weigh themself at home.

3. The athlete and sports psychologist jointly review and comment the eating self-records.

4. Nutritional education: a varied and regular weekly diet is established (if the patient's diet has been seriously altered, begin by working on the least deteriorated areas, gradually working towards an entire day's intake), gradually guiding the athlete towards an appropriate diet for his/her sporting activity.

5. Giving up laxatives, diuretics, vomiting and any other compensatory behaviour: self-records are used here, and the patient is informed about the adverse effects of these techniques and their inefficiency as weight control methods.

6. Guidance with the athlete's family.

Session 4

1. The athlete is weighed and the weight is noted down on their weight card.

2. The patient (athlete) and therapist (sports psychologist) jointly review and discuss the eating and exercise self-records.

3. The progress made is reinforced and the patient is taught how to praise themself for their improvements.

4. Prohibited foods are slowly introduced.

5. Explanation of the cognitive and behavioural changes resulting from the illness, and the relationship between situation-thought-emotion and behaviour.

6. Presentation of the cognitive self-records.

7. Family guidance and parent involvement.

During these initial sessions, a great deal of effort should be put into forming a solid relationship with the athlete, since to a great extent, the patient's collaboration and motivation to change depends on this factor. It is vital for the athlete to feel supported and understood, as well as perceiving a secure and trusting environment. On the other hand, parents should be encouraged to talk about other matters at home, not related to the illness or sport. Often, the concern for their child is such that it brings them to constantly comment 'how thin he/she is' or 'how little he/she is eating', putting a lot of pressure on the patient, especially at mealtimes, and not offering any benefit to the treatment process (these comments can undo the positive reinforcement provided during sessions).

Stage 2   The second stage maintains all the objectives from stage 1, whilst trying to advance in more specific aspects: the diet becomes richer in calories, and cognitive restructuring of distorted thoughts related to food, weight and figure intensifies.

Session 5

1. The athlete is weighed and the weight is noted down on their weight card.

2. The patient and therapist jointly review and discuss the eating, physical activity and cognitive self-records (contrasting past and current data in order to establish the proposed future progress, and using motivating aspects from the sporting activity).

3. Cognitive restructuring I: identification of automatic thoughts; study of the situations in which they are produced and control strategies (the use of distractions, key words . . .). At this stage of the treatment process, it is recommendable to use examples from the patient's sport, since this setting produces a range of

typical situations in which automatic thoughts play an important role, and through a familiar example, can help the patient appreciate how they work (e. g. a canoeist who realises he/she is being overtaken, fails to control his/her thoughts, which unconsciously reduces his/her performance).

Session 6

1. The athlete is weighed and the weight is noted down on their weight card.

2. The patient and therapist jointly review and discuss the eating, physical activity and cognitive self-records.

3. Cognitive restructuring II: identification and correction of irrational thoughts. As with the previous session, it is very useful to employ examples of sporting situations in which irrational thoughts are produced. (E.g. A taekwondoka who is in good physical form and has to confront an inferior rival, irrationally thinks, 'If my rival is taller than me I will lose').

Session 7

1. The athlete is weighed and the weight is noted down on their weight card.

2. The patient and therapist jointly review and discuss the eating, physical activity and cognitive self-records.

3. Cognitive restructuring III: identification and correction of negative thoughts. During this session, the therapist should continue the use of examples from the sporting context in order to maintain the athlete's motivation to continue the treatment (e.g. a distance athlete may start to think, 'I'm getting tired, I can't keep going, I need to drop-out').

Session 8

1. The athlete is weighed and the weight is noted down on their weight card.

2. The patient and therapist jointly review and discuss the eating, physical activity and cognitive self-records.

3. Cognitive restructuring IV: review of previous phases. Here, the patient may be presented with different examples of typical thoughts that occur in athletes, helping to identify their existence and learn how to adapt thinking in each situation.

Session 9

1. The athlete is weighed and the weight is noted down on their weight card.

2. The patient and therapist jointly review and discuss the eating, physical activity and cognitive self-records.

3. Body image I: analysis of the current aesthetic models and systematic de-sensitivity and relaxation techniques. In this section, it is important to deal with the

'typical' body images in sport, helping the athlete form his/her own perception of these, as well as becoming aware of the existence of different body morphologies in each sport.

Session 10

1. The athlete is weighed and the weight is noted down on their weight card.

2. The patient and therapist jointly review and discuss the eating, physical activity and cognitive self-records.

3. Body image II: the patient's body perception is assessed, comments about perceptive distortions and recognition of her own body. Depending on the sport in question, the therapist should be aware that the patient might be more concerned about certain parts of his/her body (e.g. distance athletes prefer to have very thin legs, a marked jaw line, etc.).

Session 11

1. The athlete is weighed and the weight is noted down on their weight card.

2. The patient and therapist jointly review and discuss the eating, physical activity and cognitive self-records.

3. Body image III: cognitive restructuring of distorted thoughts related to the patient's body image.

Session 12

1. The athlete is weighed and the weight is noted down on their weight card.

2. The patient and therapist jointly review and discuss the eating, physical activity and cognitive self-records.

3. Self-esteem (figure and weight are the only factors the patient uses to boost their self-esteem). Having worked on the athlete's thoughts and body image, it is important to help them understand that to a great extent, self-esteem is a combination of the two factors. Likewise, at this point, the athlete may be taught social skills to help prevent the negative effects of other people's comments.

Session 13

1. The athlete is weighed and the weight is noted down on their weight card.

2. The patient and therapist jointly review and discuss the eating, physical activity and cognitive self-records.

3. Self-esteem (as with the previous session).

Session 14

1. The athlete is weighed and the weight is noted down on their weight card.

2. The patient and therapist jointly review and discuss the eating, physical activity and cognitive self-records

3. Social skills I: the use of social models and learning adequate behaviours for different social situations. Here, the work will revolve around the sports context, where conversations tend to revolve around the athlete's speciality, focusing on the situations in which it will be easier for the patient to form social relationships.

Session 15

1. The athlete is weighed and the weight is noted down on their weight card.

2. The patient and therapist jointly review and discuss the eating, physical activity and cognitive self-records.

3. Social skills II: practice through role-playing different situations. It is fundamental for the athlete to role-play the situations he/she is more likely to encounter given the context of their particular event. For example, a middle-distance athlete should be ready for the conversations that crop up while stretching following a training session.

Session 16

1. The athlete is weighed and the weight is noted down on their weight card.

2. The patient and therapist jointly review and discuss the eating, physical activity and cognitive self-records.

3. Prevention of relapses: detecting risk factors and strategies to confront them. If the patient is going to continue practicing the same event, it is important to remind them of the many potentially dangerous situations they will confront.

Session 17

1. The athlete is weighed and the weight is noted down on their weight card.

2. The patient and therapist jointly review and discuss the eating, physical activity and cognitive self-records.

3. Treatment evaluation and generalisation of the acquired skills.

6.4 Types of treatment

The very existence of so many different types of treatment can be considered a step forwards in the fight against eating disorders. The effectiveness of these methods is difficult to quantify and they should be selected according to their suitability for the individual characteristics of each case and the degree to which the illness has developed. However, it is highly important to be familiar with all the treatment options in order to choose the most fitting one for each stage of treatment and for each individual patient. In the *Handbook of Treatment for Eating Disorders*, Garner and Garfinkel (1997) discuss the different treatment options, focusing on anorexia and bulimia in the general population. This publication may prove a useful guide for dealing with athletes suffering from eating disorders, being sure to adapt the treatments to the peculiarities of this context.

Given the great variety of symptoms eating disorders present, the most effective and complete therapeutic approach is that which combines medical, pharmaceutical and psychological techniques simultaneously (Halmi, 2005). This multidisciplinary vision provides the necessary overall treatment to solve every aspect that may be directly or indirectly influencing the illness. For example, if a gymnast were suffering from an eating disorder, provoked by the pressure exerted by her coach and parents, simply normalising her weight by making her eat more would prove useless if the factors causing her illness are not dealt with first.

Taking this multidisciplinary approach into account, the following treatments should be considered.

6.4.1 Individual treatment

The treatment administered directly to an athlete is essential for their recovery. Many treatment alternatives are available, and the selection will depend on the focus given by the sport psychologist and the particularities of the case at hand:

Medical treatment Given the physical complications involved with the majority of eating disorders, medical input is always necessary, although not sufficient on its own. Therefore, a multidisciplinary approach is required, in which doctors and psychologists work side by side.

Following the diagnosis, the first step is to perform a general physical examination of the patient, in order to deal with any medical complications that may arise. In addition to treating any physical problems and correcting malnutrition (both reversible in the majority of cases as weight and healthy eating habits are recovered), it is recommendable to count on the involvement of a dietician, who can provide advice and monitor dietary matters, adapting them to the needs and preferences of the patient. Along these lines, relating their knowledge to sport, dieticians can help boost athletes' nutritional training, providing guidance about the appropriate elements that can serve to improve performance and well being.

Cognitive behavioural treatment (CBT) This is possibly the most broadly employed alternative with eating-disorder patients (Burke & Schramm, 1995; Ricca *et al.*, 2000) and consists of relating the athlete's thoughts to their behaviours.

- *Behavioural treatment*: Closely related to cognitive treatment, this aims to reinforce adapted behaviours (e.g. avoiding eating foods that could provoke weight gain). This is an arduous and complicated task, involving a constant effort on behalf of both the therapist and the patient, which is as difficult to achieve, as it is necessary. In order to accomplish this much feared weight gain, it is vital to appropriately deal with all of the phobic and anxiety aspects that complicate the process, which will emerge throughout the treatment process.

- *Cognitive treatment*: The principal objective of cognitive therapy is to modify all false/inappropriate thoughts and beliefs related to food, weight and body image.

Education and nutritional advice   Nowadays, access to information related to eating disorders is simple, since new sources, principally the Internet, provide a constant flow of data. Therefore, throughout the treatment process, the function of the therapist is to channel the information the patient receives, explaining in a clear and concise manner, everything related to the illness, its symptoms and its risks.

Such nutritional education is highly recommended. Moreover, when treating athletes, information regarding correct nutrition should be associated wherever possible with sports performance. Advice on how to look after diet at different stages of the competitive season, what athletes should avoid doing, and the positive consequences of a balanced diet (both in terms of sports performance and health) should be focused on during sessions.

Other individual therapies   Other therapies that can be used are psychoanalytic therapy (the therapist focuses on determining the origin of the eating disorder through analysing the athlete's past experiences, focusing on the different moments of their childhood), and interpersonal therapy (the psychologist examines difficulties relating to others).

6.4.2   Family and/or couple therapy

In the majority of cases, as a cause or effect, the family environment surrounding a patient suffering an eating disorder is usually much deteriorated. Families often feel somewhat disorientated regarding the illness at hand, not knowing exactly how to act and feeling guilty for the problem. Therefore, it becomes necessary to conduct interventions with the family, parallel to individual therapy. Likewise, in certain cases, it is necessary to treat family problems directly with the patient, since they may be influencing both the continuance of the illness, as well as their chances of recuperation.

6.4.3   Group therapy

The therapist should choose whether to conduct an individual or group therapy. Nevonen and Broberg (2006) compare the effectiveness of these two treatment options, concluding that there are no significant differences between the results obtained from the two sets of patients. In some cases, group therapy can complement and reinforce individual therapy. With a fundamentally educative focus, and directed by a therapist, the group serves to improve social skills and increase awareness of the patients' illnesses. Nevertheless, and despite the numerous advantages, it is important to be very careful with negative competitiveness, a phenomenon that may emerge between the group's components. Along these lines, it is advisable to include some partially recovered patients in the group, who can act as role models for the remaining members.

Group therapy can also be used with parents and the partners of athletes. This constitutes a useful source of information, understanding and union. In short, it can provide a much needed 'escape valve'. Similarly, 'support groups' are frequently formed, made up of individuals, coaches, and athletes who have some degree of experience with eating disorders and wish to share their perspective of these problems in order to help reinforce the treatment process.

6.4.4 Pharmaceutical therapy

The use of drugs in the treatment of eating disorders has been justified in recent years by confirming the relationship between these conditions and others, in which pharmaceuticals have proved effective (emotional and anxiety disorders...). Nevertheless, although some investigations have indicated the effectiveness of some pharmaceuticals in suppressing certain eating disorder symptoms, there remains a degree of scepticism regarding their suitability. Antidepressants are the most widely accepted drug in the treatment of these illnesses.

In the majority of cases, drugs are used to alleviate the symptoms of depression, anxiety, lack of sleep, or hyperactivity. However, considering that the majority of these related symptoms disappear as patients recover weight and normalise eating habits, perhaps the best 'drug' is food.

6.5 Conclusions

This chapter has presented the most important aspects involved in treating eating disorders, and has described the various methods or strategies that may be employed.

The ultimate aim of treatment in the sports context is to reintegrate athletes into their respective sporting activities, encouraging the acquisition of adequate eating habits, which allow them to maintain a long sporting career with results worthy of their physical and psychological potential.

Follow-up is important with athletes, since the conditioners surrounding them make relapses frequent. Once again, adequately informing coaches, parents and other individuals involved in the sporting environment, serves to prevent both the development of eating disorders, as well as possible relapses. Furthermore, incorporating specialist sport psychologists into teams and clubs would lead to more successful treatment.

7 Cyberpsychology and Eating Disorders in Sport

Joaquín Dosil and Isabel Díaz

Marcus gave up competitive cycling two years ago. Over the last few months, he has started thinking about taking cycling up again, and getting back into the shape he was in before. However, whenever Marcus thinks about going out for a ride, he always ends up not doing so. The problems start as soon as he puts his cycling suit on: he looks at his legs and feels really fat. Having searched on the Internet, he finds a website offering on-line sport psychology guidance given by an eating disorder specialist and he decides to get in contact. From that moment on, he begins consulting with this specialist via an on-line chat facility, who helps him understand his inappropriate thoughts, providing strategies to control them.

7.1 Introduction

Over the last decades, technological advances, particularly those related to the Internet, have made a significant impact on social life and scientific development. The first time a computer was used to transmit information was in the 1960s, during the Cold War, when it was principally employed as a method of calculation. In the 1970s, four North American universities managed to connect to one another via computers, in order to share data and carry out a joint investigation. In 1972 the amount of universities connected to what had become known as the ARPA-Net,

Eating Disorders in Athletes Joaquín Dosil
© 2008 John Wiley & Sons, Ltd

rose to 40. Initially, only the largest institutions had access, but by the mid 1970s, smaller and medium-sized entities were also able to hook up, forming part of an ever-growing network. In 1990, access to the newly named 'Internet', was granted governmental support, boosting its growth and diffusion in an extraordinary manner, and resulting in the appearance of the first free commercial operations. Between 1990 and 1995, the number of computers connected to the Internet climbed from 160 000 to some 5 000 000, allowing millions of people to access the network of all networks (Laszig & Rieg, 2000; Riva *et al.*, 2002; Zabinski *et al.*, 2003a). These data allow us to reflect on the many possibilities of the Internet, in a broad array of contexts, ranging from business and politics, to education and more interestingly, psychology (or more specifically, sport psychology and eating disorders).

This chapter discusses how the Internet relates to eating disorders in sport, introducing the concept of *cyberpsychology*, discussing the specific information that can be found on the Internet about these illnesses, and the possibility of 'on-line' treatment. Although this form of therapy is still at the developmental stages, its great potential as a treatment alternative, both with athletes and the normal population, make it a fundamental part of this publication.

7.2 Psychology and new technologies: cyberpsychology

Cyberpsychology is an area of psychology emerging from the convergence of new technologies, congress communications, publications and journals, and the jobs related to these areas (Prieto, 1999). In 1994, discussions began regarding the use of new technology in clinical consultancies, in the field of applied psychology. From that moment on, communications, posters, conferences and symposiums on this subject became commonplace in congresses related to many diverse areas of psychology. Moreover, the first publications began to surface, including the following important texts: *Cyberpsychology* by Gordo-Lopez and Parker (1999), *Towards Cyberpsychology* by Riva and Galimberti (2001), *E-Therapy: case studies, guiding principles, and the clinical potential of the internet* by Hsiung (2002), *Technology in Counselling and Psychotherapy,* by Goss and Anthony (2003), and *On-line Counselling: A Handbook for Mental Health* by Kraus *et al.* (2004) or *The Oxford Handbook of Internet Psychology* by Joinson *et al.* (2007).

In a recent review, Dosil and García-Prieto (2004) highlight the three major areas of psychology that have taken most interest in the use of the Internet: educative psychology, social psychology and psychotherapy. In the latter, various investigations have researched into the effectiveness of the Internet for conducting psychotherapeutic interventions and on-line assessment.

Currently, more specific methods of 'on-line' intervention have been developed, such as those designed by Vincelli *et al.* (2003), which analyse the effectiveness of cognitive–behavioural therapy in the on-line treatment of panic disorders with agoraphobia. These authors used *experimental cognitive therapy*, combining cognitive techniques to achieve thought modification, and virtual reality for exposure techniques, in order to prevent inappropriate responses. Along these lines, similar studies by Ritterband *et al.* (2003) confirm the practicality of Internet treatment, obtaining better results from on-line interventions than personal therapy, with children suffering encopresis.

In the treatment of post-traumatic stress, Lange *et al.* (2003) developed a treatment procedure using the Internet, consisting of psycho-education, surfing the internet for information, on-line counselling and measuring treatment effects. Through this type of intervention they obtained some positive results in 50 per cent of the patients opting for this treatment method. Stroem *et al.* (2000) also used e-mail to treat patients suffering from migraines; likewise, other authors, such as Griffiths and Cooper (2003), and Bermejo (2001), turned to this form of on-line treatment for some forms of addiction.

Many publications dealing with the use of the Internet in psychology have focused on analysing its advantages and disadvantages, as well as the resources it can provide (Dosil & García-Prieto, 2004). The possible resources include:

- *On-line training*: An increasing number of companies, universities or psychology centres offer training programmes through the Internet. On-line campuses are being developed as a resource for those who are unable to attend educational courses in person. Tutors run these courses through the use of forums, maintaining contact with students via real-time conversations or e-mail, in the form of 'virtual tutorials'.

- *Professional forums*: Currently, there are several forums in which psychology and psychiatry professionals share their experiences, discuss their doubts and present their studies on the web. This type of forum should always be controlled and coordinated by experts, only granting access to information and studies based on valid and reliable results, so not to hinder the quality of professional work. A specialised Webmaster, or a group in charge of filtering information, is necessary for these types of professional forums and meeting places.

- *Information*: A fast growing number of new websites appear, providing information related to psychology studies or topics. Nevertheless, to find the best websites, it is important to carryout correct searches, since not all offer adequate and up-to-date information. The Internet offers an immense quantity of information, but does not filter it, and can even supply counteractive data.

- *Prevention*: Several websites for institutions and organisations provide guidelines for the prevention of certain illnesses, inadequate habits, such as smoking, and even inappropriate eating or addictive behaviours. Moreover, some associations related to eating disorders, offer prevention guidelines for parents, youngsters, teachers and coaches. These websites allow users to get in contact with the relevant professionals, in order to seek guidance and counselling for specific cases. Zabinksi *et al.* (2003a, b), for example, offer an Internet-based prevention of eating disorders.

• *Self-help programmes*: Many individuals now prefer to turn to self-help programmes offered through the use of modern technology (see for example: Williams, 2003). In 1985, Huon gave the first details of patients who had employed this method to commence psychological treatment. Likewise, Carter and Fairburn (1998) conducted an investigation into eating disorders, comparing a conventional one-to-one self-help programme with 24 individuals suffering from binge-eating disorders, with another programme, in which 24 subjects used guided self-help via e-mail. Both treatment options were compared to a control group of patients. The group using guided self-help via e-mail obtained the most significant improvement in terms of diminished binge eating and psychiatric symptoms, as well as significantly reducing restricted eating.

• *Virtual reality*: Vincelli (1999), having experimented with recreation through psychotherapeutic virtual reality, confirmed this method as being the future of clinical psychology. Along similar lines, Perpiñá *et al.* (2003), use virtual reality to treat problems related to body image disturbers and binge eating.

• *On-line therapy*: Today, many psychologists offer their services via the Internet (Dosil, 2004). Regarding eating disorders in athletes, the Internet is considered an ideal method at various stages of the treatment process, although it is sustained by the capability of the therapist and athlete to appropriately use the service.

7.3 Cyber-sport-psychology and eating disorders

Cyber-sport-psychology may be defined as: 'An emerging concept which studies physical exercise and sport psychology in the telecommunications context (Information and Communication Technologies ICT), principally the Internet' (Dosil, 2004; p. 102). Sports psychology has begun to take advantage of the many resources offered by the Internet, so to conduct psychological guidance and interventions with coaches, athletes and clubs at ease. E-mail and chatrooms have become extremely effective forms of communication with coaches, offering a fast and easy way of providing information about sports results and performances, as well as expressing problems arising with the team, individual athletes or the coaching role. Through this resource, sports psychologists are able to carryout assessments, maintaining direct and dynamic contact, both with coaches and athletes. Likewise, psychological guidance in sport has extended to other members of the sporting context, such as directors, who optimise their management skills by using psychological strategies acquired in person, through e-mail, in the form of advice and/or on-line conversations.

Not all sports clubs are able to employ a full-time sports psychologist and few athletes and teams count on the physical presence of a sports psychologist during every training session. Sports psychology professionals are often unable to conduct continued interventions ('on-site') because of economic or time restrictions. Faced with this reality, the Internet has opened up numerous treatment possibilities that were not previously viable.

Through the Internet, athletes are able to maintain contact with sports psychologists wherever they train or compete. Some sports psychologists already maintain a professional on-line relationship with athletes who are thousands of miles away. Moreover, many cases which are currently treated in the clinical context, may be treated on-line, such as anxiety problems, self-confidence issues, depression, general health problems, psychological burnout and even social or schooling problems, which may be affecting an athlete's sporting performance.

Within the field of cyberpsychology, on-line education and guidance/intervention are the two main areas of interest for athletes suffering from eating disorders.

For example, in terms of training professionals to become eating disorders specialists, the Internet establishes distance training courses, making use of virtual tutorials, forums, and meetings, etc., which serve to increase the knowledge of sports psychology professionals wanting to become familiar with this matter. Many sports psychology association websites already offer discussion forums in which professionals are able to share their experiences and conduct virtual enquiries, establishing fluid, up-to-date and ongoing communication with other sports psychologists from all over the world. In the case of eating disorders, cultural differences are an important factor, which may serve to enrich this form of continuous education.

On-line assessment can be of benefit to both athletes suffering from eating disorders as well as coaches or club members wishing to acquire preventative guidance. In the sports setting, those seeking psychological assistance often demand improved athlete, coach or team performances, and in many cases, these matters can be dealt with via e-mail or real time conversations.

7.4   The Internet: information about eating disorders in sport

Over recent years, numerous websites have appeared which make continuous references to eating disorders in athletes. In the description of eating disorder characteristics, aspects related to physical activity and eating problems in athletes are included (risk factors, guidelines for parents and coaches, etc.). The continuous increase in the number of websites dedicated to eating disorders echoes the degree of concern these illnesses have provoked all around the world. In this sense, the Internet has become a resource of mass global access, where the information provided is a direct reflection of the demand.

Therefore the Internet may be considered a potentially positive space for informing the general population and preventing eating related problems. Nevertheless, exactly *how* the 'network of all networks' is used determines whether it is a positive or negative activity. Dosil and García Prieto (2004) detail some of the advantages and disadvantages of using the Internet in the field of sports psychology:

Advantages:

- It promotes sports psychology and offers easy access to many subjects related to this discipline.
- Such information is gradually becoming more numerous and more easily located on the Internet.
- It facilitates collaboration between institutions and professionals, providing access to debate forums, meetings and even professional courses and congresses.
- It allows for distance learning.
- It aids communication between coaches/athletes from different areas.
- It provides a new treatment option: On-line therapy for athletes.

Disadvantages:

- The potential intrusion of non-specialist sports psychology professionals or non-qualified professionals.
- Given the sheer quantity of information provided some may be of poor quality or lack reliability.
- Specialist services may be inappropriately promoted.
- Lack of rigorous controls over the professional services provided.
- Loss of verbal information, so valuable in the field of psychology.
- Potential intrusion by Internet addicts.

In order to perform a search for websites containing information on eating disorders in athletes, the correct keywords must be inserted in any of the popular search engines (e.g. Google, Yahoo, Lycos, etc.). Next, the various websites containing information about eating disorders in sport appear. Those that best fit the search requirements include:

- www.aedweb.org [accessed 16 August 2007]: This is the website for the Academy for Eating Disorders. It mainly offers internal information about the academy, its members, activities, publications, etc, and some external data regarding the different types of eating disorders, including obesity. It also offers some statistics regarding the current prevalence of eating disorders and future forecasts, as well briefly describing the risk factors contributing to the development of eating disorders and their consequences. Moreover, it specifies the most adequate forms of treatment for eating disorders, detailing some brief characteristics of each. However, it fails to make any specific reference to eating disorders in sport.

• www.anad.org [accessed 16 August 2007]: This is the website for the National Association for Anorexia Nervosa and Associated Disorders, and offers both internal and external information. Furthermore, it informs about the statistics related to eating disorders, as well as the general characteristics and causes of these, and guidelines for their detection. It also makes a small reference to eating disorders in athletes. Similarly, it offers information about the different types of treatment available, as well as including information about self-help groups in different countries. Interestingly, this particular association promotes the possibility of developing on-line self-help groups.

• www.anred.com [accessed 16 August 2007]: Anorexia Nervosa and Related Eating Disorders Inc. was founded in 1970, and its website contains eating disorders information that is constantly updated. Moreover, there is a section dedicated to eating disorders in athletes, including basic and concise information about how these illnesses can affect sportspeople, as well as how they can be prevented and treated.

• www.b-eat.co.uk [accessed 16 August 2007]: The Eating Disorders Association (UK) presents an extensive website, which covers mostly external information. It provides information and advice for both adults and youngsters about eating disorders: symptoms and how to recognise them, possible treatments (providing the relevant contact details), and how to help sufferers. Moreover, it emphasises the role friends can play in the detection of eating disorder in youngsters. It also includes an ample section about eating disorders in athletes and excessive exercise. Likewise, it provides information for coaches, monitors, and those individuals involved in sport, including parents, friends and the athletes themselves. In addition, it supplies three different guides about eating disorders in sport, available in PDF format: for coaches, family members and friends, or athletes.

• www.edreferral.com [accessed 16 August 2007]: The International Eating Disorder Referral Organization is an entity that provides information and demonstrates different therapeutic resources, aimed at both those suffering from an eating disorder, as well as those directly implicated, such as family, friends, teachers and coaches. It offers some internal information, but mainly provides external data. It includes a definition of each disorder and fully describes all the risk factors, stressing the impact of gender and age. Furthermore, it offers practical information to parents and teachers, both regarding the prevention of eating disorders, as well as guidance in the search for the most adequate treatment options. It also contains a special section for eating disorders in athletes, highlighting the high-risk sports, risk factors and medical complications. Moreover, it offers guidelines for coaches and contains an interesting section with links to other associations or interesting eating disorder sites.

- www.eatingdisorderscoalition.org [accessed 16 August 2007]: This website offers general information about eating disorders, and aims to gain their recognition as a public health priority.

- www.eatingdisorderinfo.org [accessed 16 August 2007]: This is the website for the Alliance of Eating Disorders Awareness, offering general information about eating disorders and how to identify potential eating disorders. It also includes personal testimonies from individuals who have suffered an eating disorder.

- www.iaedp.com [accessed 16 August 2007]: This is the official website for the International Association of Eating Disorder Professionals. The most noticeable aspect of this particular website is being able to directly contact the professional members of this international association. However, no reference is made to eating disorders in sport. Principally, it represents a guide for professionals.

- www.nationaleatingdisorders.org [accessed 16 August 2007]: This is the website for the National Eating Disorders Association, and offers mainly internal information. This particular website focuses on the promotion of eating disorder treatment and prevention programmes in the form of CD-sand self-help books, along with association articles. It also offers a broad range of information about eating disorders: anorexia, bulimia and binge eating, as well as their risk factors, causes and protection dynamics. Moreover, it includes information for sufferers, parents, teachers, friends, and classmates, highlighting the role of each individual in detecting eating related problems and helping sufferers. It also offers guidelines for professionals. This particular website also dedicates a section to eating disorders in sport. It provides some simple descriptions of the risk and protection factors for eating disorders in sport, emphasising the Female Athletic Triad. Moreover, it provides a link to the International Olympic Committee website, containing an article about female athletes and health risk factors. Finally, it details 10 prevention guidelines for coaches.

- www.something-fishy.org [accessed 16 August 2007]: This website is dedicated to raising awareness and providing support to people with eating disorders. This site stands out for having relevant information about eating disorders in different languages, assisting users in finding the adequate professionals for their treatment, as well as providing reliable links to related websites.

- www.swedauk.org [accessed 16 August 2007]: The website for the Somerset & Wessex Eating Disorders Association offers both internal and external information.

Table 7.1 Eating disorders websites. Reproduced from Villa and Navas (2002), courtesy of McGraw-Hill, Madrid

Website	Address (URL)
Argentina Society of Obesity and Eating Disorders	www.saota.org.ar (in Spanish)
Attention-Defence of Anorexia and Bulimia Nervosa Association	www.adaner.org (in Spanish)
Compulsive Eaters Anonymous – H.O.W.	www.ceahow.org
Eating Disorders Association (NZ)	www.everybody.co.nz
Eating Disorders Association N-Ireland	www.eatingdisordersni.com
Eating Disorders Association of South Australia	www.edasa.org.au
Eating Disorders Association Resource Center	www.eda.org.au
Eating Disorders Professionals (IAEDP)	www.iaedp.com
Eating Disorders Research Society	www.edresearchsociety.org
Food Addicts Anonymous	www.foodaddictsanonymous.org
Harvard Eating Disorders Center (HEDC)	www.hedc.org
Healing Connections, Inc.	www.healingconnections.org
HUGS International Inc.	www.hugs.com
Multiservice Eating Disorder Association (MEDA)	www.medainc.org
National Alliance on Mental Illnes (NANI)	www.nami.org
National Association to Advance Fat Acceptance, Inc. (NAAFA)	www.naafa.org
National Eating Disorder Association	www.edap.org
National Eating Disorders Information Center	www.nedic.ca
Ophelia's place	www.opheliasplace.org
Overeaters Anonymous	www.oa.org
Promoting Legislation & Education About Self-Esteem, Inc. (PLEASE)	
Somerset & Wessex Eating Disorders Association	www.swedauk.org
Spanish Association for the study of eating disorders	www.aeetca.org (in Spanish)
The Eating Disorders Action Group	www.e-d-a-g.com
The National Center for Eating Disorders	www.eating-disorders.org.uk
The Renfrew Center Foundation	www.renfrew.org
WINS (We Insist on Natural Shapes)	www.winsnews.org

All websites accessed 16 August 2007.

Through small articles written by different professionals, it refers to the different characteristics of eating disorders: symptoms, detection, and physical and psychological complications in both men and women. Moreover, it includes a section in which professionals develop an investigative activity: introducing questionnaires and surveys, which users can fill-in and send. One of these investigations deals with the possibility of on-line guidance for eating disorders. In the section 'Other Eating Disorders', it refers to both athletic anorexia and bigorexia, although only very briefly. Finally, it includes an interesting article about the characteristics of gym-goers in relation to eating disorders.

As it would be impossible to cover all the eating disorders websites referring to sport in one way or another, Table 7.1 lists some more relevant ones.

7.5   On-line diagnosis and treatment of eating disorders in sport

The treatment of psychological problems related to eating has undergone much analysis in recent years. Researchers have defended various methods to eradicate eating disorders, but have yet to arrive at an agreement over which method is the most successful. As seen in the previous chapter, it should be the sports psychology specialist who selects the most appropriate form of treatment, according to the specific requirements of the athlete in question. When deciding on the treatment, it is essential for the therapist to create a specific profile of the athlete, in order to better understand the case at hand and apply the most adequate solutions for the sporting discipline. Likewise, it is important to take into account the degree to which the illness has developed. If the disorder has advanced beyond its initial stages, an athlete's treatment must be principally clinical.

In sport, the most frequent types of psychological guidance are *clinical* and *field*. Nevertheless, in recent years, with technological advances, more and more on-line treatments have become available (Dosil, 2006):

- *Clinical guidance*: this constitutes the most traditional method, in which the athlete attends a sports psychology office or unit.

- *Field guidance*: with this method, guidance takes place in the training setting, in the athlete's own environment.

- *On-line assessment*: this method is applied via e-mail or simultaneous chat facilities.

A fourth alternative is the *mixed model*, in which two types of guidance can be combined: on-line and in person (clinical or field). The decision to use one method or another will depend on the characteristics of the case at hand, the seriousness of the disorder and the availability of both the athlete and the therapist. Yager (2003), considering other illnesses, highlights the advantages of on-line treatment for people suffering from eating disorders:

- anonymity, facilitating inhibition on behalf of the patient;
- the speed at which information can be communicated;
- easy access, both geographically and in terms of time;
- the low cost of using the Internet.

In some cases, eating disorders in sport must be treated in person, since on occasions it is necessary to rigorously control the conditions and physical state of the sufferer.

The intervention itself may be directed towards the athlete, the coach or the parents. Yager (2003) presents his experiences of treating eating disorders via e-mail. In some cases, parents were included in the on-line therapy, parallel to the athlete's on-line treatment. In this form of treatment, via e-mail, Yager also introduced cognitive–behavioural therapies and nutritional guidance, obtaining some very satisfactory results. Along these lines, Grunwald and Busse (2003) carried out a form of on-line therapy that encompassed family members and friends as part of the patient's treatment, given that on many occasions these individuals sought information about the disorder. Therefore, it is often highly important to maintain contact with family members and friends in order to gain information about the patient and their environment, which could aid their treatment process.

Similarly, in the sporting context, the person who detects a problem is often the coach, since he/she usually spends the most time with athletes, observing any changes in their behaviour during training and competitions. In these cases, sports psychologists can guide coaches in what to do if they suspect one of their athletes is suffering from an eating disorder. An on-line session, whether by e-mail or instant chat, serves as a good way of orientating coaches in this aspect. This method can also be used with parents, if they are the ones who detect a problem with an athlete's eating habits. If, on the other hand, it is the athlete who gets in contact with a sports psychologist, then treatment may commence following a *screening* of the case.

As previously seen, there are various forms of intervention: on-line, mixed, in person, etc. However, if the athlete develops considerable physical complications, on-line treatment is not a feasible option. In more severe cases, the best option is to treat the patient in person, and therapists may have to consider partial or even total hospitalisation.

7.5.1   *Commencing on-line treatment of an eating disorder in sport*

First, to initiate on-line treatment, it is essential to have the right equipment to do so. Therefore, depending on the form of on-line therapy proposed, a therapist can choose more or less complementary treatments. However, the basic equipment includes: a good Internet connection, the appropriate programs to conduct treatments via the web, and a microphone and/or a camera. Logically, the better the quality of the Internet connection, the easier it will be to use certain methods. The four most commonly used methods are:

- *Electronic mail (e-mail).* A case is put forward in an extensive written message, sent to the therapist via e-mail. The therapist responds in a determined period of time, which is agreed from the first session. The fact that this form of treatment is not immediate sometimes poses problems, although it does give therapists time to thoroughly analyse the case presented to them, providing the best treatment options.

- *Real time chat (instant messaging).* The therapist conducts a form of interview with the patient via short typed messages in real time (immediate). Patients present their cases and the therapist guides them, providing potential solutions and action guidelines. The advantage of this method, as opposed to e-mail, is the fact that the response is instantaneous. Also, more than two people can participate in conversations, enabling therapists, co-therapists, coaches, parents, etc. to access the same information at the same time. Being able to work with a co-therapist aids a broader and more rigorous treatment process, analysing the information from a different perspective and complementing treatment solutions. However, it is important for therapists to control the access to these conversations, and ensure that the athlete is fully aware at all times of who is participating, so not to appear intrusive. Nevertheless, just as therapists can maintain one conversation with several individuals, the nature of this technology also allows them to hold two or more *separate* conversations at the same time. For example, in one 'window' a therapist can chat with the athlete, and in another, they can consult with the co-therapist. This benefits a close and coordinated relationship between the therapist and co-therapist, which translates into a better quality intervention for the patient.

- *Real time conversations (verbal).* A real time interview is appropriate in those eating disorder cases where an initial base has already been established and only brief weekly contact is required. This method is quicker than chat and does not depend on the capacity to type quickly. The therapist and patient can speak, similarly to a telephone conversation, although they cannot see each other. Various programs currently allow conversations without any cost at all.

Figure 7.1

Table 7.2 The use of different Internet resources in on-line therapy

Therapeutic resource	Corresponding on-line resource
Structured questionnaire	E-mail
Specific questionnaire	E-mail
Open and specific questions.	Instant messaging
Intersession diaries	E-mail
Self-records: thoughts, nutrition, activities	Instant messaging and electronic mail

- *Videoconferences*. This is a real time conversation with visual contact, produced via web cameras connected to the computer. Being real time, information is transmitted instantaneously. Perhaps this is the on-line method that gets closest to a face-to-face interview, allowing the therapist to obtain both verbal and non-verbal information, such as facial expressions or gestures.

The ideal scenario for effective on-line therapy is to combine all the different types of on-line intervention, especially in those cases where physical variables need to be monitored (see also Table 7.2). Based on experiences with three of the methods described, the following action guide is proposed:

1. First, the initial assessment can be carried out via e-mail, sending the patient a structured questionnaire to complete and return. This provides the necessary information in order to carry out an evaluation of the problem and an analysis of the case.

2. Next, this assessment may be complemented with an interview, using a real time messaging facility, and if possible, a videoconference, which allows the therapist to observe the patient, both in terms of physical aspect, as well as attitudes and behaviour during the interview, etc.

3. Finally, any extended work may be conducted in sessions held via chatrooms, real time conversations or videoconferences, depending on the characteristics of the athlete and the case. In the meantime, the patient sends completed intersession tasks to the therapist via e-mail, so they can be evaluated and modified as and when necessary. Such intersession tasks may include weekly activity records, eating guidelines or exercise plans.

7.5.2 *Contact with professionals*

Sport psychology teams can provide their services on the Internet via a website. Many sport psychology units or private practitioners use this method as a way of making themselves known and distributing their services more broadly. However, these methods often incite some negative aspects: intrusion, lack of professionalism, or fraudulent behaviours. Nevertheless, these downfalls could be avoided if the official psychology colleges and/or national and international sport psychology associations regulated these practices, providing accreditations to those professionals wishing to use on-line methods.

The first step to establishing on-line therapy through a website is ensuring that the psychology professional can be easily contacted. Emperador (2001) suggests creating a brief entry form, which provides access to the consultancy website. Being able to contact the sport psychologist through this channel offers potential clients easy and practical access, and maintains their anonymity.

An easy entry form model, to obtain some simple data for the initial case assessment, is detailed in Table 7.3.

Once this initial contact has been made through the form, the therapist sends a survey to the athlete via e-mail. Internet treatment allows therapists to perform an initial screening interview, in which they can decide whether or not a case is suitable for on-line treatment.

Table 7.3   Basic data for on-line assessment

Please fill in the following form in order for us to assess your case. We will then contact you accordingly:

Name or nick name:
Age:
Contact e-mail address:
Contact telephone number:
Sporting discipline:
Level of participation:
What is your reason for contacting us?
Have you had any previous contact with sport psychologists or other mental health specialists? If so, what was the reason for this contact?

Observations:

Table 7.4   Criteria for ruling out treating a case through on-line therapy

Extremely low body weight: BMI below $18 \, kg/m^2$
Being under age
Low motivation to change and commence therapy
Being under pharmaceutical treatment
Uncontrollable binge eating and vomiting. The consumption of alcohol or other drugs which could endanger the patient's life
Extremely elevated risk of suicide and significant symptoms of depression
Significant self-injury behaviours
The patient has failed to respond to previous clinical treatments
Medical complications: amenorrhoea, osteoporosis, heart or stomach problems, electrolyte disturbance, etc.
Important weight loss over recent weeks
Inexistent social and family support
History of addictions: important to avoid Internet addiction (see Ferraro *et al.*, 2007)
Serious problems in sentimental and family relationships: physical abuse, addictions in the family

According to the textbooks on good practice in the treatment of eating disorders such as anorexia nervosa or bulimia nervosa, the criteria for ruling out treating a case through on-line therapy is as in Table 7.4.

Sports psychologists should have broad knowledge of the available treatment resources, hospitals, doctors, and eating disorder specialists near a patient, in case they require urgent medical attention, hospitalisation, or a physical check-up. If a patient's symptoms worsen or the previously detailed exclusion criteria emerge, he/she must be immediately referred to a nearby clinic, or if the therapist practises in the same geographical region, he/she may coordinate a mixed therapy programme.

As detailed in the previous chapter, it is important to consider the motivation for an intervention before commencing any psychological treatment. In the case of on-line therapy, given its many peculiarities, patients' motivation for treatment must be even greater, since it requires a higher degree of involvement and dedication on their behalf compared to other treatment methods. On some occasions, signing some form of contract, in which a patient commits to maintain on-line treatment sessions, or continue treatment in person, may serve to increase motivation and help maintain the intervention process.

7.5.3 The initial assessment

One possible model for an on-line interview has two parts: the first assesses general aspects, similar to a diagnostic interview; whilst the second focuses on specific aspects related to eating disorders, sport and nutrition.

This assessment may be completed with complementary tests, such as the questionnaires described in the chapter on diagnosing eating disorders in sport: the Eating Attitudes Test (EAT-40), the Eating Disorders Inventory (EDI), the Body Shape Questionnaire (BSQ), the Obligatory Running Questionnaire, the Exercise Dependence Questionnaire, (EDQ) or the Exercise Dependence Scale (EDS). Moreover, these surveys may be complemented with the Athlete's Habits Questionnaire (Dosil & Diaz, 2002).

Family members and coaches should be interviewed at the beginning of treatment process; in order to complete the information provided by the athlete, and if necessary, include them within the intervention programme. Throughout the intervention, the following sessions may be incorporated: coach–athlete–sports psychologist, or, family member–athlete–sports psychologist.

Throughout the initial assessment, the psychological condition of athletes should be evaluated. In many cases, this comorbidity will be dealt with in the athlete's treatment, given that the therapeutic objectives can be modified if the patient presents a certain personality trait, or a potential depressive or anxiety disorder conducive of eating disorders. It is essential to conduct an accurate diagnosis, using specific tests.

During the second interview, once the initial assessment has been carried out, the data lacking from the initial stage should be completed. This second interview

Table 7.5 Data in the second on-line interview

Principal occupation away from the sport
Periods of time when the patient has felt better
Has the patient made an attempt to get better? Has anyone tried to help?
Home environment: family nutrition/eating habits
Importance given to the sport and eating/nutrition at home
Meals: timetables, type of food consumed, quantities consumed

is conducted via on-line sessions, in which the therapist is responsible for guiding the meeting towards the most important questions, gathering the necessary information to form the therapeutic objectives.

The following data (Table 7.5) may be drawn together in the second interview.

7.5.4 The objectives of on-line therapy

Once the initial assessment of the athlete has been concluded, the therapy should be orientated by specific therapeutic objectives, clearly set out at the beginning of the on-line intervention. Following the guidelines developed in the previous chapter, the subsequent objectives may be established:

- *Recover weight*: Bearing in mind the athlete's diagnosis, one of the principal objectives at the beginning of any therapeutic process is regaining a healthy weight. In order to achieve this objective, it is necessary for somebody close to the patient, such as a family member or GP, to monitor and control the weight recovery process. In the majority of cases, recovering and maintaining a healthy weight determines being able to return to physical activity.

- *Normalise eating guidelines*: Here, the main objective is to achieve adequate eating behaviour and nutrition through educating the patient about healthy eating and modifying any unhealthy habits and behaviours. In this respect, it is vitally important to maintain contact with the family, who can confirm the athlete's progress. The athlete may be asked to keep a weekly food intake record to send to their therapist via e-mail, in order to observe the quantity and quality of these meals. Likewise, coaches should look out for any anomalous behaviour related to food during training camps or competitions, etc. The therapist should not give athletes dietary guidelines during the initial stages of treatment, unless a rapid weight recovery is required, or if they are suffering from bulimia nervosa.

- *Eliminating inadequate weight loss methods*: It is important to eradicate any purgative behaviour, such as vomiting, thermal methods, laxatives or diuretics. Using such techniques to lose weight is common in eating disorders, and can have serious consequences on an athlete's health. In the case of athletes who resort to excessive exercise as a weight loss method, it may be necessary to reduce their training load, or even eliminate exercise completely until their weight stabilises, before gradually reintroducing physical activity. Educating athletes in healthy eating habits represents one of the key strategies to successful treatment.

- *Modifying distorted thoughts*: Patients suffering from eating disorders harbour a series of unrealistic thoughts regarding their weight, figure and eating habits, which serve to feed their disorder. Cognitive restructuring, along with self-records, reality checks, thought detection training and self-instructions are some of the cognitive strategies that can be applied during treatment sessions.

- *Eliminating binge eating and vomiting*: With bulimia nervosa and purgative anorexia, removing these practices becomes the principal objective at the beginning of the intervention. The therapeutic process can progress through stimuli control training, restructuring eating habits and planning activities.

- *Eliminating isolation*: Those suffering from eating disorders tend to isolate themselves at the onset of their condition. In some cases, the lack of physical contact in on-line therapy runs the risk of favouring such isolation, meaning therapists must be on the look out for any signs of this. If it occurs therapists should maintain face-to-face sessions, or suggest group therapy as another treatment alternative. Along these lines, removing sporting activity may mean sacrificing an athlete's social network, and if he/she displays signs of isolation, it may become advisable to consider this decision. Similarly, it is essential to work on organising and planning the athlete's time.

- *Social skills training*: This technique can help prevent isolation, teaching athletes the different communication strategies, activity plans, or assertive skills. This form of training can be carried out during on-line sessions or in face-to-face sessions, as and where necessary.

In cases where home nursing is established as a treatment resource, the Internet and on-line therapy may prove an appropriate option (Morandé, 1999). Home nursing is often used when there is a lack of hospital resources, or when objectives have not been attained through other treatment options. The person undergoing 'hospital' treatment at home is restricted in terms of going out and physical exercise, and the family maintains a high degree of supervision. Therefore, being able to communicate quickly and easily with a therapist on a daily basis may favour a patient's progress in these circumstances.

7.5.5   On-line sessions

An example of how to conduct an on-line session with an athlete suffering from an eating disorder is described in Table 7.6.

Table 7.6 Guidelines for an on-line session

Greeting
Review of weekly tasks: self-records, activities, guidelines, etc.
Presentation of the session objectives
Approach each objective in order, as indicated to the patient beforehand
Session summary in terms of the established objectives

Having explained the aspects that will be dealt with during the session ahead, specific objectives will be established for each one. It is advisable to end each session with a summary, explaining the tasks to be carried out at home during the week, agreeing on a date and time to review these and provide feedback.

With on-line therapy, it is essential to maintain the athlete's motivation towards the treatment process. Along these lines, it is important to deal with any questions the athlete poses, making sure to fully respond to his/her needs and doubts, and trying to modify inadequate habits from the beginning. This allows the athlete to observe positive changes and has encouraging effects on how they approach future objectives. It is fundamental to maintain an established order during on-line sessions, so as to avoid the athlete gaining control over the therapy. The therapist should be seen as being approachable but firm, making it clear who directs the session. Jointly establishing specific, realistic and attainable goals and objectives during the sessions is another way of approaching this initial contact, since for many athletes, being able to take an active part in their own treatment process is very motivating. Nonetheless, on other occasions, when the situation is more serious, or given the characteristics of an athlete, only the therapist may propose the objectives.

Rewarding athletes' achievements, however small, through verbal or written encouragement, serves to motivate and improve their adherence to on-line treatment. Moreover, taking the coldness out of sessions with affective and sincere communication, with which the patient feels comfortable, being comprehensive and providing security and trust, are necessary to commence and maintain a fruitful on-line therapy process.

7.5.6   The sports psychologist and on-line treatment

Before commencing on-line treatment with athletes it is important to fully understand the scientific support for this type of intervention. Heinicke *et al.* (2007) demonstrated the feasibility of an on-line therapy programme with girls who had body image and eating problems, consisting of six, 90-minute weekly small group and synchronous on-line sessions, facilitated by a therapist and a manual, obtaining excellent results to support this type of therapy. Moreover, Gollings and Paxton (2006) conducted an interesting study in which they compared the treatment of eating disorders via the Internet with face-to-face techniques, finding no significant differences between the two forms of intervention. Other research, such as that carried out by Winzelberg *et al.* (2000) has shown how Internet-based programmes for reducing risk factors for eating disorders prove effective, even more so than those techniques developed in the classroom (Celio *et al.*, 2000). Therefore, on-line treatment can prove highly appropriate for the treatment of eating disorders in athletes.

In terms of the qualities and qualifications required of sport psychologists to successfully conduct this form of intervention with athletes, Calvo (2002) describes some fundamental characteristics:

- *An exhaustive knowledge of the characteristics of the sport in question and its relationship with eating behaviour disorders*: physical, psychological and behavioural factors.

- *Capacity to create an environment of security and trust*, in which the patient can appreciate the psychologist's domain over the key factors of the sport.

- *Written expression*: During on-line sessions, this becomes highly important; the psychologist's capacity to express him/herself clearly and concisely helps develop communication and trust in the patient–therapist relationship (sending positive, not punitive messages; encouraging the patient to express his/her emotions). Moreover, given the lack of verbal communication, the sport psychologist must be capable of interpreting a lot of information from the different characteristics of the written language, including its different tones and expressions.

- *Tolerance of frustration*: This includes knowing how to accept the athlete's failures and errors during the treatment process. Eating behaviour disorders are conditions with a prolonged and unstable development. The recovery process is slow, and on occasions, athletes suffer relapses or display changes to their initial symptoms, making it difficult to establish new objectives. It is important for the sport psychology professional to accept these setbacks and not feel frustrated if the treatment progress fails to advance as initially expected.

- *Directness*: Communication should be sincere and the therapist must establish the limits. Chat facilities, given their anonymous nature, can produce a 'distancing' in the patient–therapist relationship, especially in terms of response time. For example, a patient may write, but fail to properly read the reply given by the therapist. In these cases, the therapist must establish certain time limits, or a number of phrases that can be used during each session. What is more, the therapist should make the communication rules clear from the beginning of the on-line treatment process.

- *Tolerating resistance to change*: Athletes suffering from eating disorders are often reluctant to stick to treatment, challenging their progress. The therapist is responsible for motivating the athlete and guaranteeing he/she adheres to the treatment process.

- *Reinforcement during interviews*: The sports psychologist should reinforce the athlete during the entire treatment process, especially when the athlete becomes reluctant to maintain sessions or communicate adequately. It is important to reward every effort made by the athlete to improve communication and expression.

In conclusion, sports psychologists using on-line therapy to treat athletes with eating disorders must have specific training in both the treatment of this illness and sport psychology.

7.5.7 Paying for on-line sessions

Naturally, sports psychology professionals must charge for their services, regardless of the type of therapy provided, and it is recommended they do so in accordance with the guidelines established by the professional associations. During the initial contact with the patient, whether by e-mail or telephone, the terms of payment must be established, given that the lack of face-to-face contact could complicate the payment process later on and hinder the treatment.

First, it is important to evaluate the patient's suitability to on-line therapy during the initial interview via e-mail, since as previously indicated, not all cases are suitable for this form of intervention. Once a patient has been cleared to commence treatment, the sessions can be charged for via a bank transfer or a postal giro. Payment may be made before each individual session or patients can opt to pay for a set number of sessions in advance. The latter option favours the patient's commitment to a certain number of sessions and increases their adherence to the course of treatment.

7.5.8 The advantages and disadvantages of using on-line therapy to treat eating disorders in sport

Treating any psychological problem through on-line therapy has its potential benefits and downfalls, and eating disorders in athletes are no exception. The most important advantages of on-line therapy treatment of athletes with eating disorders are as follows (summarised in Table 7.7):

Table 7.7 Summary of the advantages of on-line therapy

Accessibility
Intersession tasks
Co-therapists
Intervention with family and coaches
Extensive assessment
Information available prior to treatment sessions
Training of new sports psychology professionals

- *Flexible timetable and access to the treatment service*: Access to a computer with an Internet connection is extremely easy nowadays, whether at home, at a sports club, or even an Internet café. Treatment sessions can be easily adapted to the timetables of both the athlete and the therapist, since there is no need to attend a clinic or sports psychology unit in person, avoiding interfering with an athlete's training schedule. On the other hand, if an athlete has had to temporarily give up sporting activity, sessions can be scheduled to coincide with the training times. Moreover, athletes need not abandon treatment sessions during training camps and trips to competitions since the Internet is generally accessible everywhere.

- *Intersession tasks*: Self-records, activity plans and the like, can be sent in daily or weekly e-mails, allowing the therapist to monitor the athlete's progress and provide the relevant feedback quickly. The therapist and athlete should agree on the frequency of these e-mail updates, setting the treatment guidelines and committing to a regular follow-up.

- *Intervention of a co-therapist*: The co-therapist, as previously described, assists the principal therapist in providing treatment, both during on-line sessions, as well as helping to evaluate the intersession tasks sent by e-mail. Given that chat communication may be slowed down by reading time, the co-therapist can help the principal therapist establish objectives, maintaining fluid conversation with the athlete, whilst simultaneously consulting with the principal therapist in a separate window.

- *Intervention with family members and coaches*: Being able to include more than two people in an on-line conversation is an important aspect of on-line therapy. The collaboration of family members and/or the coach often proves fundamental in the treatment of eating disorders, especially with athletes, since the coach's input is vital when it comes to using physical exercise as part of the treatment process. Chat facilities enrich this process, making it possible to have joint family sessions or coach–athlete sessions, in which collective decisions can me made, allowing all parties to participate in the treatment process. However, it is important to be cautious, limiting the information provided by family members, who often have a tendency to give more information than is necessary for treatment purposes, and without the knowledge of the patient. Therefore, the therapist should limit this aspect at all times, clarifying the type of information family members should put forward, and establishing a time and place to do so, avoiding information being given without the consent of the athlete (if over the age of consent). The use of modern treatment resources such as the Internet can favour this type of communication. The family should be guided to ensure the athlete is present or, ask the athlete's permission to engage in a private conversation with the therapist.

- *Broad assessment possibilities*: With on-line therapy, a patient can be sent a survey via e-mail, giving them time to reflect over the questions before answering. Therefore, the information provided through this form of assessment is usually accurate, and if the survey is well structured and exhaustive, can save a lot of time at the beginning of the therapy process. Moreover, sending additional questionnaires can complement the information gained in the initial survey.

- *Information is obtained from the athlete prior to treatment sessions*. Thanks to the speed of e-mail, the patient can send their intersession tasks to the therapist in real time, allowing them to prepare the following session accordingly, adapting it to the athlete's progress and focusing on the problems at hand.

- *Sessions can be archived*. Being able to store sessions allows the therapist to review the process as and when necessary, correcting any errors in the intervention and reassessing the information provided by the patient during consultations. This allows the therapist to maintain a degree of control over the entire process, helping to plan subsequent sessions and objectives.

- *The Internet provides a new training possibility*. On-line therapy offers new work experience opportunities for those studying sports psychology, allowing inexperienced professionals to work as co-therapists, enriching their professional development and sport psychology training.

Various difficulties may arise during the on-line treatment of eating behaviour disorders. Nevertheless, there are various solutions a therapist can consider in order to minimise potential problems during the intervention:

- *Weight*: Recovering a healthy weight constitutes one of the principal treatment objectives with athletes suffering from eating disorders, and must be constantly monitored by the therapist. However, in some cases, athletes will be unable to take responsibility for weighing themselves. For example, some athletes resort to weighing themselves five or six times a day to check they are not 'getting fat', and in such circumstances, a family member must be put in charge of monitoring an athlete's weight, or the athlete should attend regular weigh-ins at a clinical facility.

- *The order of interventions with group sessions*: During on-line treatment sessions in which more than two people participate, it is important for the therapist to establish a set order for the interventions. This may involve participants using some form of visual signals, available on chat facilities, to indicate that they wish to intervene in the conversation. The rules should be made clear from the beginning of the session and repeated when they are not complied with, even sanctioning or expelling participants who repeatedly break the rules.

- *The lack of non-verbal communication*: One of the biggest downfalls of on-line therapy is the loss of non-verbal communication. However, using webcams may counteract this, although the visual information received must be interpreted with care, since the images produced may be delayed or distorted.

- *Poor written expression*: Not everyone has the same capacity to express thoughts and emotions in writing. To resolve this difficulty, the therapist should direct sessions towards effectively expressing emotions, posing closed questions, so to avoid ambiguous answers, obtaining the necessary information for the intervention.

- *Time control*: In some cases, patients may try to breach their programmed session time. To avoid this occurring, it is essential to maintain rigorous time control, clearly stipulating the start and finish time of treatment sessions, defining the objectives at the beginning of each one, and sticking to the programmed order of interventions.

Once again, it is important to stress that on-line therapy may be inappropriate for patients with extremely low weight or who engage in frequent binge eating or self-induced vomiting. If a patient is seen to be suffering from serious symptoms or if their condition appears to be deteriorating, the therapist must contact a family member immediately to organise clinical treatment. Likewise, on-line therapy may prove counterproductive for some patients suffering a high degree of isolation. Nonetheless, on-line sessions can provide guidelines for dealing with this factor, incorporating them into a mixed therapy regime.

7.6 Conclusions

The development of today's academic world is ever more influenced by and dependent on the progress of new technologies. Recently, in the case of sports psychology and eating disorders, there has been a clear proliferation of websites covering both matters. Depending on how these technological advances are employed, they may prove beneficial or damaging. The Internet is an ideal scenario for the prevention of eating disorders, since it can be used to inform athletes of the risks involved with poor nutrition and diet, excessive concern with weight and figure, and maintaining harmful habits in the quest for the 'ideal' body for a specific sporting activity. On the contrary, the Internet, often unregulated, can produce some negative effects, for example, the existence of websites promoting eating disorders.

On-line therapy is still at the development stage, but as described throughout this chapter, there is already scientific evidence to verify the benefits of its use in certain cases of athletes with eating disorders. In light of this, the following years should see continued research into this area, in order to perfect the treatment possibilities that can be offered to athletes suffering these illnesses.

8 Case Studies of Eating Disorders in Sport

Joaquín Dosil and Olga Díaz

8.1 Introduction

This chapter details four cases of athletes who have suffered from eating disorders, carried out pathological weight loss behaviours, or felt 'overcome' by excessive concern for their figure, weight or food. The individuals described in these cases have been chosen from 'high risk' sports, in terms of eating disorders. Likewise, a fifth case study has been added, in which sport has formed the basis of treatment, constituting a key element in overcoming an eating disorder.

The following structure has been followed throughout the chapter: initially, the case description provides basic information regarding the eating-related problem; next, the situation is analysed by a psychology professional, highlighting the key aspects and possible causes-solutions (without entering into diagnostic elements: semi-structured interview, etc.); and finally, the treatment and follow-up establish the action to be taken by the psychologist, family, coach and athlete, in order to eradicate the disorder.

The case studies presented are intended to represent examples of eating disorders in sport, typical situations which may be encountered in this context and which require special treatment. Therefore, certain information has been emitted if it is not considered relevant to understanding how to direct treatment. Likewise, to

Eating Disorders in Athletes   Joaquín Dosil
© 2008 John Wiley & Sons, Ltd

avoid repetitiveness, once certain treatments have been described, they are not dealt with again. The main objective is to present the key elements in the treatment of each case. Finally, although all the case studies are based on real life situations, in order to conserve the privacy of the athletes, some elements that could potentially identify them have been varied.

8.2   A case study of eating disorders in athletics

Figure 8.1

8.2.1   Case description

Dani is 12 years old. He is in the first year of secondary education at a private school. His grades are good and he forms part of the school athletics team. He trains three times a week under the watchful eye of the athletics coach, who is a professional athlete. Given the impressive results the coach has achieved in the last season, all members of the athletics team (10 boys and 5 girls) look up to him.

Although he does other extracurricular activities, Dani intends to become an elite athlete, 'like those on the television'. He likes distance events and when he sees African runners, he dreams of one day having a 'lean' body like theirs, and being able to run as fast as they do. For the time being, Dani is certainly not so lean and fast, and is perhaps a little bulkier than he should be for his age and stature. His teammates have already teased him about this, and his coach has suggested on various occasions that he could be thinner.

His eating problems began after a competition, when his coach told him: 'It would be better if you put your efforts into throwing the shot putt or hammer, you don't have the right qualities to be a distance runner, and I'm sure you'd do well in throwing events'. These comments hurt Dani a lot. When he got home, he promised himself that nobody would ever say anything like that to him again, and he decided that the best solution was to stop eating, or to eat as little as possible. The results soon became evident: his weight loss was rapid. All the family noticed it, he just wasn't the same as before ('I don't fancy eating that, I'm full up, I don't want any more . . .') His parents quickly turned to a specialist for advice, the situation was getting out of control, and they didn't know how to confront it.

8.2.2 Analysis of the situation

At first sight, a case like Dani's seems to have an easy solution, and since treatment is usually simpler the younger the patient is, his age is a favourable factor. Nevertheless, many issues could be affecting the seriousness of his eating disorder; being unfamiliar with the situation at hand or disregarding certain dynamics could make the problem acute and difficult to treat (late detection, parents or coach who fails to notice abnormal behaviours, etc.). Early diagnosis is always the best guarantee of successful treatment.

In every case, therapy should begin with an exhaustive analysis of the variables contributing towards the problem. Therefore, an interview is usually used to define the environment in which the athlete operates. Along these lines, in this specific case, the priority contexts in Dani's life are: family, school and sport. Considering it is the parents who attend the consultancy, the information they provide is used to analyse these three contexts. For the time being, the aim is not to reproduce all of the information given, but to pick out which is most important and relevant to Dani's treatment:

• The family environment: Dani's parents stress how he has radically changed his eating habits in a relatively short period of time, significantly reducing his food intake and losing several kilos over the last few months. They have tried to talk to him on repeated occasions to find out what is going on, but Dani claims there is nothing wrong and that he simply does not feel like eating ('. . . he says he feels full up and won't eat anything . . .'). His parents begin to suspect that his behaviour is because he wants to be thinner, but they fail to understand his motives, which has brought them to investigate the possible causes behind his change in behaviour: problems in class, with his class mates, in athletics, etc.

• The school environment: once aware the problem existed, the first step Dani's parents took was speaking to his school teacher, who failed to shed any light on the situation, stating he had not seen any changes in Dani's behaviour in class. Nevertheless, he had noticed the physical changes, putting them down to 'the body's natural development' at his age. Moreover, the teacher indicated that Dani maintains a good relationship with his class mates: 'he is always with the same group of friends and there is no visible tension in class, quite the contrary, there is real companionship at all times; and regarding his academic performance, it remains as good as ever, high grades and a positive attitude . . .' Armed with this information, Dani's parents ruled out problems at school and turned their attention to athletics.

- The sports environment: the second step was to speak to the athletics coach. To begin with, he did not warn of any problems and even displayed satisfaction with Dani's current sporting conduct, indicating that '. . . now he has an adequate weight to do athletics, before he didn't have the right qualities to be a distance runner and not long ago I even advised him to change events . . .' This information concerned Dani's parents, but at the same time it clarified where the problem lay (their hypothesis: faced with the coach's comments, Dani was afraid of not being able to do the athletic discipline he liked). Dani's parents and coach opted not to take any action before consulting with a psychology professional.

8.2.3 Treatment and follow-up

The proposed intervention is directed towards Dani's parents and coach. The objective is to achieve an adequate weight without preventing him from doing athletics. In order to achieve this, a series of guidelines must be followed, as detailed below:

- Guidelines directed towards the parents: the coach should explain the problem and solution to Dani (given how much Dani admires him). It is important for his parents to be present during this explanation, so to arrive at some form of joint agreement regarding his treatment. Likewise, Dani's parents should explain the steps they have taken to him, procuring to transmit their understanding of what has happened and their desire to help.

With respect to eating guidelines, it is important to arrive at some form of joint agreement (as indicated previously: coach, child and parents) regarding daily intake, and display a comprehensive and supportive attitude, especially during mealtimes, avoiding stressful situations, which do not contribute to overcoming the problem (asking a lot of questions about his food intake, for example). Along these lines, when Dani's parents observe him making an asserted effort to meet the stipulated agreement, even though it seems impossible, they should give him brief messages of support. In these situations, the following phrases usually help: 'Go on, you can do it!', 'We know it's hard for you but . . .', or 'That's it, just a little bit more'. On the other hand, in certain circumstances, if Dani is seen forcing the situation and putting too much effort into the task, which can be just as unproductive, the criteria should be made more flexible. However, in these cases, it is important to reason with Dani, making him understand why the criteria has been adapted on this specific occasion, avoiding him using this resource as an excuse in the future. Moreover, it is important not to neglect the use of verbal reinforcements when he manages to achieve a stipulated agreement, with phrases such as: 'You've done really well, we know it was hard for you'.

- Guidelines directed towards the coach: as previously stated, the coach's intervention is fundamental in this case. The psychologist should make an appointment with the coach to explain the problem and the intervention guidelines. The coach must be made aware that as a role model, he has great influence over his athletes' behaviour and can help them in issues that go beyond the sporting activity. Focussing on Dani's case, the proposed objectives are established, as well as the best way to achieve them. The coach's attitude is favourable and he commits to carrying out the programmed actions (the therapist provides him with a model to follow).

Regarding the other guidelines, it is important to highlight the importance of encouraging adequate behaviours, such as: having achieved the agreed criteria or having put on the necessary weight. Moreover, in groups, during training sessions, it is useful to provide basic information on nutrition, stressing how a healthy and balanced diet is essential to perform well in sport, minimizing the importance given to body shape and size, etc.

The follow-up to this problem is carried out through the parents, either by telephone or in person, as and when doubts arise. On the other hand, frequent contact is maintained with the coach, establishing collaborative psychological guidance with the entire group. As time goes by, the situation stabilizes and Dani maintains adequate eating habits for his age, stature and activity.

An Example of the Psychologist–Coach Interaction

Situation: A meeting between the psychologist and Dani's coach is held in the athletics stadium at the end of a regular training session. The coach is aware that the psychologist is coming to see him, as the parents have informed him beforehand.

The interview will be divided into various sections.

Step 1: Gathering general information about the case and the coach's point of view
P = Psychologist
C = Coach

P   Good afternoon, Alex? Are you Dani's Coach?

C   Yes, that´s me, you must be Steve.

P   Listen, I'm here to talk to you about Dani. Did his parents mention to you that I was coming?

C   Yes, they said you were coming, but they didn't say too much about what it was about. They mentioned he's not eating well, but I haven't seen any problems in his training . . . in fact, he's running better than ever now he's thinner. I don't know, perhaps his parents think he's eating little, but maybe they are not too familiar with an athlete's diet.

P   So you're quite happy with Dani's physical changes, and with his athletic performance?

C   Yes, I'm more than happy! Before, Dani was never going to get anywhere as a distance athlete. Now, his physique is allowing him to really train well. I've got high hopes for him this season.

P   OK, and how do you think he managed to make such a drastic physical change?

C   Well, I think he probably just realised that athletes need to eat a very healthy and balanced diet, and perhaps he wasn't eating so healthily before . . . and well, the results are evident.

P   And what type of guidance do the athletes receive regarding nutrition and diet? I mean to say, how do the athletes know what constitutes a healthy and balanced diet?

C   Hmm, to be honest, we just don't have the means to provide them with a nutritionist. And, lets be honest, these are just kids, it's not like we are going to start lecturing them at such a young age about food. That's up to the parents.

(As can be appreciated here, the coach contradicts himself. On the one hand, he explains that athletes need to maintain a healthy and balanced diet. However, on the other hand, he confirms that his athletes receive no information or guidance on this matter, claiming this is the parents' responsibility).

P   And does the athletics club send home any information to the parents regarding general lifestyle habits (what coaches call 'invisible training'), you know, about sleeping enough, resting, eating well, etc.?

C   Well, to be honest, no. Normally, when parents have a problem, they come and speak to me, and I give them advice on what they should do.

Step 2: Working with Dani's specific case

P   In Dani's case, I believe his parents already came to speak to you? They're quite worried about him.

C   Yes, they came to see me, and I'm more than happy to help. What do you suggest I do?

P   OK, I'm glad you're willing to collaborate. I think that in this case, it could be the key to Dani getting better.

C   Ok, perfect, but what exactly is wrong with him?

P	Well, you see, one of Dani's dreams right now is to become an elite athlete, doing distance events, and he has decided to do whatever he can to achieve his objectives. So, he's convinced that the thinner he is, the better he will be.
C	Yes, but I have to say, I don't disagree with Dani on that point! He's doing exactly the right thing to be a good athlete.
P	Yes, you're not totally wrong, it's important to be thin to become an elite athlete, but you have to be well nourished too. The problem with Dani, is how he's going about it.
C	OK, but what do you mean? Where is Dani going wrong?
P	Well, Dani doesn't have all the knowledge that you have as an elite athlete, and he doesn't realise what a balanced diet involves. So, to lose weight, he has simply reduced the amount he is eating, not eating at all on some occasions. So, whilst he may be running well at the moment for having lost weight, what he is doing is not healthy and there is no way his body can sustain it over time.
C	Ah, I see. But, how much is little for you? I mean, perhaps he was eating a lot before, and now he is eating the right amount, and it just seems little to his parents.
P	Yeah, naturally sometimes parents exaggerate out of worry. But, I have looked into it, and he is displaying certain behaviours, which indicate he is suffering from symptoms of an eating disorder.
C	Ah, so it's quite serious then?
P	Yes, it could be, but I think we have caught the problem early enough and we still have time to nip it in the bud. His age and the fact that the problem hasn't been around long are going to help us sort this out much more quickly.

(In this second phase, the psychologist has earned the trust of the coach, and has also managed to make him aware of the seriousness of Dani's problem).

Step 3: Collaborating with the coach to solve the problem

C	So what should I do then?
P	The first thing you should bear in mind is that for Dani, you are the most important reference point in athletics. He looks up to you, and he values everything you say.
C	So I should speak to him then? But, what should I say?
P	OK, it's important that you speak to him in private, not in front of his team mates, and we are going to approach the problem indirectly, connecting it to his general development as an athlete, because if we are too direct with him he could become over defensive. What do you think?

C   OK, that sounds good to me. So what exactly should I say?

P   Well, you should speak to Dani and explain that you are pleased with him, tell him how he is improving a lot. But then, you need to talk to him about 'invisible training', what he does outside of training. This will involve you talking about sleeping enough, whether he sleeps well . . . and then gradually entering into speaking about a balanced diet, as just another factor forming part of this 'invisible training'. Do you understand what I mean to say?

C   Yes, OK, I think I know what you mean. So I need to explain to him about all these matters, without putting too much emphasis on food and eating?

P   Yes, exactly. What we want is for somebody like you, who he trusts and admires, to inform him of appropriate lifestyle behaviours, that way, he is more likely to pay attention to what is being said.

C   OK, I understand all of that. I'll try and speak to him after one of the training sessions. Perhaps I can organise for his parents to come 10 minutes later to pick him up. But after I speak to him, how will I know it has worked? What should I do after?

P   Well, this is where collaborating with his parents comes into it. They can call you, email you, or even come and speak to you in person, and you will be able to work jointly with them on this problem. And I will be at hand, so that if you or his parents have any problems, you can consult me. OK, so to begin with we will see how it goes with you speaking to him. Let's see if we can induce some changes in his attitude. I'll call you in a week and we can see how it went, and see how well this strategy is working. Does that seem ok to you?

C   Ok, that all sounds fine to me, we'll speak in a week then.

8.3   A case of eating disorders in taekwondo

Figure 8.2

8.3.1   *Case description*

Mario is 22 years old. He is in the fourth year of a law degree and competes in taekwondo at elite level. In recent years he has won medals in every Spanish Championships and has a real possibility of going to the Olympics, something he has dreamt of all his life. Unfortunately, his exams have coincided with the regional championships and his recent performances have been less than satisfactory. He is currently competing in a higher weight category than what he believes would be ideal for him. He has argued with his coach all week (for having put on weight), and there are just five days left before the Spanish Championships, where Mario will be fighting for the chance to go to the Olympic Games.

Over this last week, Mario has gone on a restrictive diet, cutting out all fatty foods, but it does not seem to be enough, and his coach relentlessly pursues the matter various times a day ('I don't understand how you can weigh this much', 'you've let yourself go', 'the Championship is getting away from us' . . .). Now, Mario is thinking of taking laxatives and diuretics, going to a sauna and training in plastic clothing. He thinks this is the only way he can lose the necessary kilos in time. His coach, knowing nothing about Mario's plans, and not knowing how to focus the coming competition and the pressure of the situation, makes an appointment with a psychologist in the Taekwondo Federation.

8.3.2   *Analysis of the situation*

A situation such as this can be considered 'urgent'. When an important competition is so close, the interventions a psychologist applies should be limited to basic aspects, which interfere as little as possible in the athlete's performance.

The coach's sincerity reveals his great concern with the current state of taekwondo. On various occasions, he regrets the situation they are in, blaming himself for many things that have 'gone wrong'. His greatest fear is 'throwing away the numerous years of hard work at peak level they have put in, just so he can have the chance of competing in the Olympics'. Therefore, he frequently doubts whether Mario is currently in the ideal category for his weight. During the interview, special emphasis is placed on clearly defining in which category Mario should compete to achieve peak performance, an aspect considered key in the intervention. Following a broad debate and the use of decision matrices, the coach concludes that given the circumstances, the most adequate solution is to stay in the same category, since objectively speaking, Mario has greater possibilities of performing better.

Meanwhile, assessing the seriousness of the situation, the psychologist suggests Mario attends an interview as soon as possible, or if necessary, he will go to his training facilities (there is a high possibility that Mario is already using weight-loss strategies that could prove dangerous to both his health and his sports performance). Without creating a sense of alarm, the psychologist informs the coach that they should take joint action 'urgently'.

The coach contacts Mario by telephone and they make an appointment for an hour later, at a time that does not interfere with his physical preparation (during the telephone conversation, Mario is observed trying to get around the appointment, but eventually gives in to the insistence and 'authority' of his coach). He arrives at the clinic, displaying a somewhat defensive attitude and fails to understand why he needs to attend a psychologist so close to the competition. To begin with, the coach is not present, helping Mario answer the questions more sincerely.

The psychologist, well aware of the previous tension during the telephone conversation, and confronted with Mario's unreceptive attitude, initially sets out to gain his confidence, something fundamental to carrying out any intervention. The strategy used is dialogue, speaking about his sporting career, focusing especially on the good times he has had, the successes he has achieved, and trying to relate them to other subjects (hobbies, friends, etc.), in order to create a relaxed and trusting environment, the most adequate context for achieving the objectives of the session. Once the climate of the interview is considered ideal, the psychologist tries to broach the key aspects of the problem: the idealness of his category and his weight-loss methods. Mario explains how he does not feel physically or mentally well enough to compete, and goes on to describe how the solution is losing weight, so he can compete in the next weight category down; he has already restricted his diet and is considering using other methods such as laxatives, sauna, etc . . .

Once arriving at this point in the interview, and taking into consideration the coach's opinion, the psychologist discusses with Mario the possibility of competing in the category he is in, analysing all the advantages and disadvantages. They eventually decide on staying within the same category, a decision that is reinforced when Mario discovers that his coach shares this opinion.

The interview is ended with both the athlete and coach present, so to design a joint intervention plan.

8.3.3 'Urgent' treatment

Given the proximity of the competition, in this case the treatment is considered 'urgent' and focuses on two aspects:

- Reducing the stress under which Mario and his coach are submitted, and improving the communication between them. It is fundamental to reduce pre-competitive anxiety, and the coach should act as an ally rather than a 'stressor'.

- Determining the adequate food intake and training for peak performance in the competition (depending on the category they have decided to compete in).

Having made the decision to remain in Mario's current category, all efforts are directed towards this goal, avoiding doubting the decision, which would only prove unproductive at such a late stage. Self-affirmations and motivating statements are used to increase confidence in the decision made and the athlete's capabilities to achieve a good result, etc. The coach's role is fundamental throughout this process, providing the adequate backup and reassurance, especially when Mario begins to feel discouraged. Likewise, they remain in contact with the psychologist in order to follow-up the problem.

Regarding results, communication was improved between the coach and athlete, and an adequate food intake was produced before, during and after the competition. More importantly, Mario's sports performance was magnificent and the psychologist went on to form a permanent part of Mario's support team throughout the season.

8.4   A case of eating disorders in gymnastics

Figure 8.3

8.4.1   Case description

Maria is 13 years old and is a professional gymnast. Everyday she is submitted to 8-h training sessions in the Technical Centre, where her studies are adapted around the demands of the sport. Lately, her performance has dropped and her coach has reproached her on various occasions. All members of the team eat together, and there appears to be some form of 'competition' to see who eats less. The coach does not seem to think this matter is important and at no point intervenes or comments on what is really occurring. The coach believes that 'they should learn to look after themselves and know what is better or worse for their personal performance'. Maria's mother was also a professional gymnast and thinks her daughter should make every effort to reach the same level she did. Moreover, she sees sacrificing food as something normal, just another part of her training. Nevertheless, her father is worried about the situation and has already warned of her anomalous behaviour at mealtimes, as well as the performance problems she is having, and turns to a specialist sport psychologist for advice.

8.4.2 Analysis of the situation

Of all the sports, gymnastics has been the most associated with eating behaviour disorders. Nevertheless, as seen throughout this publication, other sporting disciplines display even higher prevalence rates. Unfortunately, whilst more adequate training of gymnastics' teachers and coaches has helped reduce the number of gymnasts suffering from eating disorders, some cases still emerge. The 'authoritarian coach equals sporting success' model continues to reign in certain teams, and submitting young gymnasts to diets and excessive pressures is still employed and even considered as 'beneficial' to high performance. In the case presented here, the coach disregards his gymnasts' diet at an age where eating properly is essential for their physical and mental development. At these ages, the coach's function has to go beyond the purely competitive facet; in fact, he/she should constitute a role model to be followed, whilst the sport itself, although highly competitive, should remain an educative activity.

During the interview with Maria's father, there are indications of family problems. The perception is that '. . . there just isn't any communication, and speaking about food is out of the question. Her mother puts excessive pressure on Maria, who in turn, only wants to please her'. The relationship between the couple has been affected by these circumstances and they appear to have grown apart.

On the basis of this information, a family session is considered necessary. Initially, this session is approached from an applied psychology perspective, focusing on strategies that help improve athletes' performance: improved concentration during training sessions and competitions, establishing objectives, confronting situations, etc. Consequently, this creates an adequate environment to broach more delicate aspects.

8.4.3 Treatment

As indicated previously, the session held with Maria and her parents is directed towards strategies to improve her performance. Information is gathered to help decipher exactly what is going wrong, arriving at the conclusion that Maria is being put under too much pressure, both by her mother and her coach. Consequently, during training sessions, although she tries to do well, she commits illogical errors because of her insecure thoughts: 'I'm not capable . . . I'll never do it, etc.'

On the one hand, the proposed therapy is directed towards the parents, with the aim of them learning to communicate more effectively within the family, and arrive at unanimous conclusions regarding Maria. Special emphasis is put on reducing the pressure they place on her and encouraging her to have more confidence in her positive qualities. This involves changing her perception of the situation; that is to say, helping her use self-affirmations such as: 'if I concentrate, I can do it' . . . 'I have sufficient qualities to do this well, I just need to focus' . . . On the other hand, the proposed therapy is also directed towards Maria A debate is carried out with her, regarding her qualities and downfalls in training, making her see exactly how her thoughts are affecting her performance, and teaching her to control them. This involves Maria identifying adequate self-affirmations to use during training sessions when she detects defeatist thoughts (also applicable during competitions). Likewise, a self-report is completed to help her become more aware of defeatist thoughts and put into practice the adequate self-instructions.

The matter of food is broached in later sessions, once the therapist considers the mother is ready to speak about it. The process used is similar to that applied with other issues, although in this case, it becomes important to have good knowledge of diets, the necessary calorie intake according to the athlete's stature, age and physical exercise, weight loss strategies used, etc. A nutritionist can provide this information beforehand or, this specialist may even attend the session in person, always with the family's consent.

In conclusion, it is important to reiterate that the matter of food, or indeed any other, should always be approached delicately and without impositions; it should be the patients themselves who arrive at the conclusion that a change is necessary.

8.5 A case of eating disorders in aerobics

8.5.1 Case description

Rosa is 18 years old and has just started studying at university. It is the first time that she has lived away from home, sharing a student flat with two other girls of the same age. At first she has a wonderful sensation of freedom, especially since she has been waiting to move out for some time. Her two flatmates have some peculiar eating habits, dedicating a lot of their time to gathering information from magazines, the television or the Internet about beauty, image, diets and anything related to aesthetics. They seem to be 'obsessed' with their figures, constantly trying to achieve smaller sizes, trying to lose weight and maintain their form.

Rosa weighs 58 kg and is 1.62 m tall. Gradually, she lets herself get carried along with the situation and has begun to excessively worry about her figure. She is a little overweight for her stature and decides to take measures. She signs up to a local gym, where for a fixed monthly quote she can attend any type of activity for as long as she wants each day. To begin with, she goes to the gym three times a week. The results can be seen quickly, with a rapid reduction in weight (and daily food intake): 55 kg. This spurs her on and she decides to start going to the gym on a daily basis, but at the end of the first week she has not lost any more weight, despite having increased the frequency. Therefore, undeterred, she starts attending two or three classes in a row, every day. She has to lose weight! In the flat, her friends constantly encourage her: 'how lucky, you've lost weight', 'you look great', etc., but now the scales are her only rival. She weighs herself when she gets up, before and after going to the gym and before she goes to bed. It has become a ritual. More significantly, it is a ritual with some predefined objectives that, in the case of not being met, create an enormous sense of unease.

After a month and a half without seeing her, Rosa's parents do not understand how she has changed so much and express their concern. Initially, they think it must just be carelessness . . . 'I bet they study all day long and don't even have time to go shopping . . .', but after spending a few days with Rosa, they soon appreciate that there is a serious problem: she hardly eats and now weighs just 52 kg.

8.5.2 Analysis of the situation

Commencing university education usually implies an important change for adolescents. Many new students must move away from home and their parents to study. This means they have to adapt to a new situation, with different elements: independence, freedom of timetable, etc. The relationship between eating disorders and these changes often emerges when, in addition to breaking away from everything they knew before, adolescents get into inappropriate situations: neglecting nutrition and mealtimes, negative influences from flatmates, etc . . .

In this case, Rosa has gone from not worrying at all about her figure and weight, to suffering clear symptoms of an eating disorder. People like Rosa are easily influenced, and changes in lifestyle – accompanied by environmental 'pressures' – increase the probability of eating disorders.

On the advice of her parents, Rosa decides to see a psychologist. As with previous cases, the first session is approached with one clear objective: winning the patient's trust. The interview covers any aspect that could have anything to do with her current problem.

8.5.3   Treatment

Following an initial assessment, the treatment focuses on normalising Rosa's habits. Although the patient has lost a lot of weight, she has not yet reached the limits that indicate her health is in immediate danger. Therefore, the intervention will focus more on the acquisition of self-control strategies and appropriate habits, rather than a pressing weight increase. The following strategies and techniques are applied during the first week:

- Information about her problem, introducing intervention mechanisms and strategies focused on cognitive–behavioural techniques.

- Stipulating the number of meals she should consume, as well as the type and quantity of food. Initially, Rosa is recommended to eat three meals a day, with the possibility of increasing food intake with a piece of fruit or something similar at mid-morning and mid-afternoon. To begin with, the type of foods will be mainly low in calories, in quantities that are normal for her stature and the calories she burns during physical exercise. A diet is planned out for the first week and the patient is recommended to share mealtimes with someone who can support her. Considering her flatmates are not the most adequate people for this function (for what has been commented previously), it is agreed that a friend, who knows about her problem, will accompany her at mealtimes. She is also encouraged to keep self-records of what she eats.

- Regarding physical exercise, it is jointly agreed that she will attend just one daily activity at the gym.

- The patient agrees to only weigh herself in the clinic. Moreover, given the considerable levels of anxiety provoked by anything related to the scales, she is taught distraction and relaxation strategies such as: muscular relaxation and the use of imagery, which she will have to employ when worrying thoughts enter her mind. Also, she is shown how these strategies will prove useful to confront other situations and/or stimuli that produce unease.

As the patient begins to normalise her habits, automate the techniques, and is more capable of rationalising situations, other aspects will be approached such as: increasing her weight to a more adequate level, ideal quantities and types of food, etc . . .

8.6   Sport: a solution to combat anorexia

Figure 8.4

8.6.1   Case description

Maria is 14 years old and has started to display a series of worrying behaviours: she has lost several kilos in weight and every mealtime ends in a row, since she refuses to eat even the smallest quantities of food. What is more, a meal may consist of just one croquette and a yogurt. Her parents have tried everything to convince her that this food intake is not sufficient, but she insists that she is not hungry and refuses to go to a doctor. Meanwhile, she has also increased her physical exercise, walking great distances and asking her parents to sign her up to a gym.

As far as her friends are concerned, she has totally blocked them out, using her studies as an excuse ('I don't have enough time to see them . . .').

8.6.2   Treatment

Faced with this situation, her parents turn to a specialist doctor, who recommends she be hospitalised. Following a month without obtaining satisfactory results, her parents decide to take her home and take charge of her treatment, consulting with both a psychologist and a nutritionist. The following guidelines are established:

1. Agree and commit to a certain level of food intake, which will vary according to the advice of the nutritional expert.

2. Speak as little as possible about food, and only during stipulated moments.

3. Explain to the rest of the family the importance of not discussing food with the Maria.

4. Seek ideal situations to introduce certain food items, whether in a relaxed environment at home, in a cafeteria, etc.

5. Transmit understanding of the problem, appreciating the suffering it provokes.

6. Find activities to distract Maria's attention from the problem, which may prove interesting and enjoyable at the same time.

7. Encourage getting back in touch with friends.

It is clear that this form of intervention requires time and a certain level of preparation on behalf of the parents. In this particular case, it is the mother who assumes most of the responsibility.

As previously indicated, the strategies make use of multiple distracting elements, searching for an activity which could prove both gratifying, as well as allowing her to calm her anxiety to do exercise. Moreover, such an activity encourages her to reinitiate social relations. In this case, the chosen activity was skiing; some of her friends were already involved in this sport and were members of a club that made frequent trips to the mountains during the snow season.

The skiing coach proved to be a key figure, who, with the help of Maria's mother, managed to motivate her. Initially, he encouraged her to do the sport and gradually helped her introduce normal food items into her diet. This whole process was slow and subtle, above all when referring to food. Every week, the coach took advantage of group sessions to mention some aspects related to a balanced diet, and put them into practice during the trips to the mountains. Therefore, gradually and without forcing the situation, Maria began to reacquire adequate eating habits, as well as gradually increasing her relationship with the ski group.

The process of recuperation, right through to total remission, took approximately 2 years. Today, 2 years later, Maria is a skiing instructor and is fully aware of the important role her training group plays in the lives of each child, not just in nutritional matters, but in aspects related to the development of each individual, such as self-esteem, self-image, etc.

8.7 Conclusions

The diversity of cases described in this chapter reflects the importance of personalizing treatment to each individual athlete. Although not by any means exhaustive, it aims to provide basic guidance, based on a series of ideas defended throughout the book:

- *Sports psychologists* should acquire an in-depth knowledge of the specific sporting modality with which they are to work, in order to adapt to the demands of each situation. Likewise, it is important for sports psychologists to use initial sessions for gaining athletes' trust, increasing their acceptance of subsequent treatment. Moreover, taking the coach, the parents and the athlete's immediate surroundings into account, provides an overall vision of the problem, and allows for coordinated action to be taken.

- *Parents*, given that they are able to see the patient's behaviour within the home setting, play a fundamental role in the prevention of eating-related problems. The majority of eating-related behaviours are carried out at home, meaning parents should be aware of how certain practices may be related to eating disorders. On this premise, information is the best form of prevention; parents should encourage healthy and varied eating habits in their children from a young age, and know how to identify problematic conducts. The family climate can positively or negatively affect the prevention, development, duration and eradication of eating disorders.

- *Young athletes.* It is fundamental to provide guidance about eating issues in grass-roots sport. Likewise, any doubts or concerns about diet, weight or figure should be resolved. Young athletes need reference points close to them (principally, coaches and parents), who can provide security and confidence, so their sporting activity takes on a principally educative character.

- *Coaches.* The role of coaches goes beyond simply transmitting technical, tactical and physical knowledge. They should be perceived as role models for appropriate behaviour and serve as a reference point for young athletes, being fully aware of the importance and influence their comments and behaviours have.

- *Directors* of teams and clubs should encourage the participation of parents; provide training courses for coaches, parents and athletes; as well as select qualified coaches, who are capable of educating athletes in nutritional and psychological aspects.

References

Abraham, S. (1996). Characteristics of eating disorders among young ballet dancers. *Psychopathology* **29**(4), 223–229.

Acheson, K.J., Schutz, Y., Bessard, T., Anantharaman, K., Flatt, J.P., and Jequier, E. (1988). Glycogen storage capacity and de novo lipogenesis during massive carbohydrate overfeeding in man. *American Journal of Clinical Nutrition* **48**, 240–247.

Ackard, D.M., Brehm, B.J., and Steffen, J.J. (2002). Exercise and eating disorders in college-aged women: Profiling excessive exercisers. *Eating Disorders: The Journal of Treatment and Prevention* **10**(1), 31–47.

Ahrendt, D.M. (2001). Ergogenic aids: counselling the athlete. *American Family Physician* **63**(5), 842–843.

Ainsworth, B.E., Haskell, W.L., Leon, A.S., Jacobs, D.R. Jr, Montoye, H.J., Sallis, J.F., and Paffenbarger, R.S. Jr (1993). Compendium of Physical Activities: classification of energy costs of human physical activities. *Medicine & Science in Sport & Exercise* **25**, 71–80.

Alderman, B.L., Landers, D.M., Carlson, J., and Scott J.R. (2004). Factors related to rapid weight loss practices among international-style wrestlers. *Medicine & Science in Sport & Exercise* **36**(2), 249–252.

Alvarez, T.D., Franco, P.K., Mancilla, D.J.M., Alvarez, R.G., and López, A.X. (2000). Factores predisponentes de la sintomatología de los trastornos alimentarios. *Revista de Psicología Contemporánea* **7**(1), 26–35.

American College of Sports Medicine (2000). Joint position statement: nutrition and athletic performance. American College of Sports Medicine. American Dietetic Association, and Dietitians of Canada. *Medicine & Science in Sport & Exercise* **32**, 2130–2145.

American Dietetic Association (2000). Position of the American Dietetic Association, Dietitians of Canada, and the American College of Sports Medicine: Nutrition and athletic performance. *Journal of American Dietetic Association* **100**, 1543–56.

American Psychiatric Association (2000). *Diagnostic and statistical manual of mental disorders (4th edition revised)*. Washington: American Psychiatric Association.

ANRED (Anorexia Nervosa and Related Eating Disorders) (2007). Athletes with eating disorders. Overview. www.anred.com.

Arnhein, D. (1994). *Medicina deportiva: fisioterapia y entrenamiento atlético*. Barcelona: Mosby.

Eating Disorders in Athletes   Joaquín Dosil
© 2008 John Wiley & Sons, Ltd   ISBN 0-470-1170-6

Bachner-Melman, R., Zohar, A.H., Ebstein, R.P., Elizur, Y., and Constantini, N. (2006). How anorexic-like are the symptom and personality profiles of aesthetic athletes?. *Medicine & Science in Sport & Exercise* **38**(4), 628–636.

Bale, P., Doust, J., and Dawson, D. (1996). Gymnast, distance runners, anorexics, body composition and menstrual status. *Journal of Sports Medicine and Physical Fitness* **36**(1), 49–53.

Balsom P., Ekblom B., Sjodin B., and Hultman E (1993). Creatine supplementation and dynamic high-intensity intermittent exercise. *Scandinavian Journal of Medicine and Science in Sports* **3**, 143–149.

Bamber, D., Cockerill, I.M., and Carroll, D. (2000). The pathological status of exercise dependence. *British Journal of Sports Medicine* **34**, 125–132.

Barbany, J.R. (2002). *Alimentación para el deporte y la salud.* Barcelona: Martínez Roca.

Bässler, K.H., Golly, I., Loew, D., and Pietrzik, K. (2002). *Vitamin-Lexicon.* München: Urban-Fisher Verlag.

Baum A. (2006). Eating disorders in the male athlete. *Sports Medicine.* **36**(1), 1–6.

Beals, K.A., Brey, R.A., and Gonyou, J.B. (1999). Understanding the female athlete triad: Eating disorders, amenorrhea, and osteoporosis. *Journal of School Health* **69**(8), 337–340.

Becvar, D.S. and Becvar, R.J. (2000). *Family Therapy A Systemic Integration.* Boston, MA: Allyn & Bacon.

Beebe, D.W., Holmbeck, G.N., and Grzeskiewicz, C. (1999). Normative and psychometric data on the body image assessment-revised. *Journal of Personality Assessment* **73**(3), 374–394.

Belko, A.Z., Obarzaneck, E., Kalkwarf, H.J., *et al.* (1983). Effects of exercise on riboflavine requeriments on young women. *American Journal of Clinical Nutrition* **37**, 509–517.

Benardot, D. and Retton, M. (1994). *Nutritional Readiness.* Indianapolis: United States Gymnastics Federation.

Benson, J.E., Allemann, Y., Theintz, G.E., and Howald, H. (1990). Eating problems and calorie intake levels in Swiss adolescent athletes. *International Journal of Sport Medicine* **11**(4), 249–252.

Benson, R.A. and Taub, D.E. (1993). Using the PRECEDE model for causal analysis of bulimic tendencies among elite women swimmers. *Journal of Health Education* **24**(6), 360–368.

Bergstrom, J. and Hultman, E. (1967). A study of the glycogen metabolism during exercise in man. *Scandinavian Journal of Clinical Laboratory Investigation* **19**(3), 218–238.

Bergstrom, J., Hermansen, L., Hultman, E., and Saltin, B. (1967). Diet, muscle glycogen and physical performance. *Acta Physiological Scandinavica* **71**(2), 140–150.

Bermejo, A. (2001). Valoración y aplicación de la terapia psicológica via Internet. *Información Psicológica* **75**, 65–71.

Beshgetoor, D., Nichols, J.F., and Rego, I. (2000). Effect of training mode and calcium intake on bone mineral density in female Master cyclists, runners, and non athletes. *International Journal of Sport Nutrition, Exercise and Metabolism* **10**(3), 290–301.

Blasco, M.P., García Mérita, M.L., Balaguer, I., Pons, D., and Atienza, F. (1992). Técnicas de recogida de información en la evaluación de trastornos alimenticios en deporte. *Congreso Científico Olimpiadas* 92. Andalucía.

Bloom, P.C., Costill, D.L., and Vollestad, N.K. (1987). Exhaustive running: inappropiate as a stimulus of muscle glycogen supercompensation. *Medicine & Science in Sport & Exercise* **19**(4), 398–403.

Blouin, A.G. and Goldfield, G.S. (1995). Body image and steroid use in male bodybuilders. *International Journal of Eating Disorders* **18**, 159–165.

Blumenthal, J.A., O'Toole, L.C., and Chang, J.L. (1984). Is running an analogue of anorexia nervosa? *JAMA* **252**, 520–523.

Bouissou, P., Defer, G., Guezennec, C., Estrade, P., and Serrurier, B. (1988). Metabolic and blood catecholamine responses to exercise during alkalosis. *Medicine & Sciencie in Sport & Exercise* **20**, 228–232.

Bratman, S. and Knight, D. (2001). *Health Food Junkies: Orthorexia Nervosa: Overcoming the Obsession with Healthful Eating.* USA: Broadway.

Brewer, B.W. and Petrie, T.A. (2002). Psychopathology in sport and exercise. In J.L.Van Raalte & B.W. Brewer (eds.), *Exporing Sport and Exercise Psychology.* Washington: American Psychological Association.

Brooks-Gunn, J., Warren, M.P., and Hamilton, L.H. (1987). The relation of eating problems and amenorrhea in ballet dancers. *Medicine & Sciences in Sports & Exercise* **19**(1), 41–44.

Brotherhood, J.R. (1984). Nutrition and sports performance. *Sports Medicine* **1**, 350–389.

Brouns, F. (1995). *Necesidades nutricionales de los atletas.* Barcelona: Paidotribo.

Brownell, D.K., Rodin, J., and Wilmore, J.H. (1992). *Eating, Body Weight and Performance in Athletes: Disorders of Modern Society.* Philadelphia, PA: Lea and Febiger.

Brownell, K.D. and Rodin, J. (1992). Prevalence of eating disorders in athletes. In K.D. Brownell, J. Rodin, and J.H. Wilmore (Eds.), *Eating, Body Weight, and Performance in Athletes.* Malvern, PA: Lea & Febiger.

Burke, L.M. and Read, R.S. (1993). Dietary supplements in sport. *Sports Medicine* **15**(1), 43–65.

Burke, L., Desbrow, B., and Minehan, M. (2000). Dietary supplements and nutritional ergogenic aids. In L. Burke and V. Deakin (Eds.), Clinical Sports Nutrition (2nd ed., pp. 455–528). Sydney: McGraw-Hill.

Burke, R.C. and Schramm, L.L. (1995). Therapists' attitudes about treating patients with eating disorders. *South Medicine Journal* **88**(8), 813–818.

Byrne, S. and McLean, N. (2002). Elite athletes: Effects of the pressure to be thin. *Journal of Science and Medicine in Sport* **5**(2), 80–94.

Caballero, J.A., Vives, L., and Garcés de los Fayos, E. (2001). Análisis bibliométrico de las investigaciones sobre trastornos alimentarios en la actividad física y el deporte (1992–2000). *Actas VII Congreso Nacional de Psicología de la Actividad Física y del Deporte.* Pontevedra: Asociación Gallega de Psicología del Deporte.

Calvo, R. (2002). *Anorexia y Bulimia: Guía para padres, educadores y terapeutas.* Barcelona. Planeta Prácticos.

Caracuel, J.C., Arbinaga, F., and Montero, J.A. (2003). Perfil socio-deportivo de ususarios de gimnasios: Un estudio piloto. *Edupsykhé. Revista de Psicología y Psicopedagogía* **2**(2), 273–308.

Carron, A.V. and Hausenblas, H.A. (2000). Group influences on eating and dieting behaviors in male and female varsity athletes. *Journal of Sport Behavior* **23**(1), 33–41.

Carter, J.C. and Fairburn, C.G. (1998). Cognitive-behavioral self-help for binge eating disorder: A controlled effectiveness study. *Journal of Consulting and Clinical Psychology* **66**, 616–623.

Castro, J., Toro, J., Salamero, M., and Guimera, E. (1991). The eating attitudes test: Validation of the Spanish version. *Psychological Assessment* **2**, 175–190.

Catalina, M.L., Bote, B., García, F., and Ríos, B. (2005). Orthorexia nervosa: a new eating behavior disorder? *Actas Españolas de Psiquiatría* **33**(1), 66–68.

Celio, A.A., Winzelberg, A.J., Wilfley, D.E., Eppstein-Herald, D., Springer, E.A., Dev, P., and Taylor, C.B. (2000). Reducing risk factors for eating disorders: comparison of an Internet- and a classroom-delivered psychoeducational program. *Journal of Consulting and Clinical Psychology* **68**(4), 650–657.

Choi, P.Y., Pope, H.Jr, and Olivardia, R. (2002). Muscle dysmorphia: a new syndrome in weightlifters. *Bristish Journal of Sports Medicine* **36**(5), 375–376.

Choma, C.W., Sforzo, G.A., and Keller, B.A. (1998). Impact of rapid weight loss on cognitive function in collegiate wrestlers. *Medicine & Science in Sports & Exercise* **30**(5), 746–749.

CIE-10. Guia de Bolsillo de la Clasificacion. (2001) London: Churchill Livingstone.

Clarkson, P.M. (1993). Nutritional ergogenic aids: caffeine. *International Journal of Sport Nutrition* **3**(1), 103–111.

Clinton, DN. (1996). Why do eating disorder patients drop out? *Psychotherapy and Psychosomatics* **65**(1), 29–35.

Cogan, K.D. (2005). Eating disorders: when rations become irrational. In S. Murphy (Ed.), *The Sport Psych Handbook* (pp. 237–254). Champaign, IL: Human Kinetics.

Coksevim, B., Ustdal, M., Saritas, N., and Karakas, E.S. (1997). Judocuda hizli kilo kaybinin guc, kuvvet, dayaniklilik, esneklik ve ceviklik uzerine etkisi. *Spor hekimligi dergisi* **32**(2), 55–61.

Cooper, P.J., Taylor, M., Cooper, Z., and Fairburn, C.G. (1987). The development and validation of the Body Shape Questionnaire. *Journal of Eating Disorders* **6**(4), 485–494.

Couchman, P. and Bayly, M. (1992). *Women bodybuilding*. Videocassete. Australian Broadcasting Corporation.

Coyle, E.F. (1995). Substrate utilization during exercise in active people. *American Journal of Clinical Nutrition*, **61**(suppl), 968S–979S.

Dale, K.S. and Landers, D.M. (1999). Weight control in wrestling: eating disorders or disordered eating?. *Medicine & Science in Sports & Exercise* **31**(10), 1382–1389.

Davis, C. and Cowles, M. (1989) A Comparison of weight and diet concerns and personality factors among female athletes and non-athletes. *Journal of Psychosomatic Research* **33**, 527–536.

Davis, S.E., Dwyer, G.B., Reed, K., Bopp, C., Stosic, J., and Shepanski, M. (2002). Preliminary investigation: the impact of the NCAA wrestling weight certification program on weight cutting. *Journal of Strength and Conditioning Research* **16**(2), 305–307.

De la Torre, D.M. and Snell, B.J. (2005). Use of the preparticipation physical exam in screening for the female athlete triad among high school athletes. *Journal of School Nursing*, **21**(6), 340–345.

DeBate, R.D., Wethington, H., and Sargent, R (2002). Sub-clinical eating disorder characteristics among male and female triathletes. *Eating and Weight Disorders*, **7**(3), 210–220.

Decombaz, J., Reinhardt, P., Anantharaman, K., Von Glutz, G., and Poortmans, J.R. (1979). Biochemical changes in a 100 km run: free amino acids, urea and creatinine. *European Journal of Applied Physiology and Occupational Physiology* **41**(1), 61–72.

Degoutte, F., Jouanel, P., Beque, R.J., Colombier, M., Lac, G., Pequignot, J.M., and Filaire, E. (2006). Food restriction, performance, biochemical, psychological, and endocrine changes in judo athletes. *International Journal of Sport Medicine* **27**(1), 9–18.

Del Castillo, V. (1998a). La alimentación del deportista. *Lecturas Educación física y deportes (Revista Digital)*, 9. www.efdeportes.com.

Del Castillo, V. (1998b). Deporte y trastornos de alimentación. *Lectura de Educación Física y Deportes (Revista Digital)*, 9. www.efdeportes.com.

Delgado, M. (1998) La alimentación en la optimización del rendimiento en gimnasia. In J. López-Bedoya, M. Vernetta, and F. Panadero (eds). *Investigación y Gimnasia. Su aplicación práctica* (pp. 21–28). Granada: Universidad de Granada.

Delgado, M., Gutierrez, A., and Castillo, M.J. (1999). *Entrenamiento físico-deportivo y alimentación. De la infancia a la edad adulta.* Barcelona: Paidotribo.

Diagnostic and Statistical Manual of Mental Disorders (DSM-IV-TR) (2001) New York: American Psychiatric Association.

Díaz, I. (2005). Propuesta de un programa de prevención de trastornos de la conducta alimentaria para entrenadores. *Cuadernos de Psicología del Deporte* **5**(1–2), 63–76.

Díaz, O., González Díaz, O., and Dosil, J. (1998). *Trastornos de la alimentación*. Madrid: Concapa.

Dick, R.W. (1991). Eating disorders in National Collegiate Athletic programs. *Athletic Training* **26**, 136–140.

Donili, L.M., Marsili, D., Graziani, M.P., Imbriale, M., and Cannella, C. (2004). Orthorexia nervosa: a preliminary study with a proposal for diagnosis and an attempt to measure the dimension of the phenomenon. *Eating Weight Disorders* **9(2)**, 151–157.

Donili, L.M., Marsili, D., Graziani, M.P., Imbriale, M., and Cannella, C. (2005). Orthorexia nervosa: validation of a diagnosis questionnaire. *Eating Weight Disorders* **10(2)**, 28–32.

Dosil, J. (2000). *Estudio de la incidencia de los trastornos alimentarios en diferentes deportes*. Santiago de Compostela: FUNDEHSGA.

Dosil, J. (2002a). *El psicólogo del deporte: Asesoramiento e intervención*. Madrid: Síntesis.

Dosil, J. (2002b). Motivos de práctica de actividades físicas y deportivas en profesores de educación secundaria. *Revista Galego-Portuguesa de Psicoloxía e Educación* **6(8)**, 171–178.

Dosil, J. (2003). *Trastornos de la alimentación en el deporte*. Sevilla: Wanceulen.

Dosil, J. (2004). *Psicología de la actividad física y del deporte*. Madrid: McGraw-Hill.

Dosil, J. (2006). *The Sport Psychologist's Handbook: A Guide for Sport-Specific Performance Enhancement*. Chichester, UK: John Wiley & Sons.

Dosil, J. and Díaz, O. (2002). Valoración de la conducta alimentaria y de control de peso en practicantes de aeróbic. *Revista de psicología del deporte* **11(2)**, 183–195.

Dosil, J. and Díaz, I. (2006). Cuestionario de hábitos alimentarios en el deporte (CHAD): versión preliminar. *Revista de Psicología General y Aplicada* **59(4)**, 509–524.

Dosil, J. and Garcés de Los Fayos, E.J. (2007). *Ser psicólogo del deporte*. Noia: Toxosoutos.

Dosil, J. and García-Prieto, D. (2004) Asesoramiento on-line en psicología del deporte. *Cuadernos de psicología del deporte* **4(1–2)**, 19–28.

Draeger, J., Yates, A., and Crowell, D. (2005). The Obligatory Exerciser. *The Physician and Sportsmedicine* **33(6)**. www.pshyssportsmed.com/issues/2005/0605/yates.htm.

Drummer, G.M., Rosen, L.W., Heusner, W.W., Roberts, P.J., and Councilman, J.E. (1987). Pathogenic weight-control behaviours of young competitive swimmers. *The Physician and Sportsmedicine*, **15**, 75.

Duncan, M.J., Dodd, L.J., and Al-Nakeeb, Y. (2005). The Impact of Silhouette Randomization on the Results of Figure Rating Scales. *Measurement in Physical Education and Exercise Science*, **9(1)**, 61–66.

Duncan, M.J., Al-Nakeeb, Y., Nevill, A.M., and Jones, M.V. (2006). Body dissatisfaction, body fat and physical activity in British children. *International Journal of Pediatric Obesity* **1(2)**, 89–95.

Durstine, J.L. and Haskell, W.L. (1994). Effect of exercise training on plasma lipids and lipoproteins. In: J. Holloszy (ed.), *Exercise and Sports Science Reviews* (pp. 684–690). Baltimore: Williams & Williams.

Ecónomos, C.D., Bortz, S.S., and Nelson, M.E. (1993). Nutritional practices of elite athletes. Practical recommendations. *Sports Medicine* **16(6)**, 381–399.

Elliot, D.L., Goldberg, L., Moe, E.L., Defrancesco, C.A., Durham, M.B., and Hix-Small, H. (2004). Preventing substance use and disordered eating: initial outcomes of the ATHENA (Athletes Targeting Healthy Exercise and Nutrition Alternatives) Program. *Archives of Pediatric and Adolescent Medicine* **158(11)**, 1043–1049.

Elwood, P.C., Yarnell, J.W.C., Pickering, J., Fehily, A.M., O'Brien, J.R. (1993). Exercise, fibrinogen, and other risk factors for ischaemic heart disease. Caerphilly Prospective Heart Disease Study. *British Heart Journal* **69**, 183–187.

Emperador, L. (2000) Psicoconsulta: una Terapi@ on-line. www.psicología-on-line.com.

Epling, W.F. and Pierce, W.D. (1996). *Activity Anorexia: Theory, Research, and Treatment.* New Jersey: LEA.

Epling, W.F., Pierce, W.D., and Stefan, L. (1983). A theory of activity-based anorexia. *International Journal of Eating Disorders* **3**(1), 27–46.

Epstein, Y. and Armstrong, I.E. (1999). Fluid electrolyte balance and exercise: concepts and misconceptions. *International Journal of Sport Nutrition* **9**, 1–12.

Estok, P.J. and Rudy, E.B. (1996). The relationship between eating disorders and running in women. *Research in Nursing and Health* **19**(5), 377–387.

Fairburn, C.G. and Beglin, S.J. (1994). Assessment of eating disorders: interview or self report questionnaire? *International Journal of Eating Disorders* **16**, 363–370.

Fairburn, C.G. and Wilson, G.T. (eds.) (1993). *Binge Eating: Nature, Assessment and Treatment.* New York: Guilford Press.

Ferraro, G., Caci, B., DÁmico, A., and DiBlasi, M. (2007). Internet Addiction Disorder: Australian Study. *CyberPsychology and Behavior* **10**(2), 170–175.

Ferrand, C., Magnan, C., and Philippe, R.A. (2005). Body-esteem, body mass index, and risk for disordered eating among adolescents in synchronized swimming. *Perceptual and Motor Skills* **101**(3), 877–884.

Filaire, E., Maso, F., Degoutte, F., Jouanel, P., and Lac, G. (2001). Food restriction, performance, psychological state and lipid values in judo athletes. *International Journal of Sports Medicine* **22**(6), 454–459.

Fink, J. (2004, July). Silent witness: Some of Australia's best sportspeople continue to cope with mental illness in silence. *Inside Sport* **151**, 68–75.

Finkenberg, M.E. and Teper L. (1991). Self-concept profiles of competitive bodybuilders. *Perceptual and Motor Skills* **72**, 1039–1043.

Fitzgibbon, M.L., Blackman, L.R., and Avellone, M.E. (2000). The relationship between body image discrepancy and body mass index across ethnic groups. *Obesity Research* **8**, 582–589.

Franseen, L. (2000). Preventing and manging eating disorders. *Synchro Swimming* **8**(2), 23.

Furnham, A. and Boughton, J. (1995). Eating behavior and body dissatisfaction among dieters, aerobic exercisers and a control group. *European Eating Disorder Review* **3**(1), 35–45.

Garcés de Los Fayos, E.J. and Vives Benedicto, L. (2003). *Una aproximación a la vigorexia desde los trastornos alimentarios: Importancia, implicación e impacto en los desórdenes conductuales.* Memoria del Proyecto de Investigación financiado. Murcia: ADANER.

Garner, D.M. and Garfinkel, P.E. (1979). The eating attitudes test an index of the symptoms of anorexia nervosa. *Psychological Medicine* **9**, 273–279.

Garner, D.M. and Garfinkel, P.E. (1980). Socio-cultural factors in the development of anorexia nervosa. *Psychological Medicine* **10**(4), 647–656.

Garner, D.M. and Garfinkel, P.E. (1997). *Handbook of Treatment for Eating Disorders.* New York: Guilford Press.

Garner, D.M., Olmsted, M., and Polivy, I. (1983). Development and validation of a multidimensional Eating Disorders Inventory for anorexia anorexia nervosa and bulimia. *International Journal of Eating Disorders* **2**, 15–34.

Garner, D.M., Rosen, L.W., and Barry, D. (1998). Eating disorders among athletes: Research and recommendations. *Child and Adolescent Psychiatric Clinics of North America* **7**(4), 839–857.

Gilbert, S. (2005). *Counselling for Eating Disorders.* London: Sage.

Girard, S. (2000) Timing fuel for peak racing. In S. Girard (ed.). *Endurance Sports Nutrition* (pp. 51–79). Champaign, IL: Human Kinetics.

Gladding, S. T. (2002). *Family Therapy History, Theory, and Practice*. Columbus, OH: Merrill Prentice Hall.

Goldfield, G.S., Blouin, A.G., and Woodside, D.B. (2006). Body image, binge eating, and bulimia nervosa in male bodybuilders. *Canadian Journal of Psychiatry* **51**(3), 160–168.

Gollings, E.K. and Paxton, S.J. (2006). Comparison of internet and face-to-face delivery of a group body image and disordered eating intervention for women: a pilot study. *Eating Disorders* **14**(1), 1–15.

Gomez, P. (1996). *Anorexia Nerviosa. La prevención en la familia*. Madrid: Pirámide.

González-Alonso, J., Mora-Rodriguez, R., Below, P.R., and Coyle, E.F. (1997). Dehydration markedly impairs cardiovascular function in hypertehermic endurance athletes during exercise. *Journal of Applied Physiology* **82**(4), 1129–1136.

Gonzalez-Gross, M., Miguel-Tobal, F., Gutierrez, A., and Castillo, M.J. (2001). Dinking patterns of Spanish soccer players. *Archivos de Medicina Deportiva* **85**, 428.

Gordo-Lopez, A. and Parker, I. (1999). *Cyberpsychology*. London, UK: Routledge.

Gordon, R.A. (1999). *Anorexia and Bulimia: Anatomy of a Social Epidemy*. Oxford: Blackwell.

Goss, S. and Anthony, K. (2003). *Technology in Counselling and Psychotherapy*. New York: Palgrave Macmillan.

Govero, C. and Bushman, B.A. (2003). Collegiate cross country coaches' knowledge of eating disorders. *Women in Sport and Physical Activity Journal* **12**(1), 53–65.

Graham, T.E. and Spriet, L. (1991). Performance and metabolic responses to a high caffeine dose during prolonged exercise. *Journal of Applied Physiology* **71**(6), 2292–2298.

Greenhaff, P. (1995). Creatine and its application as an ergogenic aid. *International Journal of Sport Nutrition* **5**, S100–S110.

Greenleaf, J. (1992). Problem: thirst, drinking behavior, and involuntary dehydratation. *Medicine Science in Sports and Exercise* **24**(6), 645–656.

Griffin, J. and Harris, M.B. (1996). Coaches attitudes, knowledge, experiences, and recommendattions regarding weight control. *The Sport Psychologist* **10**(2), 180–194.

Griffiths, M. and Cooper, G. (2003). On-line therapy: Implications for problem gamblers and clinicians. *Brithish Journal of Guidance and Counselling* **31**(1), 113–135.

Grunwald, M. and Busse, J.C. (2003). On-line consulting service for eating disorders – analysis and perspectives. *Computers in Human Behaviour* **19**, 469–477.

Guimerá, Q. and Torrubia, B. (1987). Adaptación española del Eating Disorders Inventory (EDI) en una muestra de pacientes anoréxicas. *Anales de Psiquiatría* **3**, 185–190.

Guthie, S.R. (1986). The prevalence and development of eating disorders within a selected intercollegiate athlete population. *Dissertation Abstracts International* **46**, 3649A.

Guthie, S.R., Ferguson, C., and Grimmett, D. (1994). Elite women bodybuilders: ironing out nutritional misconceptions. *The Sport Pscychologist* **8**(3), 271–286.

Halmi, K.A. (2005). The multimodal treatment of eating disorders. *Wolrd Psychiatry* **4**(2), 69–73.

Harris, J.A. and Benedict, F.G. (1919). *A Biometric Study of Basal Metabolism in Man*. Washington, DC: Carnegie Institute.

Harris, M.B. (2000). Weight concern, body image, and abnormal eating in college women tennis players and their coaches. *International Journal of Sport Nutrition and Exercise Metabolism* **10**(1), 1–15.

Harris, M.B. and Greco, D. (1990). Weight control and weight concern in competitive female gymnast. *Journal of Sport and Exercise Psychology* **12**, 427–433.

Hausenblas, H.A. and Carron, A.V. (1999). Eating disorders indices and athletes: an integration. *Journal of Sport and Exercise Psychology* **21**(3), 230–258.

Hausenblas, H.A. and McNally, K.D. (2004). Eating disorder prevalence and symptoms for track and field athletes and nonatheletes. *Journal of Applied Sport Psychology* **16**(3), 274–286.

Hausenblas, H.A. and Symons, D. (2000). How much is too much? The development and validation of the exercise dependence scale. *Psychology and Health* **17**, 387–404.

Haworth-Hoeppner, S. (2000). The critical shapes of body image: the role of culture and family in the production of eating disorders. *Journal of Marriage and Family* **62**(1), 212–227.

Heffner, J.L., Ogles, B.M., Gold, E., Marsden, K., and Johnson, M. (2003). Nutrition and eating in female college athletes: a survey of coaches. *Eating Disorders* **11**(3), 209–220.

Heinicke, B.E., Paxton, S.J., McLean, S.A., and Wertheim, E.H. (2007). Internet-delivered targeted group intervention for body dissatisfaction and disordered eating in adolescent girls: A randomized controlled trial. *Journal of Abnormal Child Psychology* **23**(3), 379–391.

Henderson, M. and Freeman, A. (1987). Self-rating scale for bulimia. The BITE. *British Journal of Psychiatry* **150**, 18–24.

Hermansen, L., Hultman, E., and Saltin, B. (1967). Muscle glycogen during prolonged severe exercise. *Acta Physiologia Scandinavica* **71**(2), 129–139.

Herrin, M. (2003). *Nutrition Counselling in the Treatment of Eating Disorders*. New York: Brunner-Routledge.

Hildebrandt, T., Schlundt, D., Langenbucher, J., and Chung, T. (2006). Presence of muscle dysmorphia syptomology among male weightlifters. *Comprehensive Psychiatr,* **47**(2), 127–135.

Hinton, P.S., Giordano, C., Brownlie, T., and Haas, J.D. (2000). Iron supplementation improves endurance after training in iron-depleted, nonanemic women. *Journal of Applied Physiology* **88**(3), 1103–1111.

Hobart, J.A. and Smucker, D.R. (2000). The female athlete triad. *American Family Physician* **61**, 3357–3364.

Hopkinson, R.A. and Lock, J. (2004). Athletics, perfectionism, and disordered eating. *Eating and Weight Disorders* **9**(2), 99–106.

Hsiung, R.C. (2002). *E-Therapy: Case Studies, Guiding Principles, and the Clinical Potential of the Internet*. New York: W.W. Norton and Company.

Hulley, A.J. and Hill, A.J. (2001). Eating disorders and health in elite women distance runners. *International Journal of Eating Disorders* **30**(3), 312–317.

Huon, C. F. (1985) An initial validation of a self-help program for bulimia. *International Journal of Eating Disorders* **4**, 573–588.

Jenkins, D.G., Palmer, J., and Spillman, D. (1993). The influence of dietary carbohydrate on performance of supramaximal intermittent exercise. *European Journal of Applied Physiology* **67**, 309–314.

Jiménez Cruz, A., Cervera, P., and Bacardi, M. (1998). *Tablas de composición de alimentos*. Barcelona: Sandoz Nutrition.

Johnson, B. (2002). Caroline Ingham: full recovery. *US Rowing* **34**(3), 18–20.

Joinson, A., McKenna, K., Postmes, T. and Reips, U.-D. (2007). *The Oxford Handbook of Internet Psychology*. USA: Oxford University Press.

Jones, R. L., Glintmeyer N., and McKenzie, A. (2005). Slim bodies, eating disorders and the coach–athlete relationship. a tale of identity creation and disruption. *International Review for the Sociology of Sport* **40**(3), 377–391.

Jonnalagadda, S.S., Ziegler, P.J., and Nelson, J.A. (2004). Food preferences, dieting behaviours, and body image perceptions of elite figure skaters. *International Journal of Sport and Nutrition Exercise Metabolism* **14**(5), 594–606.

Juhn, M. (2003). Popular sports supplements and ergogenic aids. *Sports Medicine* **33**(12), 921–939.

Karlson, K., Becker, C., and Merkur, A. (2001). Prevalence of eating disordered behavior in collegiate lightweight women rowers and distance runners. *Clinical Journal of Sport Medicine* **11**(1), 32–37.

Karlson, K.A. (2001). Prevalence of eating disordered behavior in collegiate lightweight women rowers and distance runners. *Clinical Journal of Sport Medicine* **11**(1), 32–37.

Karlsson, J. and Saltin, B. (1971). Diet, muscle glycogen, and endurance performance. *Journal of Applied Physiology* **31**(2), 203–206.

Katch, F.L. (1985). Nutrition for athletes. In R.P. Welsh and R.J. Shephard (eds.), *Current Therapy in Sports Medicine 1985–1986* (pp. 28–30). Philadelphia: BC Decker Inc.

Kenefick, R.W., Mahood, N.V., Mattern, C.O., Kertzer, R., and Quinn, T.J. (2002). Hypohydration adversely affects lactate threshold in endurance athletes. *Journal of Strength and Conditioning Research* **16**(1), 38–43.

Kerr, G., Berman, E., and De Souza, MJ. (2006). Disordered eating in women's gymnastics: perspectives of athletes, coaches, parents, and judges. *Journal of Applied Sport Psychology* **18**(1), 28–43.

Kiningham, R.B. and Gorenflo, D.W. (2001). Weight loss methods of high school wrestlers. *Medicine and Science in Sport and Exercise* **33**(5), 810–813.

Kowatari, K., Umeda, T., Shimoyama, T., Nakaji, S., Yamamoto, Y., and Sugawara, K. (2001). Exercise training and energy restriction decrease neutrophil phagocytic activity in judoists. *Medicine and Science in Sports and Exercise* **33**(4), 519–524.

Kraemer, W.J., Fry, A.C., Rubin, M.R., *et al.* (2001). Physiological and performance responses to tournament wrestling. *Medicine and Science in Sports and Exercise* **33**(8), 1367–1378.

Kraus, R., Zack, J., and Stricker, G. (2004). *On-line Counselling: a Handbook for Mental Health.* London, UK: Elsevier.

Kreider, R.B., Ferreira, M., Wilson, M., *et al.* (1998). Effects of creatine supplementation on body composition, strength and sprint performance. *Medicine and Scienie in Sport and Exercise* **30**(1), 73–82.

Kutlesic, V., Williamson, D.A., Gleaves, D.H., Barbin, J.M., and Murphy-Eberenz, K.P. (1998). The Interview for the diagnosis of eating disorders-IV: Application to DSM-IV diagnostic criteria. *Psychological Assessment* **10**, 41–48.

Lakka, T.A. and Salonen, J.T. (1992). Physical activity and serum lipids: a cross-sectional population study in eastern Finnish men. *American Journal of Epidemiology* **136**, 806–813.

Landers, D.M., Arent, S.M., and Lutz, R.S. (2001). Affect and cognitive performance in high school wrestlers undergoing rapid weight loss. *Journal of Sport and Exercise Psychology* **23**(4), 307–316.

Lange, A., Rietdijk, D., Hudcovicova, M., *et al.* (2003). Interapy: A controlled randomized trial of the standardized treatment of posttraumatic stress through the Internet. *Journal of Consulting and Clinical Psychology* **71**(5), 901–909.

Laszig, P. and Rieg, K. (2000) Informations and discussion groups in the world wide web by the example of eating disorders. *Such* **46**(2), 121–128.

Lemon, P.W.R. (1995). Do athletes need more dietary protein and amino acids? *International Journal of Sports Nutrition* **5**, S39–S61.

Leone, J.E., Sedory, E.J., and Kimberly, A.G. (2005). Recognition and treatment of muscle dysmorphia and related body image disorders. *Journal of Athletic Trainer* **40**(4), 352–359.

Letosa-Porta, A., Ferrer-García, M., and Gutiérrez-Maldonado, J. (2005). A program for assessing body image disturbance using adjustable partial image distorsion. *Behavior Research Methods* **37**(4), 638–643.

Lozano de la Torre, M. and Muñoz, R. (1995). Influencia de los hábitos dietéticos en la nutrición del adolescente. *Archive Pediatrics* **46(suppl. 1)**, 73–77.

Machado, P.P., Machado, B.C., Gonçalves, S., and Hoek, H.W. (2006). The prevalence of eating disorders not otherwise specified. *International Journal of Eating Disorders* 15 December (published on-line).

Madison, J.K. and Ruma, S.L. (2003). Exercise and athletic involvement as moderator of severy of eating pathology and psychopathology in adolescents with eating disorders. *Journal of Applied Sport Psychology* **15(3)**, 213–222.

Malczewska, J., Racynski, G., and Stupnicki, R. (2000). Iron status in female endurance athletes and in non-athletes. *International Journal Sport Nutrition Exercise Metabolism* **10(3)**, 260–276.

Malinauskas, B., Cuchiarra, A.J., and Bruening, Ch. (2005). Body dissatisfaction, anthropometric, and dietary intake differences among female college athletes and non-athletes. *Medicine and Science in Sports and Exercise* **37(5)**, Supplement :S74.

Marti, B. (1991). Health effects of recreational running in women. Some epidemiological and preventive aspects. *Sports Medicine* **11(1)**, 20–51.

Martin, C. and Bellisle, F. (1989). Eating attitudes and taste response in young ballerinas. *Physiology and Behavio* **46(2)**, 223–227.

Martin, K.A. and Lichtenberger, C.M. (2002). Fitness enhancement and changes in body image. In T.F. Cash and T. Pruzinsky (eds), *Body image: a Handbook Of Theory, Research, and Clinical Practice* (pp. 414–421). New York: Guilford Press.

Marzano, M.M. (2001). The contemporary construction of a perfect body image: bodybuilding, exercise addiction, and eating disorders. *Quest* **53(2)**, 216–230.

Mataix, J. (1992). Situación nutricional del deportista. In VVAA., *Avances en nutrición deportiva. I Congreso Mundial de Nutrición Deportiva*. Ministerio de Educación y Ciencia. Consejo Superior de Deportes.

Matejek, N., Weimann, E., Witzel, C., Moelenkamp, G., Schwidergall, S., and Boehles, H. (1999). Hypoleptinaemia in patients with anorexia nervosa and in elite gymnasts with anorexia athletica. *International Journal of Sports Medicine* **20(7)**, 451–456.

Matheson, H. and Crawford-Wright, A. (2000). An examination of eating disorder profiles in student obligatory and non-obligatory exercisers. *Journal of Sport Behavior* **23(1)**, 42–50.

Matson, L.G. and Tran, Z. (1993). Effets of sodium bicarbonato ingestión on anaerobic performance: a meta-analytic review. *International Journal of Sport Nutrition* **3**, 2–28.

Maughan, R.J. (1993). Gastric emptying during exercise. *Sports Science Exchange* **6(5)**, 1–5.

Maughan, R.J. (1995). Creatine supplementation and exercise performance. *International Journal of Sport Nutrition* **3**, 94–101.

Maughan, R. and Leiper, J. (1994). Fluid replacement requeriments in soccer. *Journal of Sports Sciences* **12(suppl.)**, 29–34.

Maughan, R.J. and Noakes, T.D. (1991). Fluid replacement and exercise stress. a brief review of studies on fluid replacement and some guidelines for the athlete. *Sports Medicine* **12(1)**, 16–31.

Maughan, R.J. and Poole, D.C. (1981). The effects of a glycogen-loading regimen on the capacity to perform anaerobic exercise. *European Journal of Applied Physiology* **9**, 211–219.

McArdle, W.D., Katch, F.L., and Katch, V.L. (1991). *Exercise Physiology Energy, Nutrition and Human Performance.* Philadelphia: Lea and Febiger.

McArthur K.E. and Feldman M. (1989) Gastric acid secretion, gastrin release, and gastric emptying in humans as affected by liquid meal temperatura. *American Journal of Clinical Nutrition* **49(1)**, 51–54.

McCabe, M.P. and Ricciardelli, L.A. (2005). A prospective study of pressures from parents, peers, and the media on extreme weight change behaviours among adolescent boys and girls. *Behaviour Research and Therapy* **43**(5), 653–668.

McNaughton, L.R. and Cedaro, R. (1992). Sodium citrate ingestion and its effects on maximal anaerobics exercise of differents durations. *European Journal of Applied Physiology* **64**, 36–41.

Michela, J. (2007). *Ergogenic aids: achieving a competitive edge.* www.ultracycling.com/nutrition/ergogenic.html

Minuchin, S. (1977). *Families and Family Therapy.* London: Routledge.

Minuchin, S., Lee, W.Y., and Simon, G.M. (2006). *Mastering Family Therapy: Journeys of Growth and Transformation* (2nd edition). Chichester, UK: John Wiley & Sons.

Monsma, E.V. and Feltz, D.L. (2006). A mental preparation guide for figure skaters: A developmental approach. In J. Dosil (ed.). The Sport Psychologist's Handbook: a guide for sport-specific performance enhancement (pp. 427–454). Chichester, UK: John Wiley & Sons.

Monsma, E.V. and Malina, R.M. (2004). Correlates of eating disorders risk among figure skates: a profile of adolescent competitors. *Psychology of Sport and Exercise* **5**(4), 447–460.

Moore, J.M., Timperio, A.F., Crawford, D.A., Burns, C.M., and Cameron-Smith, D. (2002). Weight management and weight loss strategies of professional jockeys. *International Journal of Sport Nutrition and Exercise Metabolism* **12**(1), 1–13.

Morandé, G. (1995). *Un peligro llamado anorexia.* Madrid: Temas de hoy.

Morandé, G. (1999). *La anorexia. Cómo combatir y prevenir el miedo a engordar de las adolescentes.* Madrid: Temas de Hoy.

Moriarty, D. and Moriarty, M. (1997). Eating Disorders among Athletes: Public Policy to Promote Social and Individual Behavioural Change. Paper presented at the *Annual Meeting of the American Alliance for Health, Physical Education, Recreation, and Dance* (St. Louis, MO, March 20–24).

Muñoz, A. and López Meseguer, F.J. (1998). *Guía de alimentación para el deportista.* Madrid: Tutor.

Myers, J.B., Guskiewicz, K.M. and Riemann, B.L. (2003). Syncope and atypical chest pain in an intercollegiate wrestler: a case report. *Journal of Athletic Ttraining* **34**(3), 263–266.

Myers, T.C., Swam-Kremeier, L., Wonderlinch, S., Lancaster, K., and Mitchell, J.E. (2004). The use of alternative delivery systems and new technologies in the treatment of patients with eating disorders. *International Journal of Eating Disorders* **36**(2), 123–143.

Nagel, D.L., Black, D, R., Leverenz, L.J., and Coster, D.C. (2000). Evaluation of a screening test for female collage athletes with eating disordered and disordered eating. *Journal of Athletic Training* **35**(4), 431–440.

Nasser, M. (1988). Eating disorders: the cultural dimension. *Social Psychiatry and Psychiatry Epidemiology* **23**, 184–187.

National Collegiate Athletic Association, NCAA (1998). Wrestling Weight-Certification Program. Overland Park, KS: National Collegiate Athletic Association.

Neumarker, K., Bettle, N., Neumarker, U., and Bettle, O. (2000). Age- and gender-related psychological characteristics of adolescent ballet dancers. *Psychopathology* **33**(3), 137–142.

Neumaerker, K.J., Bettle, N., Bettle, O., Dudeck, U., and Neumaerker, U. (1998). The Eating Attitudes Test: Comparative analysis of female and male students at the Public Ballet School of Berlín. *European Child and Adolescent Psychiatry* **7**(1), 19–23.

Nevonen, L. and Broberg, A.G. (2006). A comparison of sequenced individual and group psychotherapy for patients with bulimia nervosa. *International Journal of Eating Disorders* **39**(2), 117–127.

Newhouse, I.J. and Clement, D.B. (1990). Iron status in athletes: an update. *Sports Medicine* **5**, 337–352.

Nichols, J.F., Rauh, M.J., Lawson, M.J., Ji, M., and Barkai, H.S. (2006). Prevalence of the female athlete triad syndrome among high school athletes. *Archives of Pediatric Adolescente Medicine* **160**, 137–142.

Niñerola, J. and Capdevila, L. (2002). Rendimiento deportivo y trastornos de alimentación. In J. Dosil (ed.), *Psicología y rendimiento deportivo*. Ourense: Gersam.

Noakes, T.D. (1993). Ayudas nutricionales: carbohidratos. actualizaciones en fisiología del ejercicio. ayudas ergogénicas. *II Jornadas Internacionales de Fisiología del Ejercicio*, Madrid.

Noakes, T., Adams, B., Myburgh, K., Greeff, C., Lotz, T., and Nathan, M. (1988). The danger of an inadequate water during prolonged exercise. A novel concept revisited. *European Journal Applied Physiology* **57**, 210–219.

Noden, M. (1994). Dying to win: for many women athletes, the toughest foe is anorexia. Gymnast Christy Henrich lost her battle. *Sport Illustrated* **81**(6), 52–60.

O'Connor, P.J., Lewis, R.D., and Kirchner, E.M. (1995). Eating disorder symptoms in female college gymnasts. *Medicine and Science in Sports and Exercise* **24**(4), 550–555.

Ogden, J., Veale, D.M.W., and Summers, Z. (1997). The development and validation of the Exercise Dependence Questionnaire. *Addiction Research and Theory* **5**, 343–356.

Okano. G., Holmes, R.A., Mu, Z., Yang, P., Lin, Z., and Nakai, Y. (2005). Disordered eating in Japanese and Chinese female runners, rhythmic gymnastas and gymnastas. *International Journal of Sports Medicine* **26**(6), 486–491.

Olivardia, R., Pope, H., and Hudson, J.I. (2000). Muscle dysmorphia in male weightlifters: a case-control study. *American Journal of Psychiatry* **157**(8), 1291–1296.

Olmedilla, A. and Andreu, A. (2002). Propuesta de iIntervención psicológica para el control de hábitos alimentarios en deportistas jóvenes. *Cuadernos de Psicología del Deporte* **2**(2), 13–28.

Olson, M.S., Williford, H.M., Richards, L.A., Brown, J.A., and Pugh, S. (1996). Self-reports on the eating disorder inventory by female aerobic instructors. *Perceptual and Motor Skills* **82**, 1051–1058.

Oppliger, R.A., Steen, S.A., and Scott, J.R. (2003). Weight loss practices of college wrestlers. *International Journal of Sport Nutritional and Exercise Metabolism* **13**(1), 117–121.

Oppliger, R.A., Utter, A.C., Scott, J.R., Dick, R.W., and Klossner, D. (2006). NCAA rule change improves weight loss among national championship wrestler. *Medicine and Science in Sports and Exercise* **38**(5), 963–970.

Otis, C.L., Drinkwater, B., Jhonson, M., Loucks, A., and Wilmore, J. (1997). American College of Sports Medicine Position Stand: The female athlete triad. *Medicine and Sciencie in Sport and Exercise* **29**, I–IX.

Parker, R.M., Lambert, M.J., and Burlingame, G.M. (1994). Psychological features of female runners presenting with pathological weight control behaviors. *Journal of Sport and Exercise Psychology* **16**(2), 119–134.

Pasman, L.J. and Thompson, J.K. (1988). Body image and eating disturbance in obligatory runners, obligatory weightlifters, and sedentary individuals. *International Journal of Eating Disorders* **7**(6), 759–769.

Pate, D.R., Greydanus, D.E., Pratt, H.D., and Philips, E.L. (2003). Eating disorders in adolescent athletes. *Journal of Adolescent Research* **18**(3), 280–296.

Pernick, Y., Nichols, J.F., Rauh, M.J., Kern, M., Ji, M., Lawson, M.J., and Wilfley, D. (2006). Disordered eating among a multiracial/ethnic sample of female high-school athletes. *Journal of Adolescent Health* **38**(6), 689–695.

Perez Recio, G., Rodriguez, F., Esteve, E., Larraburu, I., Font, J. and Pons, V. (1992). Prevalencia de trastornos de la conducta alimentaria en deportistas. *Revista de Psicologia del Deporte*, 1, 5–16.

Perpiñá, C., Botella, C., and Baños, R.M. (2003). Virtual reality in eating disorders. *European Eating Disorders Review* 11(3), 261–278.

Petrie, T.A. and Rogers, R. (2001). Extending the discussion of eating disorders to include men and athletes. *Counselling Psychologist* 29(5), 743–753.

Picard, C.L. (1999). The level of competition as a factor for the development of eating disorders in female collegiate athletes. *Journal of Youth and Adolescence* 28(5), 583–594.

Pickett, T.C., Lewis, R.J., and Cash, T.F. (2005) Men, muscles, and body image: comparisons of competitive bodybuilders, weight trainers, and athletically active controls. British Journal of Sports and Medicine 39, 217–222.

Pope, H.G., Katz, D.L., and Hudson, J.L. (1993). Anorexia nervosa and 'reverse anorexia' among 108 male bodybuilders. *Comprehensive Psychiatry* 34(6), 406–409.

Pope, H.G., Gruber, A., Choi, P., Olivardia, R., and Philips, K.A. (1997). Muscle dysmorphia: An underrecognized form of body dysmorphic disorder. *Psychosomatics* 38, 548–557.

Pope, H.G., Phillips, K., and Olivardia, R. (2000a). *The Adonis Complex: The Secret Crisis of Male Body Obsession*. New York: Free Press.

Pope, H.G., Gruber, A., Mangweth, B., Bureau, B., Decol, C.H., Jouvent, R. and Hudson, J.L. (2000b). Body image perception among men in the three countries. *American Journal of Psychiatry* 157(8), 1297–1301.

Popovich, A.M. (1998). *Eating and dieting behaviors and weight concerns among NCAA Division I women swimmers*. University of Oregon.

Powers, P.S. and Johnson, C. (1996). Small victories: Prevention of eating disorders among athletes. *Eating Disorders: The Journal of Treatment and Prevention* 4(4), 364–377.

Prieto, J.M. (1999). Una nueva disciplina. Ciberpsicología. *Revista Infocop* 74, 23–24.

Pruitt, J.A., Kappius, R.V., and Imm, P.S. (1991). Sport, exercise, and eating disorders. In L. Diamant (Ed.), *Psychology of Sport, Exercise, and Fitness: Social and Personal Issues*. Washington: Hemisphere Publising Corp.

Pujol-Amat, P. (1998). *Nutrición, salud y rendimiento deportivo*. Barcelona: Espaxs.

Raich, R.M. (1997). *Anorexia y bulimia: Trastornos alimentarios*. Madrid: Pirámide.

Rankin, J.W. (2002). Weight loss and gain in athletes. *Current Sports Medicine Reports* 1(4), 208–213.

Ransone, J. and Hughes, B. (2004). Body-weight fluctuation in collegiate wrestlers: implications of the national collegiate athletic association weight-certification program. *Journal of Athletics Training* 39(2), 162–165.

Ravaldi, C., Vannacci, A., Zucchi, T., *et al.* (2003). Eating disorders and body image disturbances among ballet dancers, gymnasium users and body builders. *Psychopathology* 36(5), 247–255.

Ren, H., Xing, W.H., Wang, L.Q., and Li, L. (2000). Research on somatotype characteristics of female judokas. *Journal of Beijing University of Physical Education* 23(2), 215–217.

Ricca, V., Mannucci, E., Zucchi, T., Rotella, C.M., and Faravelli, C. (2000). Cognitive-behavioural therapy for bulimia nervosa and binge eating disorder. A review. *Psychotherapy and Psychosomatics* 69(6), 287–295.

Ringham, R., Klump, K., Kave, W., *et al.* (2006). Eating disorder symptomatology among ballet dancers. *International Journal of Eating Disorders* 39(6), 503–508.

Ritterband, L.M., Cox, D.J., Walker, L.S., *et al.* (2003). An internet intervention as adjunctive therapy for pediatric encopresis. *Journal of Consulting and Clinical Psychology* 71(5), 910–917.

Riva, G. and Galimberti, C. (2001). *Towards Cyberpsychology*. Amsterdam: IOS Press.

Riva, G., Bacchetta, M., Cesa, G., Conti, S., and Molinari, E. (2002). E-health in eating disorders: Virtual Reality and telemedicine in assessment and treatment. *Studies in Health Technology and Informatics* **85**, 402–408.

Romo, I. (1998). Los peligros de la báscula. *Periódico El Mundo (04-06-98)*.

Rosen, L.W. and Hough, D.D. (1988). Pathogenic weight control behavior in female college gymnasts. *Physician and Sports Medicine* **16**, 140–146.

Rosen, L.W., McKeag, D.B., Hough, D.D., and Curley, V. (1986). Pathogenic weight control behavior in female athletes. *Physician and Sports Medicine* **14**, 79–86.

Rosenvinge, J.H. and Vig, C. (1993). Eating disorders and associated symptoms among adolescent swimmers: initial screening and a controlled study. *Scandinavian Journal of Medicine and Science in Sports* **3**(3), 164–169.

Roth, D., Egli, C.M., Kriemler, S., *et al.* (2000). Female athlete triad: Diagnose, therapie und praevention von getoertem essverhlten, amenorrhoe und osteoporose. *Schweizerische Zeitschrift fuer Sportmedizin und Sporttraumatologie Bern* **48**(3), 119–132.

Routtenberg, A. and Kuznesof, A.W. (1967). 'Self-starvation' of rats living in activity wheels on a restricted feeding schedule. *Journal of Comparative and Physiological Psychology* **64**, 414–421.

Roy, B.D., Fowles, J.R., Hill, R., and Tarnopolsky, M.A. (2000). Macronutrient intake and whole body protein metabolism following resistance exercise. *Medicine and Sciencie in Sport and Exercise* **32**(8), 1412–1418.

Rumball, J.S. and Lebrun, C.M. (2005). Use of the preparticipation physical examination form to screen for the female athlete triad in Canadian interuniversity sport universities. *Clinical Journal of Sport Medicine* **15**(5), 320–325.

Saltin, B. and Karlsson, J. (1972). Muscle glycogen utilization during work of direrents intensities. In B. Pernow and B. Saltin (eds.), *Advances in Experimental Medicine and Biology. Muscle Metabolism During Exercise* (pp. 289–299). New York: Plenum.

Sanborn, C.F., Horea, M., Siemers, B.J., and Dieringer, K.I. (2000). Disordered eating and the female athlete triad. *Clinics in Sport Medicine* **19**(2), 199–213.

Santrock, J.W. (2004). *Adolescencia*. Madrid: McGraw-Hill.

Sawka, M.N., Francesconi, P.P., Pimental, N.A., and Pandolf, K.B. (1984). Hydration and vascular fluid shifts during exercise in the heat. *Journal of Applied Physiology* **56**, 91–96.

Schlundt, D.G. and Bell, C. (1993). Body image testing system: a microcomputer program for assessing body image. *Journal of Psychopatology and Behavioral Assessment* **15**(3), 267–285.

Sexton, T.L. and Whiston, S.C. (1994). The status of the counseling relationship: An empirical review, theoretical implications, and research directions. *The Counseling Psychologist* **22**, 6–78.

Sherman, R.T. and Thompson, R.A. (2003). The female athlete triad. *Journal of School Nursing* **20**(4), 197–202.

Sherman, R.T., Thompson, R.A., Dehass, D., and Wilfert, M. (2005). NCAA Coaches Survey: The role of the coach in identifying and managing athletes with disordered eating. *Eating Disorders* **13**(5), 447–466.

Siff, M. (1992). Bodybuilding anorexia?. *Fitness and Sports Review International* **27**(4), 119.

Sila, C.M. (2001). Perturbacoes alimentaries em contextos desportivos: Un estudo comparative. *Analise Psicologica* **19**(1), 131–141.

Slater, G.J., Rice, A.J., Sharpe, K., Mujika, I., Jenkins, D., and Hahn, A.G. (2005). Body-mass management of Australian lightweight rowers prior to and during competition. *Medicine and Science in Sports and Exercise* **37**(5), 860–866.

Slater, G.J., Rice, A.J., Tanner, R., *et al.* (2006). Acute weight loss followed by an aggressive nutritional recovery strategy has little impact on on-water rowing performance. *British Journal of Sport Medicine* **40**(1), 55–59.

Smith, D. and Hale, B. (2004). Validity and factor structure of the bodybuilding dependence scale. *British Journal of Sports Medicine* **38**, 177–181

Smith, D. (2006). Psychology and bodybuilding. In J. Dosil (ed.), *The Sport Psychologist's Handbook: A Guide for Sport-Specific Performance Enhancement* (pp. 617–640). Chichester, UK: John Wiley & Sons.

Smith, M.C. and Thelen, M.H. (1984). Development and validation of a test for bulimia. *Journal of Consulting and Clinical Psychology* **21**, 167–179.

Smithies, C.S. (1991). Disordered eating behaviours among synchronized swimmers. In D.R. Black (ed.), *Eating Disorders among Athletes: Theory, Issues, and Research.* Reston, VA: AAHPERD.

Smolak, L., Murnen, S.K., and Ruble, A.E. (2000). Female athletes and eating problems: a metaanalysis. *International Journal of Eating Disorders* **27**(4), 371–380.

Sours, J.A. (1992). *Starving to Death in a Sea of Objects: The Anorexia Nervosa Syndrome.* Lanham, MD: Aronson.

Spriet, L. (1995). Caffeine and performance. *International Journal of Sport Nutrition* **5**, S84–S99.

Stein, D., Lilenfeld, L.R., Plotnicov, K., *et al.* (1999). Familial aggregation of eating disorders: Results from a controlled family study of bulimia nervosa. *International Journal of Eating Disorders* **26**(2), 211–215.

Stepto, N.K., Martin, D.T., Fallon, K.E., and Hawley, J.A. (2001). Metabolic demands of intense aerobic interval training in competitive cyclists. *Medicine and Sciencie in Sport and Exercise* **33**(2), 303–310.

Stoutjesdyk, D. and Jevne, R. (1993). Eating disorders among high performance athletes. *Journal of Youth and Adolescence* **22**(3), 271–282.

Stroem, L., Pettersson, R., and Andersso, G. (2000). A controlled trial of self-help treatment of recurrent headache conducted via the internet. *Journal of Consulting and Clinical Psychology* **68**(4) 722–727.

Stunkard, A.J., Sorensen, T., and Schulsinger, F. (1983) Use of the Danish Adoption Register for the study of obesity and thinness. In: S.S. Kety, L.P. Rowland, R.L. Sidman, S.W. Matthysse (eds.) *Genetics of Neurological and Psychiatric Disorders* (pp. 115–120). New York: Raven Press.

Sundgot-Borgen, J. (1996). Eating disorders, energy intake, training volume, and menstrual function in high-level modern rhythmic gymnasts. *International Journal of Sport Nutrition* **6**(2), 100–109.

Sundgot-Borgen, J. and Torstveit, M.K. (2004). Prevalence of eating disorders in elite athletes is higher than in the general population. *Clinical Journal of Sport Medicine* **14**(1), 25–32.

Sundgot-Borgen, J., Rosenvinge, J.H., Bahr, R., and Schneider, L.S. (2002). The effect of exercise, cognitive therapy and nutritional counseling in treating bulimia nervosa. *Medicine and Science in Sports and Exercise* **34**, 190–195.

Swoap, R. and Murphy, S.M. (1995). Eating disorders and weight management in athletes. In: S.M. Murphy (ed.), *Sport Psychology Interventions.* Champaign, IL: Human Kinetics.

Sykora, C., Grilo, C.M., Wilfley, D.E., and Brownell, K.D. (1993). Eating, weight, and dieting disturbances in male and female lightweight and heavyweight rowers. *International Journal of Eating Disorders* **14**(2), 203–211.

Szmukler, G.I., Eisler, I., Gillies, C., and Hayward, M.E. (1985). The implications of anorexia nervosa in a ballet school. *Journal of Psychiatric Research* **19**(2–3), 177–181.

Taub, D.E. and Benson, R.A. (1992). Weight concerns, weight control techniques, and eating disorders among adolescent competitive swimmers: the efect of gender. *Sociology of Sport Journal* **9**(1), 76–86.

Taylor, C.B., Bryson, S., Celio, A.A., *et al.* (2006). The adverse effect of negative comments about weight and shape from family and siblings on women at high risk for eating disorders. *Pediatrics* **118**(2), 731–738.

Taylor, G.M. and Ste-Marie, D.M. (2001). Eating disorders symptoms in Canadian female pair and dance figure skaters. *International Journal of Sport Psychology* **32**(1), 21–28.

Taylor, P.N., Wolinsky, I., and Klimis, D.J. (1999). Water in exercise and sport. In: J.A. Driskell and I. Wolinsky (eds.), *Macroelements, Water and Electrolytes in Sports Nutrition.* Boca Raton: CRC Press.

Terry, A., Szabo, A., and Griffiths, M. (2004). The exercise addiction inventory: a new brief screening tool. *Addiction Research and Theory* **12**(5), 489–499.

Terry, P.C. and Waite, J. (1996). Eating attitudes and body shape perceptions among elite rowers: effects of age, gender and weight category. *Australian Journal of Science and Medicine in Sport* **28**(1), 3–6.

Terry, P.C., Lane, A.M., and Warren, L. (1999). Eating attitudes, body shape perceptions and mood of elite rowers. *Journal of Science and Medicine in Sport* **2**(1), 67–77.

Thelen, M.H., Farmer, J., Wonderlich, D., and Smith, M. (1991). A revision of the bulimia test: the BULIT-R. *Journal of Consulting and Clinical Psychology* **3**, 119–124.

Thomas, J.J., Keel, P.K., and Heatherton, T.F. (2005). Disordered eating attitudes and behaviours in ballet students: examination of environmental and invidividual risk factors. *International Journal of Eating Disorders* **38**(3), 263–268.

Thompson, R.A. and Sherman, R.T. (1993a). Reducing the risk of eating disorders in athletics. *Eating Disorders: The Journal of Treatment and Prevention* **1**(1), 65–78.

Thompson, R.A. and Sherman, R.T. (1993b). *Helping Athletes With Eating Disorders.* Champaign, IL.: Human Kinetics Publishers.

Tiggemann, M., Verri, A., and Scaravaggi, S. (2005). Body dissatisfaction, disordered eating, fashion magazines, and clothes: A cross cultural comparison between Australian and Italian young women. *International Journal of Psychology* **40**(5), 293–302.

Toro, J. (1995). *El cuerpo como delito: anorexia, bulimia, cultura y sociedad.* Barcelona: Arial.

Toro, J. and Vilardell, E. (1987). *Anorexia Nerviosa.* Barcelona: Martínez Roca.

Toro, J., Cervera, M., and Pérez, P. (1988). Body shape, publicity and anorexia nervosa. *Social Psychiatry and Psychiatry Epidemiology* **23**, 132–136.

Toro, J. Salamero, M., and Martínez, E. (1994). Assessmente of sociocultural influence on the aesthetic body shape modelo in anorexia nervosa. *Acta Psychiatrica Scandinavica* **89**, 147–151.

Toro, J., Galilea, B., Martinez-Mallén, E., *et al.* (2005). Eating disorders in Spanish female athletes. *International Journal of Sports Medicine* **26**(6), 693–700.

Torstveit, M.K. and Sundgot-Borgen, J. (2005). The female athlete triad: are elite athletes at increased risk? *Medicine and Science in Sports and Exercise* **37**(2), 184–193.

Turk, J.C., Prentice, W.E., Chappell, S., and Shields, E.W. (1999). Collegiate coaches' knowledge of eating disorders. *Journal of Athletic Training,* **34**(1), 19–24.

USOC (United States Olympic Committee) (1998). *Nutrition: Athletes, Competition and Diet.* www.olympic-usa.org.

Utter, A.C. (2002). What a wrestler needs to know about hydration and dehydration. *Wrestling* **38**(1), 20.

Van Raalte, J.L. and Andersen, M.B. (2007). When sport psychology consulting becomes a means to an end(ing): Roles and agendas when helping athletes leave their sports. *The Sport Psychologist* **21**(2).

Vardar, S.A., Vardar, E., Durmus-Altun, G., Kurt, C., and Öztürk, L. (2005). Prevalence of the female athlete triad in Edirne, Turkey. *Journal of Sports Science and Medicine* **4**, 550–555.

Vaughan, J.L., King, K.A., and Cottrell, R.R. (2004). Collegiate athletic trainers' confidence in helping female athletes with eating disorders. *Journal of Athletic Training* **39**(1), 71–76.

Villa J.G. and Navas, F.J. (2002). Manejo nutricional y otras medidas terapéuticas en la práctica deportiva y la competición. *Medicine* **8**(85), 4577–4586.

Villapiano, M. (2001). *Eating Disorders: A Time For Change: Plans, Strategies, and Worksheets.* New York: Routledge.

Vincelli, F. (1999). From imagination to virtual reality: The future of clinical psychology. *CyberPsychology and Behavior* **2**(3), 241–248.

Vincelli, F., Anolli, L., Bouchard, S., Wiederhold, B.K., Zurloni, V., and Riva, G. (2003). Experiential cognitive therapy in the treatment of panic disorders with agoraphobia: a controlled study. *CyberPsychology and Behavior* **6**(3), 321–328.

Virnig, A.G. and McLeod, C.R. (1996). Attitudes toward eating and exercise: A comparison of runners and triathletes. *Journal of Sport Behavior* **19**(1), 82–90.

Vitousek, K., Watson, S., and Wilson, G.T. (1998). Enhancing motivation for change in treatment-resistant eating disorders. *Clinical Psychology Review* **18**(4), 391–420.

Walberg, J.L. and Johnston, C.S. (1991). Menstrual function and eating behavior in female recreational weight lifters and competitive body builders. *Medicine & Science in Sports & Exercise*, **23**(1), 30–36.

Waller, G. and Katzman, M.A. (1998). Female or male therapists for women with eating disorders? A pilot study of experts' opinions. *International Journal of Eating Disorders* **23**(2), 117–123.

Warren, B.J., Stanton, A.L., and Blessing, D.L. (1990). Disordered eating patterns in competitive female athletes. *International Journal of Eating Disorders* **9**(5), 565–569.

Weight, L.M. and Noakes, T.D. (1987). Is running an analog of anorexia?: a survey of the incidence of eating disorders in female distance runners. *Medicine and Science in Sports and Exercise* **19**(3), 213–217.

West, R.V. (1998). The female athlete. The trial of disordered eating, amenorrhea and osteoporosis. *Sports Medicine* **26**, 65–71.

Wiles, J.D., Bird, S.R., Hopkins, J., and Riley, M. (1992). Effect of caffeinated coffee on running speed, respiratory factors, blood lactate and perceived exertion during 1500 m treadmill running. *British Journal of Sport Medicine* **26**, 116–120.

Williams, C. (1995). Macronutrients and performance. *Journal of Sports Sciences* **13**, S1–S10.

Williams, C. (2003). New technologies in self-help: another effective way to get better? *European Eating Disorders Review* **11**(3), 170–182.

Winzelberg, A.J., Eppstein, D, Eldredge, K.L., *et al.* (2000). Effectiveness of an Internet-based program for reducing risk factors for eating disorders. *Journal of Consulting and Clinical Psychology* **68**(2), 346–350.

Wootton, S. (1988). *Nutrición y deporte.* Zaragoza: Acribia.

Word, P.D., Stefanick, M.L., Dreon, D.M., *et al.* (1988). Changes in plasma lipids and lipoproteins in overweight men during weigth loss through dieting as compared with exercise. *New England Journal of Medicine* **319**, 1173–1179.

World Health Organization (2003). *Diet, nutrition and the prevention of chronic diseases (technical information 916)*. Geneva: WHO.

Yager, J. (2003). E-mail Therapy for Anorexia Nervosa: Prospects and Limitations. *European Eating Disorders Review* **11**(39), 198–209.

Yan, X.Q., Guo, Y.L., Wang, Z.X., Li, N., Yang, L.L., and Wang, S.W. (2000). The vitamin metabolism during the period of weight reduction in wrestlers. *Chinese Journal of Sports Medicine* **19**(2), 171–173.

Yates, A. (1991). *Compulsive Exercise and the Eating Disorders*. New York: Brunnel/Mazel.

Yates, A., Edman, J.D., Crago, M., and Crowell, D. (2001). Using an exercise-based instrument to detect signs of an eating disorder. *Psychiatry Research* **105**(3), 231–241.

Yates, A., Edman, J.D., Crago M., and Crowell, D. (2003) Eating disorder symptoms in runners, cyclists, and paddlers. *Addictive Behaviors* **28**(8), 1473–1480.

Yoshioka, Y., Umeda, T., Nakaji, S., *et al.* (2006). Gender differences in the psychological response to weight reduction in judoist. *International Journal of Sport Nutrition and Exercise Metabolism* **16**(2), 187–198.

Zabinski, M.F., Celio, A.A., Wilfley, D.E., and Taylor, C.B. (2003a). Prevention of eating disorders and obesity via the Internet. *Cognitive Behaviour Therapy* **32**(3), 137–150.

Zabinski, M.F., Celio, A.A., Jacobs, M.J., Manwaring, J., and Wilfley, D.E. (2003b). Internet-based prevention of eating disorders. *European Eating Disorders Review* **11**(3), 183–197.

Ziegler, P.J., Kannan, S., Jonnalagadda, S.S., Krishnakumar, A., Taksali, S.E., and Nelson, J.A. (2005). Dietary intake, body image perceptions, and weight concerns of female US international synchronized figure skating teams. *International Journal of Sport Nutrition and Exercise Metabolism* **15**(5), 550–566.

Zmijewski, C.F. and Howard, M.O. (2003). Exercise dependence and attitudes toward eating among young adults. *Eating Behavior* **4**(2), 181–195.

Index

Eating Disorders in Athletes　Joaquín Dosil
© 2008 John Wiley & Sons, Ltd

Index compiled by Neil Manley

CPSIA information can be obtained
at www.ICGtesting.com
Printed in the USA
BVHW012145040822
643838BV00004B/16

9 780470 011706